PRAISE FOR *CONVERSATIO*

"Priyanka Kumar's outstanding and profoundly *with Birds* [...] could help people around the world rewild their hearts and souls. [...] A landmark, most timely book."—*PSYCHOLOGY TODAY*

"Priyanka Kumar's illustrative writing style has the power to bring readers along on the journey through arroyos and Georgia O'Keeffe's mountains. The dwindling number of eagles wintering in the wetlands of New Mexico evokes a certain sadness. Kumar emboldens readers to act upon concern for all sentient beings amid widespread ecological demise."
—SAN FRANCISCO BOOK REVIEW

"Just as immersion in nature inspires a mix of profound awe and renewed curiosity about this Earth we call home, so, too, does filmmaker and novelist Priyanka Kumar's mesmerizing essay collection, *Conversations with Birds* —rendered in finely wrought prose, steeped in memory and thrumming with endless curiosity." *—BOOKPAGE* (starred)

"Priyanka Kumar wows in this sparkling exploration of her relationship with the birds that serve as her 'almanac' and help her tune 'in to the seasons' and to herself. [...] Kumar's reflections are rendered in elegant prose and are rich with vivid descriptions. [...] These outstanding reflections will inspire and enlighten, and are perfect for readers of Diane Ackerman." *—PUBLISHERS WEEKLY* (starred)

"An eloquent depiction of how birding engenders a deep love of our ecosystems and a more profound understanding of ourselves."
—KIRKUS REVIEWS (starred)

"*Conversations with Birds* does something that few other bird books do: passionately writes about that moment when a person becomes a birder. [...] A bright new voice among the usual bird literature."
—BIRD OBSERVER

"ELEGANT AND EVOCATIVE" *—NEW YORK TIMES*

PRAISE FOR *CONVERSATIONS WITH BIRDS*

"In 20 vignettes and essays, Priyanka Kumar lovingly narrates how encounters with birds have molded her outlook on life, family, and nature, bridging the mountains of her childhood in India to her adult wanderings in California and New Mexico. [. . .] Her writing is full of beauty but also tells of destruction of the interconnected ecosystems that sustain birds and people. 'Sometimes it just takes the right bird to awaken us,' she writes."

—AUDUBON, "Six Books for Bird Nerds and Nature Lovers"

"This isn't just a book about birds, it's a look at the joy and curiosity we feel when we build connections with the natural world. [. . .] With gorgeously descriptive language, Priyanka Kumar shares her fascinating discoveries about birds and uses them as a gateway to explore topics like climate change, racism, and spirituality. For anyone feeling lost in our increasingly complicated human world, *Conversations with Birds* is just the compass you need." —APPLE, "Best Books of the Month"

"*Conversations with Birds* consists of Priyanka Kumar's observations, insights, and engagement with birds and the earth in prose that feels like a gentle guide for the reader to nurture their own relationship with nature, whatever it may look like. [. . .] Kumar's writing is one of many reminders of what we have to lose, and what we must save." —SHONDALAND

"In the luminous essays of Priyanka Kumar's *Conversations with Birds*, birds are a portal to reclaiming childhood connections with nature and the lush, wild landscape of northern India's remote mountains."

—*FOREWORD REVIEWS*

"I appreciate the tenderness and honor with which Priyanka Kumar reflects on the importance of birds in her life. They mark seasons and stages, bear the wounds of climate change and still persevere with power and grace." —*MS. MAGAZINE*

"A bird the color of mangoes, a beachcomber with a crescent-moon bill, the owl who controls the dark side of nature: in unforgettable encounters with feathered neighbors like these, Priyanka Kumar charts the life-changing surprise and splendor that birds can bring. They open the heart. They widen the soul. For Kumar, a peripatetic filmmaker and often a stranger in a strange land, birds have revealed connection and created wholeness." —SY MONTGOMERY, author of *The Hawk's Way*

"Birds have guided Priyanka Kumar through danger, loss, joy, and change. In her moving collection of elegant essays, *Conversations with Birds*, she recounts her close encounters with cranes and curlews, owls and tanagers, generously sharing their wisdom and her own."
—MICHELLE NIJHUIS, author of *Beloved Beasts*

"Priyanka Kumar is attuned to the animating power that links her—and you and me—to our fellow creatures. While she has a deep affinity for birds, especially cranes and eagles and owls, she communes as well with bobcat, coyote, fox and their four-legged kin. It is a joy to travel with this versatile artist, often in the company of her husband and their two young daughters, as she roams the American Southwest in search of elusive and majestic wildlife."
—SCOTT R. SANDERS, author of *The Way of Imagination*

"Priyanka Kumar's graceful and unusual work reminds us, again, of everything we lose with each insult to the natural world. *Conversations with Birds* is a wonderful read!"
—ANDREA BARRETT, author of *Ship Fever*

CONVERSATIONS

with BIRDS

Also by Priyanka Kumar

Take Wing and Fly Here

CONVERSATIONS

with BIRDS

Priyanka Kumar

MILKWEED EDITIONS

All rights reserved. Except for brief quotations in critical articles or reviews, no part of this book may be reproduced in any manner without prior written permission from the publisher: Milkweed Editions, 1011 Washington Avenue South, Suite 300, Minneapolis, Minnesota 55415.
(800) 520-6455
milkweed.org

First paperback edition, published 2023 by Milkweed Editions
Printed in Canada
Cover design by Mary Austin Speaker
Cover illustrations drawn by John James Audubon, engraved by Robert Havell Jr.
All interior illustrations drawn by John James Audubon and engraved by Robert Havell Jr., except the bulbul on page 32, drawn by Elizabeth Gwillim
Author photo by Molly Wagoner
24 25 26 27 28   6 5 4 3 2

978-1-63955-080-7

Library of Congress Cataloging-in-Publication Data

Names: Kumar, Priyanka, 1973- author.
Title: Conversations with birds / Priyanka Kumar.
Description: First edition. | Minneapolis, Minnesota : Milkweed Editions,
    2022. | Summary: ""Birds are my almanac. They tune me into the seasons,
    and into myself." So begins this lively collection of essays by
    acclaimed filmmaker and novelist Priyanka Kumar"-- Provided by
    publisher.
Identifiers: LCCN 2022010014 (print) | LCCN 2022010015 (ebook) | ISBN
    9781571313997 (hardcover) | ISBN 9781571317452 (ebook)
Subjects: LCSH: Kumar, Priyanka, 1973- | Birds--West (U.S.) | Bird
    watching--West (U.S.) | Human-animal relationships--West (U.S.) | Bird
    watchers--United States--Biography. | Women authors, American--21st
    century--Biography. | West (U.S.)--Environmental conditions.
Classification: LCC QL672.73.U6 K86 2022 (print) | LCC QL672.73.U6
    (ebook) | DDC 598.072/3478--dc23/eng/20220727
LC record available at https://lccn.loc.gov/2022010014
LC ebook record available at https://lccn.loc.gov/2022010015

Milkweed Editions is committed to ecological stewardship. We strive to align our book production practices with this principle, and to reduce the impact of our operations in the environment. We are a member of the Green Press Initiative, a nonprofit coalition of publishers, manufacturers, and authors working to protect the world's endangered forests and conserve natural resources. *Conversations with Birds* was printed on acid-free 100% postconsumer-waste paper by Friesens Corporation.

For Michael

CONTENTS

Preface

irds are my almanac: they tune me in to the seasons, and to myself. The western tanager, *Piranga ludoviciana*, with its flaming yellow-orange plumage, and the yellow-breasted chat, *Icteria virens*, glistening with a mango sheen, mean midsummer. When a juniper tree sparks to life with a Wilson's warbler, *Cardellina pusilla*, its beady, black eyes prominent in a bright-yellow-and-olive body, I know that the aspens in the nearby Santa Fe National Forest will soon turn to gold. In midwinter, I will see dark-eyed juncos, *Junco hyemalis*, whose folk name is snowbird, pecking on the clayey, snow-plastered dirt. When specks of green mysteriously rise from the earth and a little ruby-crowned kinglet, *Corthylio calendula*, with baby-big eyes hops in a piñon pine, it will be time to celebrate spring.

When I was a small child, I lived for nearly a decade in remote mountainous areas of northern India, and almost all the worthwhile moments of my childhood were spent immersed in nature. Back then I didn't pay any special attention to birds—I mainly looked out for snakes. I was in awe of what were called leaf snakes, such as the green vine snake, *Ahaetulla nasuta*, and the shimmering skins that many kinds of venomous snakes shed in my garden formed my greatest treasure.

It wasn't until I moved to the West as a teenager that I found my life increasingly shorn from nature. So many of us are experiencing this disconnect today and our inability to see or fully experience the natural world has played a part in making our Earth a sad and vulnerable planet, where warming temperatures are reducing the breeding success of birds and habitat loss has caused sublime species such as the ivory-billed woodpecker, *Campephilus principalis*, to become extinct.

In my twenties, I started to mull over the deep connection I'd had with nature as a child. After a debilitating experience in a Northern California forest nudged me to take a closer look at birds, I realized that I had been hiking extensively through California, but not *seeing* anything. In the years to come, I befriended a string of birds and began to understand why my life in the West was lacking *rasa*, which in Sanskrit means "juice," literally and metaphorically. Gradually, the town or city became a place to move through to get to the forest, which was a radiant sanctuary—a place to discover birds, their calls, and their dances, and to comprehend why their numbers were declining. Some of these birds became such fixtures in my life that the time I spent observing them, over two decades, charts my metamorphosis into a naturalist. As I share in these pages, loving these winged marvels has been my portal into the natural world.

I recently led a group of schoolchildren into a New Mexico forest for a daylong excursion. In the morning, the children were introduced to a Swainson's hawk, *Buteo swainsoni*, one of the largest migrating raptors we get in these parts, and a burrowing owl, *Athene cunicularia*, a leggy, ground-dwelling bird who emits a "rattlesnake rasp" to scare off predators. Then we hiked on uphill until we reached a magnificent waterfall. The hawk and the owl had made a deep impression on the children and, still recalling these fierce birds, they raced to the water gushing past black basalt and began scaling the cliff face like mountain goats. It looked as though they were embracing the landscape. I stood there, mesmerized; I recognized the embrace, for nature also offered it to me as a child. A woman who was assisting me pointed out that a child might lose their footing and suffer a fall. I then called out, asking them not to climb any higher and to come back, but the children clung to the basalt rock face for a long while, the sun-inflected water haloing them, before they reluctantly scrambled down. The experience of watching these children at home in nature crystallized my belief that seeds of transformation lie dormant in all of our hearts. Sometimes it just takes the right bird to awaken us.

MANGO-COLORED BIRD

Seeing a western tanager perched on a juniper tree is like peering into the molten heart of the Southwest landscape. This sublimely colored bird must be the forest's expression of joy. Nature concentrates yellow-gold, crimson, raven black, and mango in one midsize bird who flashes like a jewel in an otherwise subdued palette of olive greens and dove blues. Seeing the western tanager is a gladdening, if aleatoric experience—walking along a dirt road, a flash is all you might see, lemon-yellow wing-bar against black, as the bird flicks past the road to perch on a dry birdbath before vanishing into a deciduous tree. Hungry for another look, you stand before the tree shimmering in the last blaze before twilight, but you sense only a flutter in the shadows or you hear a chuckle or two. The western tanager is by no means a rare bird. Well over a century back, countless strands of these birds flew freely over the Americas. Now I see tanagers only singly or in pairs. Breakneck industrialization, wanton use of pesticides, agribusinesses, and habitat loss have largely evicted these shining jewels from our parched land. The tanager, of course, is not alone; some 40 percent of the world's bird populations are in decline.

I owe a debt to this mango-colored bird; once, it quite possibly saved my life. After graduating from film school at the University of Southern California, I moved to Northern

California, where, while backpacking on the High Sierra Trail in Sequoia National Park, I had a near-death experience.

It was not my first time at this park. I relished being among the ancient sequoias, their copious, maternal trunks, the color of burnt sienna, soaring toward the shining sky. Sequoia bark is rich in tannin, which shields the trees from the maladies of rot, insects, and fire. I walked among these immortals, as John Muir once called them, with the awe I might experience among columns in a cathedral that was all the more stirring for not being bound by stone. A porous cathedral, the Earth's cathedral, and I was but a leaf undulating through it.

After a four-hour drive from Santa Cruz, where we were living, Michael and I camped overnight at the Sequoia National Park and, the next morning, we got to the permit office at nine. The air was like the kiss of a pine; in the distance, a quail cackled. We filled out the requisite forms and were handed a backpacking permit and two bear canisters and we were on our way. It was nearly ten by the time we began hiking on the High Sierra Trail. Our first steps were charged with sun-drenched hope: we planned to backpack for five or six days. I dodged an enormous pine cone in my path and inhaled the muddy, dusty, piney fragrance of the trail. From deep inside the mixed-forest canopy, a jay let out a raucous cry. The air grew balmy and my navy tee glistened in the morning light. Our knapsacks bulged with a tent, cooking equipment, water for two days, a filter for the rest, and dried and cooked food in the bear canisters.

By midafternoon, we were hiking due east where the trail rose up a V-shaped canyon. We climbed the south-facing slope with the June sun beating down on us. The hot, white light stung my eyes. The temperature was between eighty-five and ninety degrees, and only the occasional ponderosa pine offered a smudge of shade. In the sun's pelting glare, I felt that my knapsack was unconscionably heavy, but Michael's was heavier still and it pinched his shoulders uncomfortably. We trudged on, with only the sound of our boots crunching pine needles or the drone of a cricket or a fly sundering the heat-baked silence. From time to time, we exchanged anecdotes and our conversations buoyed us.

After six hours of climbing, with the trail zigzagging upward ad infinitum, my thighs were on fire and my body was limp from the sun's embrace. Worse, I was feeling uncharacteristically ill, though I couldn't pinpoint the problem. I felt nauseous, enervated, and wholly unlike myself. Instead of hiking, I was dragging myself up the trail. Still, without a specific ailment, I hesitated to complain on the first day of an almost-weeklong hike. I was slender and in tolerable health, and it sometimes amused me when *other people* acted like hypochondriacs. Now I gritted my teeth and willed myself to climb on.

I didn't know that Michael's heel had started to hurt early on in the hike. The more we walked, the more aggravated his right heel grew. He mentioned it passingly, but disoriented by my vertiginous state, I didn't take note.

We were both in our midtwenties, and we hiked daylong trails on weekends whenever we could. During a previous summer, we had spent days backpacking through Yosemite, setting camp wherever the trail led us at twilight and keeping ears open for bears as we drifted off to sleep. I loved walking under canopies of sequoias, pines, and spruces, though I had noticed that I could get overheated while doing grueling hikes in the midday sun. Michael was also an experienced and stoic mountain biker. His heel must have grown unbearably painful for him to suggest that we consider turning around.

I started, unsure if I had heard him correctly.

Yes, he was wondering if we should turn around. If his heel were to go on hurting, we might eventually get stuck in an even more remote section of the trail.

I nodded, agreeing. In the moment, his suggestion felt like a gift from the skies. The decision brought me deep relief. As we began the long hike down, I acknowledged to myself that I was feeling pretty nauseous and it would have been torture to keep climbing. Was I suffering from a heatstroke?

We clambered down to the trailhead and then to the ranger station, where we duly returned the bear canisters. The afternoon was wilting when we stopped by a Park Service café for tea before we headed out to search for a campsite.

The cashier at the café paused when he looked at my face. I saw concern flicker in his eyes before he asked: "Are you OK?"

I nodded, though I felt an ocean away from OK. I still felt clammy and the skin on my arms gleamed unnaturally, like my navy tee. Michael later told me that my face was pale and glistening all over with an olive sheen.

HAVING PLANNED TO sleep along the High Sierra Trail, we had no campground reservation and were fortunate to find a site. From our knapsacks, we pried out the gas canisters and the propane tank, and Michael began to warm up the black-eyed peas that we had cooked the night before. As the dish warmed, I smelled a rancid whiff. The tomatoes had spoiled. Abruptly, I discovered that I could no longer stand. I wavered and clutched the picnic table. Would the day's light never stop glaring at me?

I hurried into the tent and crumpled on top of the sleeping bag. Lying down, I grew aware that something sharp was piercing my forehead, drilling life out of me.

Michael sat at the picnic bench, feeling uneasy, concerned, and baffled about my collapse. Neither of us had eaten. The group next to us had a roaring fire going and they were thigh-slappingly garrulous.

It was now around 8:00 p.m. In the twilight, a singular bird darted over and perched on a tree limb right above our tent.

It was the first time Michael had seen a western tanager, but he knew enough to identify it correctly.

Our tent squatted under a colossal ponderosa pine and the tanager was perched on a crescent limb that stretched out from the tree's scaly terra-cotta trunk.

"Look at this bird."

I heard Michael's voice while drifting out of consciousness.

He wanted to come into the tent and point it out, but that would have spooked the bird. He again called softly. "Open your eyes. You have to see this bird."

Stirred by his enthusiasm, I moved my head a few inches to see what he was pointing at. I could scarcely focus. Everything was wobbly. Gravity felt like a planetary force such as I hadn't experienced before—it pinned my body to the ground, while a knifelike heaviness jabbed at my forehead.

With some effort, I poked only my head out of the tent. The vivacious colors of the male tanager, his head softly brushed with cinnabar red, stood out against the deep green of the ponderosa branch. I was transported to a childhood memory in India, gazing delightfully at mangoes my father had brought me from the farmers market. The tanager was all fruity, luscious, heartening colors. As refreshing as my father's smile. I felt a gentle breeze on my face and I located my breath again. The spot of oxygen seemed to waken my lungs. The bird was not of this world. Was I imagining it? No. Michael was just as entranced.

Later I would learn that the tanager's prime breeding season is in May and June, which explained its bridegroom glow. It's partial to open areas in evergreen forests of ponderosa pine and Douglas fir; in the Southwest, it also frequents piñon-juniper woodlands. With yellow wing-bars on raven-black wings, the male tanager may have alighted on the ponderosa branch to glean a snack of insects, while it foraged nearby for dry, spindly grasses for its coarsely woven nest.

Despite the menace clutching my forehead, the bird lit up my heart, a sunbeam poured into me, and I steadied myself. I kept on gazing with a slightly open mouth until the tanager flew away, unswervingly, as soundlessly as it had arrived.

I had been sipping tea and I asked Michael to steady me so that I might walk to the restroom. When he saw how challenging it was for me to walk and how much I needed his support, he grew troubled. He abruptly recalled that a friend's wife had suffered a debilitating condition on a backpacking trip. They had later figured out that it was altitude sickness.

Now we wondered if I was having a severe case of altitude sickness.

Closer to 11:00 p.m., I was hallucinating about what was now a lethal spider on my forehead, and now a scorpion. Feeling sure it was a scorpion, I told Michael so.

A little later, I asked him to tell my mother that I loved her.

Michael tried to reassure me but his stoicism began to fail him.

In the deepening darkness, a yellow-gold thread hovered somewhere and I let out a faint smile despite imagining that I had uttered my last words. Even if I could have called my mother, my head hurt too much to talk.

Now Michael raced over to the trailer of the camp host. He was asleep and Michael woke him up. At first put out about having his sleep disrupted, when the camp host heard about our situation, he grew irate. "You came straight from sea level to six thousand feet and immediately got onto the High Sierra Trail—and went up to ten thousand feet!" he railed. "Go sleep it off!"

The night deepened into an inky, purple welt. To stay on in the mountains, in this oppressive two-person tent, which was suffocating, strangling me, was unthinkable. In the dark, Michael stood me up, all wobbly and staggering, and helped me into our secondhand Honda. He swiftly packed up our tent and equipment. At midnight, he drove us out of the park, weaving downhill on numerous switch-backs in the coal-like darkness.

In the car, I had a vile, throbbing headache. I clutched my head in my hands and shut my eyes but nothing helped. After we had descended four thousand feet, however, all at once the pounding in my head stopped, as though a celestial being had waved a wand over me, and in my mind's eye, the nebulous yellow-gold thread blossomed into the mango-colored tanager. We were closer to sea level now.

It was still a three-and-a-half hour drive home.

BACK IN OUR tiny apartment, I convalesced on a futon for the next couple of days. I remained feverish—I had a fever in addition to altitude sickness—and daydreamed about the gloriously painted bird that had appeared out of nowhere and revived me like an oxygen tank. I had no vocabulary for what had happened: cosmic serendipity or mere coincidence?

When I consider this incident, the story mysteriously shape-shifts and the tanager assumes the central role. What is etched into me is the moment of taking in its succulent colors—seeing the western tanager for the first time, staring at it with my mouth and heart and lungs all slowly reopening. I feel certain that the bird's presence, arbitrary though it might have been, yanked me out of an eddying, tumbling, airless darkness and cracked open the door to light and life.

Was it the bird's ethereal beauty I had responded to? Simply the magnificent colors? Its colors had recalled a more sensual world that I had once belonged to—the living, breathing landscape of my childhood, sweetened with juicy guavas, jackfruits, and mangoes, when I played every minute I could in the womb of nature.

Lavished by nature, the western tanager easily wears the mantle of the landscape's soul. I was not a birder yet, but I would soon experience a thirst to know more about the tanager's life and the struggles it faces. I would learn that although it feeds on insects, the tanager also favors wild berries and it gives away its tropical origins when it sips from cut oranges. From an ecological perspective, the tanager's presence is one indicator that the insect population in an area has not catastrophically plummeted. The bird needs every beetle or wasp it can catch. After summering in the Sierra, this exquisitely colored package of hollow bones and tendons flies south to winter in the pine and oak forests of Mexico and has been known to migrate as far as Central or South America.

Why did this bird stir such aliveness in me? How did it nudge me back from the edge of life-draining darkness? As I lay recovering from altitude sickness, these questions were but seeds in my mind and I drifted into sleep not knowing whether new experiences would materialize to water these fragile seeds.

SEVEN YEARS LATER, when I longed to have a place of our own, a western tanager would stagger me once again by appearing seemingly out of nowhere at a pivotal moment. Are animal sightings simply more available to those who make it a habit to keep looking?

Having noticed the western tanager, I puzzled over the significance of its presence. Something within me was ripening. Was it my eye? "One needs an eye to see a color," writes the Indian sage Sri Nisargadatta Maharaj, whose gift is said to be to gently unwrap the mystery of the self. "The colors are many, the eye is single." I had inhaled the tanager's colors and the bird had stamped an impression on my soul. In the years that followed, before my astonished eyes, other birds flew into the center of my stories and altered the way I saw the western landscape and what place, if any, I had in it. All my hiking notwithstanding, an epiphany about the land had eluded me—until I began to notice birds.

2

A ZEN MONK AT WORK

I.

The grass glistened asparagus green. The studio we rented in a Santa Cruz apartment complex abutted a freshwater marsh with iridescent cattails, which swished gold dust in the wind and drank from the steely-green water at their feet. Between morning writing and teaching a film class at the university, I circumambulated Neary Lagoon daily. Strolling along dirt paths and wood-planked bridges, I watched ducks swim, waddle, and bicker in the pewter-green water. Past the windblown cattails, where a handful of sooty coots floated reliably, I surprised a family of mallards; their splash of emerald notwithstanding, they ran short on poise. The air smelled of swamp and the briny ocean two miles away where waves hummed and thrashed unceasingly.

Halfway into my loop, I might encounter wood ducks, *Aix sponsa*: decked out like duchesses, with fascinators on their heads, they swam in the lagoon's alcoves or strode along the mudbanks. Their gorgeousness was scarcely lessened by muddy webbed feet or waddling backsides. When the furtive ducks took note of me, they indignantly scuttled away toward the shady folds of a weeping willow. Then I remained the sole figure standing in the lagoon.

Waterfowl are socialites who can't chatter enough with one another and, in their presence, I was struck by how isolated I was in Santa Cruz. I was no stranger to solitude, I was fairly accustomed to it, but until this year I'd had some community, however tenuous—with other young filmmakers in Los Angeles—where I might experience fleeting relief. In Santa Cruz, there were only the ducks.

I was just out of film school. While doing my graduate work at the University of Southern California, I had directed a 16mm short based on a childhood incident in Assam. I loaned this short to Eli Hollander, the film chair at the University of California, Santa Cruz. At the time, Eli was making an anthropology film and he invited me to teach, as a visiting professor, the filmmaking course that he normally taught. A UCSC history professor later shared that Eli had said my work reminded him of Satyajit Ray, an iconic Indian filmmaker whom I admired.

I had acquired an MFA with a focus on directing, and my education was supposedly complete; my soul, however, felt parched. The naturalist Aldo Leopold once wrote that it is not only the volume of education that matters, but also the content. He was not mistaken. The University of Southern California in Los Angeles was considered to be one of the top film schools in the country, but all we seemed to talk about was technical stuff—a cool Dutch angle, the newest digital camera. Which was fine up to a point, since I relished mastering technical stuff and had trained myself to become a reliable cinematographer. But to what end? Rarely if ever did we engage in conversations about what stories we wanted to tell and why. After we graduated with crippling loans, there was no clear path forward except for the murky expectation that we attach ourselves to some hardheaded producer as an

assistant, serving coffee and doing drudge work for meaning-
less reality TV shows, all of which seemed to lead away from
the raison d'être for becoming an artist.

In contrast, the seaside town of Santa Cruz, like its wood
ducks, possessed an otherworldly aesthetic and its wet blue
air sometimes contained my artistic longing even as it deepened my isolation.

I WAS NEWLY married, and Michael was doing his postdoc-
toral work at UCSC. One Thanksgiving afternoon, we hiked
the nearby Wilder Ranch State Park in the gilded autumn
light. We both had tiny, two-person families in Canada and
nary a relative in America, so once again we were on our own
for Thanksgiving. The seven thousand coastal acres that
stretched desolately before us were braided with history that
echoed California's soul: in the 1500s the Ohlone people
had lived here in ingenious homes made out of bent willow
poles, but Spanish explorers seized the land in the 1700s.
The trail's bleak wildness permeated me when I hiked here
each week. One spring afternoon Michael was biking when a
pair of bobcats materialized some fifteen feet away. He slowed
down as they approached the trail. The wildcats stopped on
the trail and turned their feral faces to study him. Michael
halted. One bobcat stiffened and raised its head, reluctant to
give way. Instead, with hazel eyes the pair probed the young
man on the bicycle, and only after some time did they saunter
across the trail and vanish into the long, swaying grass on the
other side. Michael went on biking. It was that kind of a trail.

On Thanksgiving, we hiked the trail's familiar contours as
it curved along a tan coastline stretching into the blue distance.

Primeval-looking cormorants flew from one cliff top to another, issuing gruff, throaty calls and on occasion a brown pelican glided by like a scissor slashing the pale silk of the sky. The terraced cliffs, rutted sharply by rainwater, plunged into the cobalt sea. Walking along these cliffs that flanked the ocean, I felt unmoored. Thanksgiving only has a snug, homey meaning for those who have a functional family in America. My family seemed to have wasted away starting four years back, with the cruel and abrupt deaths of my father and my older brother, one jolt after another, within seventeen months. Any words I might have to articulate what had happened had frozen inside me; mostly, even my friends and colleagues did not know that my family had been devastated and my world knocked down in a twinkling. Silently, I suffered the absence of my beloved, kindhearted father—an Indian government official in his prime—and my intellectual, map-loving brother who had just begun working in Toronto after completing his international MBA, until the world peopled with humans felt inadequate. I sought instinctively the vast spaciousness of the natural world.

The wind sweeping through the bluff top cut into my face and stung my eyes until they watered. Below I saw little blurs of white and, wiping my eyes, I discerned minuscule milky-white birds, the tiniest of shorebirds, scuttling in the sand like Ping-Pong balls. The near-threatened snowy plovers, *Charadrius nivosus*, whose breeding populations have plummeted due to relentless beachfront development.

I drew closer to the edge and peered into the cove below. Sanderlings, *Calidris alba*, danced with the waves; when the water receded they moved in as one body, like giddy siblings, to scour the sand for edibles that had been washed up.

At the brink of the water, turquoise with milky sprays, the birds pirouetted and scooted away from the vigorously choppy waves. Their movements were brisk and rhythmic. I grew hypnotized by how these birds careened toward the capricious water to feed and then sure-footedly danced away from it. Watching the sanderlings flirt assuredly with the waves and scuttle up and down the beach like delirious children at play in the honey-gold light, my heart lightened.

The splashy movements of the sanderlings were a contrast to the distinctly quieter, almost camouflaged snowy plovers who stood out in the upper beach only because of the white collar that ran along the backs of their necks. In Wilder Ranch State Park, a section of the beach is closed to the public. The pale snowy plovers have adapted to the color of the sand, and they also nest on the sand where their tan-gray backs and snowy breasts blend into the beach. Such striking color adaptation provided Charles Darwin with his early insights about the mechanisms of nature. He noted that the birds on the Galápagos Islands resembled those on the mainland, except for one factor—their coloration. Unlike the brilliantly colored vermilion flycatcher, the Galápagos birds were, as Darwin wrote, "generally dusky colored." Had they adapted to the lava color of the islands?

Beach-loving humans, scarcely cognizant of avian adaptations, can keep the snowy plovers from their nests and thus thwart their breeding. As recounted in *Birds of the World*, a study by Mark A. Colwell and colleagues found that "on the northern California coast, humans have stepped on nests, driven over nests, vandalized enclosures erected to protect nests, and kept adults from brooding chicks."

The naturalist Kenn Kaufman writes that the snowy plover's nest is a "shallow scrape in the ground, lined with bits of shell, grass, pebbles, [and] other debris." I, for one, didn't want to accidentally disrupt such a lovely, ingenious, and fragile attempt to start a family.

II.

Water and land are opposing realms, with shorebirds at the edge, translating one realm to another. I identified with shorebirds; from an early age I felt at home in two realms, the East and the West, and I felt comfortable translating inscrutable India to Westerners or America to apprehensive Easterners. The pelicans I saw on my frequent walks along the Santa Cruz shoreline were slate gray with dinosaurian dimensions and plangent squawks to match. From Natural Bridges State Beach, I watched the pelicans fly from the depths of the sea toward the shore, diving headlong for fish before they wheeled around and sailed back to the depths, where, metaphorically, I wanted to be—in the core of life, art, and thought. But I had encountered only stiff winds of resistance when I tried to launch my stories, like boats, into the ocean-world. "I really love this book!" a New York editor had told my agent about my literary novel. "And I took it all the way up to our editorial meeting. But I was told that we already have an Indian author." Her words pigeonholed me; they were just one of many similar responses that repeatedly drowned my artistic self and made me feel voiceless.

III.

About a month after Thanksgiving, on a cloud-filled December morning, I took Michael on a surprise birthday hike. We headed to the Elkhorn Slough, a tidal salt marsh and estuarine research reserve some twenty-six miles south of Santa Cruz. On this first visit to the slough, a mass of ashen clouds loomed over us. What beauty the Elkhorn Slough might be said to have is of a stark, blanched variety. I zipped up my navy windbreaker as we walked up to the base of a sprawling, charcoal rock.

We were surveying the tidal mudflats below when an elderly man and a woman approached us. They were volunteers, armed with battered copies of the *National Geographic Field Guide to the Birds of North America*.

"Would you two be interested in going on a bird walk?"

We had never been on a bird walk before, but their aquatic eyes shone with such hope that I didn't care to disappoint them. I hardly realized in this moment that my way of looking at the natural world was about to undergo a seismic shift.

They led us down to the salt marsh and the four of us walked along a dirt path, skirting past gleaming pickleweed that sprouted from the ground like succulent seaweed. We began to circle the metallic-blue lagoon. Here we spotted a few tawny shorebirds. The volunteers shuffled through the worn pages of their guidebook and pointed out the name and illustration of each bird we encountered.

Around noon, I noticed a shorebird that was enormous compared to the rest. If the plight of the diminutive snowy plovers had ushered me into the domain of shorebirds, I now faced a bird who, at roughly two feet tall, was a monad of shorebirds. I was told that this solitary bird, foraging scrupulously along the edge of the blue-gray water, was a long-billed curlew, *Numenius americanus*. Intrigued, I stayed back to observe it while the others walked on.

I took in the slender lines of the curlew's neck and its marbled beige-and-umber back. I stared at its impossibly long bill, flesh colored on top and chocolate brown at the tip. Essentially the largest sandpiper in the country, the bird was half as tall as a crane, but without the crane's assured elegance. With its absurdly elongated, curved bill, the curlew looked almost unwieldy, like a pointer to another era, to the kinds of feathered creatures that might have existed in the time of dinosaurs. This bird angles its protracted bill into the burrows of mud crabs and maneuvers its prey to the surface to feed on it. In retrospect I must have seen a female, which in this species is bulkier and has a lengthier bill than the male.

The curlew was wholly at ease. The bird's unhurried pace combined with its focus and laser-sharp moves when it found an invertebrate to eat was nothing short of arresting. I might have been watching a Zen monk at work. Here was a bird that embodied Milarepa's saying: Hasten slowly and you shall soon arrive.

Observing the long-billed curlew, I thought about how my Neary Lagoon walks were taken in a similarly languid mood, and were bookended by writing or teaching sessions during which I pecked away at words in the monkish, meditative way in which the curlew probed the water for crustaceans. Weaving daily along the glittering lagoon, I had come to experience a measure of contentment while watching the wood ducks and my isolation was somewhat allayed. Now my chance initiation into the life of this exquisite curlew and my hunger to know more about the bird was like a bridge that would one day lead me back to nature's elusive womb. Contrary to the mythology about Eve, nature doesn't cast us out. Eating from the tree of knowledge, the knowledge of nature's inner working, far from being a sin, only deepens our filial love for the Earth. I can't say how much time passed. The sun blazed through the clouds and time melted like the haze. I came to myself when, out of the corner of my eye, I spotted a crab racing toward me, with the dreadful passion of a soldier on a battlefield. I had been immobile long enough that the crab had evidently decided I was fair game. I darted out of the crab's warpath and left the indelible curlew behind.

A FEW DAYS after our first bird walk, Michael and I parked our Honda in downtown Santa Cruz and began to walk over to a Sri Lankan restaurant. The owner of the Asian Rose likely took us to be underfed students for he would generously bring over an extra dish smothered with coconut or mango sauce to our table. On our way to the restaurant, I heard some chirping and traced it to a bare tree on which were perched several sparrowlike birds with bright-reddish heads. In the near twilight, the tree might have looked miserably bare, but the presence of the birds lent it animation and charm. Strangely, my heart began to beat in rhythm with the chirps. What birds were these? We both grew excited, thinking that we had chanced upon some remarkable flock.

I acquired a *National Geographic Field Guide to the Birds of North America* from the nearby Bookshop Santa Cruz, only to discover that I was a hopeless amateur. The birds we'd seen with red smudges on their heads were common house finches, *Haemorhous mexicanus*. So common that real birders scarcely deign to look at them. Are house finches really not worth a second look? It was Darwin's study of the Galápagos finches, after all, that catalyzed his insight that evolution occurs through natural selection. Considering the matter through another lens, Renaissance painters brush-stroked the European goldfinch, *Carduelis carduelis*, as a Christian symbol. I, in any case, felt ready to admire the finches that presented themselves. I seemed to be stumbling upon birds. They invigorated me, at a time when the barriers I faced as an artist had a dispiriting, estranging effect on me.

SOON AFTER THE Elkhorn Slough tour, an inner shift occurred. There's a concept in Zen Buddhism called instant enlightenment. A master taps you on the head or asks you to decode a koan; your cranial bones receive an otherworldly stimulus and light enters. It is the aha moment in overdrive. In my case, the snowy plovers had guided me to the master—a long-billed curlew, assisted by a feisty crab. Theodore Roosevelt may have felt like this when, after his struggle with nearsightedness, at thirteen he put on a pair of glasses and his eyes were at last able to see lucidly the birds that he already loved.

Now the natural world, its Western incarnation, swung open its doors to me, and I entered an animated, even kaleidoscopic experience. Whereas before I had seen American landscapes in shades of greens and browns, on vague aesthetic terms, now my senses began to truly engage with the life that was before me.

Birds ushered me into the heart of the landscape. Now my hikes meandered through the treasures hitherto hidden in the land's greenish-brown alcoves. By this time, I had already hiked expansively in California. Soon after my father's death, I had undertaken a punishing climb in Yosemite, where, on the knife-edge of Clouds Rest, along a ridge at 9,900 feet, the drop-off was terrifyingly steep; I realized that one wrong move could mean my own death. Later, I trekked past redwoods with a wealth of diameters and camped in a multitude of state and national parks, and I would soon slide down icy paths to enter the sulfurous womb of a volcano in Lassen Volcanic National Park. Despite immersing myself in these landscapes, the distance between the natural world and me had agonizingly persisted. Until the plover and the curlew bridged that gulf, I hadn't truly seen Yosemite or Lake Tahoe or even the nearby Forest of Nisene Marks.

IV.

A few months later, the Huntington Library and Gardens in San Marino put on a major exhibit of John James Audubon's paintings of American birds. I went eagerly, to see the curlew through the master's eyes. In Audubon's painting titled *Long-billed Curlew*, two curlews stand at the edge of a marsh. One curlew's bill is about to skim the water, its eye taut with attention. The second curlew's head is turned away from the water, as though listening warily for approaching danger.

I turned away from the painting, overwhelmed by its intensity.

After I had recovered, I gazed silently at the rest of the masterpieces. I walked through the large hall mounted with Audubon's work, feeling as though I were inside a basilica. Audubon's mature work shimmers with life. His birds interact with one another and their habitats. Audubon mounted the birds he shot (later I would be dismayed to learn how many) onto a soft board with pins in lifelike poses as models for drawings that seem to fly off the page. I shuffled through the enormous hall where the paintings were hung, but in the crowded space I got only fleeting glimpses of the forests Audubon had traipsed through and the birds he had seen. I wanted to study his work with quiet concentration. At the time I was also reading a biography of the poet Percy Bysshe Shelley, who spent the latter part of his brief life in the Italian countryside, and I craved to know more about Shelley's relationship with nature. Fortuitously, the research library at Huntington had specialized collections on both these artists.

I approached the library staff, who regularly let scholars and writers in to study their collections. I was given a form, which I filled out diligently, listing my master's degree and my teaching experience at the University of Southern California and at the University of California, Santa Cruz.

I didn't hear back for several weeks. Wondering what was the matter, at last I phoned the librarian to check on the status of my application.

"It was rejected," she said.

Surprised, I asked why.

"You don't fit our profile," she said.

I felt myself grow numb and at the same time I experienced a familiar pain. This sentiment had been flung at me

several times, ever since I moved to North America as a teenager but never was it so clearly articulated.

"In what way?" I whispered.

"You don't have a PhD."

Her tone was frigid, sclerotic, it was clear she wanted
to hang up. My mouth was too dry for me to prolong the
call. She hadn't asked a single question about my interest in
Audubon. Did intellectual curiosity not count for anything?
I might have told her that an MFA is a terminal degree in my
field, but her tone had blocked any doorway to a conversation. I wondered if a PhD in any field (math?) would suffice
as an entry to the hallowed library she guarded.

The conversation recalled experiences I had tried to brush
aside in the past. I had not been aware of race as any kind of
a deciding factor until at fifteen when I left India temporarily
for Britain. I had been awarded a scholarship to study at a
private British school for a semester. Officially I was the same
as any other student in the almost all-white school, some fifty
miles from London, but I noticed right away that I was perceived as being of a different species. The sentiment crystallized when one afternoon those of us who had expressed
interest in eventually applying to Oxford went on a field trip
to the university to talk with professors in our areas of interest. On the drive back in a chartered bus, smartly uniformed
boys, who were acquaintances from school, grinned at me,
while chanting repeatedly, "Paki, Paki, Paki, Paki!"

I wanted to clarify that I was from India, not Pakistan—as
descendants of the region's colonizers, they ought to know
the difference—but I remained as tongue-tied as I would
with the Huntington librarian. I did and didn't realize that

they were using a racial slur. I had gone to Britain imagining that I would have frank conversations with young people there about the moral thorniness of colonization and the brutalities it had unleashed on my country; little did I realize that I would summarily be boxed up and labeled with a slur.

What made things complicated is that such incidents arose from unexpected sources, from intelligent people, from people I admired, from people who ought to have known better; only after years of denial did I admit to myself that I was up against a systemic problem. When I was a film student at USC, on the strength of a new novel I was completing, the chair of the Master of Professional Writing Program, James Ragan, arranged for me to take some advanced classes in his department. "I would accept you into the program just based on the first paragraph," he said about my novel. One class was led by the nonfiction writer Gay Talese, who at the time was visiting from New York. I showed Talese the first couple of chapters of my novel about a young Indian girl navigating unknown waters in America, and on the appointed day I sat at a seminar table and awaited his response.

Talese had only one comment: "Can she hold the stage?"

I started.

"The girl," he added, shrugging. "You think she can hold the stage? I'm not sure. I don't think so."

He spoke in a low voice, as if the conversation was hardly worth having. I felt stung by the smug expression on his face and his casually dismissive tone. He is sowing doubt in me, I thought. He's telling me that an Indian girl cannot be the protagonist of her own story, that she can't be taken seriously, that I might erase bits of her and import a more recognizable protagonist who would be better able to "hold the stage." Would he ask the same question, I wondered, if one of the British schoolboys on that bus had written about his tumultuous experiences in North America?

PAINFUL THOUGH SUCH experiences were, I didn't want to dwell on them. I wanted to go on imagining that they were anomalies and I would soon transcend them. I wanted to hold instead the image of an infinitely long shoreline awaiting me with arms stretched in a maternal embrace. After we had left Santa Cruz and moved to Pasadena, on an early-morning trip to Leo Carrillo State Park in Malibu, the sky was drowsy and velvet gray, and I raced down the silken beach to the ocean. I stopped abruptly and experienced a catch in my throat. A long-billed curlew stood at the water's milky edge, its distinctive bill probing the soft, wet sand and in between rock crevices, for shrimp maybe. The bird belonged so genuinely to the pastel, watery landscape; how wonderful it must be to belong! Soon the curlew's back, caressed by the sun's first rays, turned golden. Even the fantastical bill no longer looked odd; it had its place. Years later I would see a curlew use its bill to threaten to spear a hawk and effectively save the life of its young.

V.

One April, Michael and I were chasing wildflowers when we stumbled upon curlews again, during visits to Carrizo Plain National Monument, a remote wetland in Southern

California. Bureau of Land Management (BLM) policies have historically indulged the ranchers in this area and the denuded land, its grasses devoured repeatedly by cattle, was now covered with desert scrub such as spiny saltbush. This grassland is home to a species of concern, the San Joaquin antelope squirrel whose numbers are declining because of habitat loss, and who swiftly won me over with its baby-brown eyes, but there were scarcely any signs of the native grasses that had once thrived here.

Grasslands are of vital importance to long-billed curlews who breed in them and feed their chicks grasshoppers and beetles all summer. Over the years at least two supervisors at Carrizo Plain had objected strongly to the overgrazing that the BLM sanctioned, but they were both suspended (one was later fired, and the other went on to die by suicide). A gloom hung over the land though we saw some species of birds such as a Savannah sparrow on the warm ocher ground and a western kingbird and Lawrence's goldfinches perched on wires.

For two glorious weeks in April, the gloom lifted and the land was painted over with masses of wildflowers: goldfields, lupines, baby blue eyes, fiddle-necks. One afternoon we stood in a sea of gold and purple while a great robust flock of long-billed curlews, in undulating waves, flew over us like a blessing, a benediction. The russet line of migrating curlews glided by in three distinct waves. They were leaving their wintering areas in coastal and inland California to head for summer breeding grounds in arid grasslands across the Southwest. We stood transfixed in saffron ribbons of color, watching curlew silhouettes with their incredible bills transforming the luminous gray sky into a realm as rich as the flower-strewn earth.

That curlews are faintly unwieldy does not prevent them from flying gracefully but it does make them more visible to louts. A few years later, Dr. Jay Carlisle, a biologist who studies long-billed curlews, would tell me that the birds are being "accidentally" shot in alarming numbers when people target practice on ground squirrels (the latter activity is legal in states such as Idaho) or when curlews mob people who walk up too close to their chicks. People shoot them just like that. For fun.

In those early years when I fell hard for birds, it's not as though I consciously bonded with them because they, too, are in a sense voiceless; they, too, have been the targets of easy cruelty. From the start, however, I felt a great deal of empathy for birds, in addition to being magnetized by their beauty; I felt surprised even when I first learned that people obsessively tick them off lists as if they are somehow inferior and are fated to be objectified and cataloged, as if they cannot be expected by themselves to hold the stage.

3

THE RASA OF BULBULS

I.

The Sanskrit term *rasa* means "juice," literally, but it alludes to charm without which life is, to put it bluntly, dry. The *Natyashastra*, an ancient treatise on theatre and dance, says that the eight *rasas* or "sentiments," such as the Sensual, the Comic, the Pathetic, the Heroic, and the Odious, are so called because we can taste them—in our minds. *Rasa* is an intricate, elusive concept you might suffer *rasa*'s absence as I at first did in Santa Cruz, or discover a stream, as I did in Ravi Shankar's house in Encinitas, Southern California.

When I arrived at the Shankar house for a scheduled interview, Mrs. Sukanya Shankar told me tersely: "OK, you have ten minutes to do the interview."

I was stunned. I had driven with my film editor for almost 350 miles from Santa Cruz to Los Angeles, stayed overnight at a colleague's house, picked up my cinematographer the next morning, loaded our camera equipment, and driven south for another 100 miles. All for ten minutes? I was directing a feature documentary on Satyajit Ray, the Indian filmmaker whose storytelling moved me deeply and who was awarded the Academy's Honorary Oscar for Lifetime Achievement in 1991. Ravi Shankar had composed the music for Ray's masterpiece, *The Apu Trilogy*, and I would learn only after Shankar's death that he had never previously been interviewed about this experience. When I glanced anxiously at his secretary, Madeline, who had arranged the interview, she obligingly said, "Mrs. Shankar, Priyanka wanted a photo of Mr. Shankar and Mr. Ray to use in the film. Let's go look for it." And she gracefully whisked Mrs. Shankar away. To Madeline's credit, she kept Mrs. Shankar occupied for the next two hours looking over old black-and-white photos.

Meanwhile, the interview lasted more than an hour, with Ravi Shankar glowing ever more as he reminisced about composing music for Ray, how he scored fleeting but resonant images like water striders dancing on the surface of a pond, and how a deep friendship ensued between the two men that lasted a lifetime. After the interview, my small crew gathered around Ravi-ji (as he asked me to call him) over a tray of chai. He spoke about his sitar practice sessions each morning and gave us a tour of his practice room. Then, in the courtyard, he lowered his voice to speak to me of his anxieties about the daughter he'd had before this marriage, the then-unknown Norah Jones—"She works in jazz clubs"—and the death of his older son in an accident, before he went on to inquire about my life, and somehow into all this talk was woven a robust dose of philosophy, warmth, intimacy, and laughter. The *Natyashastra* suggests that such *rasa* is what gives speech its flavor and even its meaning. As I left, Ravi-ji affectionately called out, "Next time you come, let us know in advance, so we can have lunch together."

Later, Ravi-ji sent me invitations to his "goodbye concerts," before he left California for India. (Did he also miss *rasa*?) As a child living in India, I had drunk deeply from the well of *rasa*. As evanescent as the silvery air on a spring day or an unexpected encounter with a bird, *rasa* can also spring from a chai-fueled conversation with close friends. Postconcert, Michael and I joined Ravi-ji backstage to continue where we had left off. The flavor of Ravi-ji's greeting, his eyes gleaming like jewels, made us feel welcome. While the conversation flowed, his wife, Sukanya, and their daughter, Anoushka, smilingly looked on. Ravi-ji believed that the magic of Indian classical music springs from "its hypnotic, intense singleness of mood." In order to invoke this mood, an artist must decide which one of the eight *rasas* will dominate a piece. It is not simply technical mastery, but also the *rasa* in Ravi Shankar's music that moves us.

II.

That summer, Michael found a temporary position at the California Institute of Technology, and we left Santa Cruz and drove south with our belongings in our respective secondhand cars. Abruptly, while driving up a grade, I saw a fire raging along the Golden State Freeway (I-5) or as it's called, the Grapevine, too luscious a word for this dreary stretch (wild grapevines once grew abundantly here). The surreal inferno flared out from the middle of the freeway and stretched its fiery arms into the lane I was to drive through. The air broiled and flames moved to tongue my car; there was no way to turn around and nowhere to stop. I inched my black Honda into a narrow crevice left untouched by the fire and drove parallel alongside a wailing wall of flames, so close that I instinctively hunched behind the wheel as smoke singed my window. Michael followed closely behind. I had been bracing myself for hotter days, but not for burning days. In the era of climate change, this was perhaps the au courant way to plunge into Southern California. From my rearview mirror I saw the fire erupt, hissing and bellowing as I steered south.

At first glance, Pasadena was all blazing light and sun-dried concrete. In the evenings, we strolled around the periphery of the California Institute of Technology where the hedges were thick and coated liberally with dust. In the southeast corner of the campus, blooming jasmines perfumed the evening air, momentarily blotting the hiss of traffic. Otherwise the snore of trucks and cars filtered all day into our apartment, which was just a block away from the northern edge of campus.

In the late afternoons, I would walk a mile to the local Peet's Coffee & Tea. Outside our three-story apartment complex, I would reliably see a black phoebe, *Sayornis nigricans*, in a black dinner jacket with tails worn over immaculate white trousers. Cheeping its name—*fee-bee*—from a pencil-tip beak, the elegant phoebe looked disheartened to find itself surrounded by concrete. Light glared onto its velvety black head and its chessboard body as the bird perched in a row of young, straggly trees. This flycatcher frequented my desolate street only because of its hidden treasure: two massive mature trees—a bauhinia and a bay—in an untenanted property that faced my living room window.

From the depths of the bauhinia tree, *Bauhinia variegata*, with abundant heart-shaped leaves and fragrant pink flowers, a northern mockingbird nightly sang a melodious, whistling—if piercing—song from its impressive repertoire. Woken abruptly on many a night by the mockingbird, whose scientific name, *Mimus polyglottos*, means "many-tongued thrush," Michael had an urge to toss a pebble at the operatic bird. Unperturbed by the havoc it wreaked on our sleep, the bird would whistle the same song obsessively and insistently until I wasn't sure in the morning whether the melody was being sung yet again or simply playing in my head. The mockingbird followed me to film sets as well. When I interviewed Peter Rainer, film critic for the *Christian Science Monitor*, for the documentary, a mockingbird stationed itself on the tree Peter sat next to and sang so lustily that the sound recordist shook her head and told me that we would have to start over.

The mockingbird is a relatively common bird, slate gray with white wing-bars that are prominent during flight but it's another species that helped Darwin intuit the mechanism of evolution. When aboard the *HMS Beagle*, Darwin realized that the Galápagos mockingbirds were not quite the same on all the islands and it was then that he began to wonder if the discrepancies between the birds were of special significance. "When I see these Islands in sight of each other . . . tenanted by these birds, but slightly differing in structure & filling the same place in Nature, I must suspect they are only varieties [subspecies]," Darwin wrote in *Ornithological Notes*.

At the end of the block tenanted by the phoebe and the mockingbird, I crossed into Caltech. The campus grounds were attractive by conventional standards, with a wedding-cake auditorium flanked by a well-watered lawn and lotus ponds encased in concrete. I found the effect to be sterile, but unsightliness descended in earnest when I walked out of the mollycoddled campus and onto the roads of the city. The sooty California Boulevard heaved and bellowed under a wilderness of traffic and smelled like the remains of an oily apocalypse.

I learned to retreat into side streets but I had to eventually face the width of Lake Avenue, which was similarly bloated with traffic. I crossed swiftly, sidestepping the Jehovah's Witnesses or the Christian missionaries—both were equally shocked to learn about my status as a Hindu and shouted after me to reconsider. I sought refuge in Peet's, where I ordered a pot of Ti Kwan Yin (Iron Goddess of Mercy) tea, wanting the floral aroma to blot out the roomful of chattering strangers as I waited to dive miraculously through the portal of writing into a roomier, more expansive world.

Lake Avenue was flanked on one side by a hulking Macy's, a yogurt place, a taco place, and a Borders that later went out of business. On the other side of the screeching road, a store sold French tablecloths and soap dispensers, next door to a rotating cast of dimly lit restaurants. Any scrap of land that wasn't devoured by a parade of stores was determinedly paved over. Why are we always buying a barrelful of things? What I had experienced of festivals in India was the getting together of family and friends, loving, radiant faces amid the too-sweet sweets. But what I'd experienced of Christmas in North America was a getting of gifts. Things became a substitute for the sustenance of conversations and love. And here were these banal stores, marring the landscape, and unceasingly offering more things. I tried to imagine native plants growing in the last remaining smidgens of land that was otherwise embalmed in concrete but my imagination sputtered.

My thoughts were leafy green but all around me was the roar of a petrochemical civilization. The only relief came from gazing at the San Gabriel Mountains in the distance. The heart of the matter was that there was no place to get lost in.

III.

As a child when I had lived at the feet of the Himalayas, in the northeastern state of Assam, I loved to get lost in a bamboo grove after coming home from school. In the early evening, I often rustled through the bamboos to get to a friend's house. For an almost-seven-year-old, a forty-minute walk is not a wink, but the swaying stalks held me in a gentle embrace as I strolled in their midst. Time became elastic.

The numberless rings around the bamboo stalks were the eternity of minutes spread out before me. The wind whistled through the stalks, and I hummed a song the Italian nuns who ran my school had recently taught me:

He loves me too, He loves me too,
I know He loves me too.
Because He loves the little bird,
I know God loves me too.

I would visit my friend, a local Assamese girl older than me by a few years, with whom I was choreographing a dance performance, and then I would walk through the grove again on my way home to dinner. Fast-growing bamboo thrives in Assam's humid zones—the young shoots of this ancient grass are edible and the plant is useful in more ways than one. Today, the state of Assam grows some two-thirds of the bamboo used in India for construction. Mercifully, nothing was being constructed in the parts where I lived. I found concord among my bamboos such as I hadn't experienced before.

My walks reflected the pace of my life: unhurried (except on weekday mornings when I raced a couple of miles to catch my school bus), with room for stillness, even void. The delicate stalks bent in the wind but rarely snapped. Slender leaves haloed the stalks like luminous specks of green light. Later I wasn't surprised to learn that the green bamboo is seen as a sacred plant in India. The cowherd god Krishna plays tunes on a bamboo flute so enchanting that the *gopis*, the milkmaids, grow incoherent with love for him.

AT SEVEN, I had experienced oneness with the natural world. But so far when I had hiked in the Los Angeles area, in humdrum areas such as Runyon Canyon, that feeling of oneness had vaporized, indistinguishable from the smog. It was not possible to get lost in greenness in Pasadena. With the grating snore of traffic ever present in our apartment, we were soon walking farther away from the edges of Caltech in the evenings, turning down roads where the traffic might cease to chase us. So it was that we ambled into neighboring San Marino with its faux Greco-Roman mansions and pedicured gardens. The hedges weren't dusty here like the neglected ones girdling Caltech. This was an excursion in contrasts.

A law must have proclaimed that only mansions can be built in San Marino. Despite their pristine lawns, the colossal structures appeared oddly uninhabited, even spectral.

Set back from the road, many loomed behind tall gates. One house displayed door-sized signs in bold red—one placed against a tree in the front yard and another above a first-floor window—blaring the name of its security system. We almost never saw anyone, except once when a man walked out to the curb in his bare feet to throw away some leaf litter.

One evening while walking along the Wonderland-like roads in San Marino, I glimpsed an exquisite crested bird and, before I could blink, I saw another. Was I dreaming? Then as though a curtain parted, half a dozen whimsical crested birds materialized in the glossy, deciduous trees fronting a gated mansion. What birds were these? The answer had to be teased out of my mind. The threads did not loosen until I recalled that these were in a class of fantasy birds from my Indian childhood. I had once been fond of what in the West might be thought of as exotic birds, such as mynahs, bulbuls, and talking parrots. When I was seventeen, my father was posted as a diplomat from Delhi to Toronto; right before the big move, my desire was to acquire a mynah, which I aimed to take with me, past the astonished eyes of immigration officials, to my new Canadian home. There I would teach the bird to talk with my posse of new friends. This awkward teenage dream suffered a silent death.

The dream reminded me, however, that I had imagined I would find community with relative ease in Canada. I had naively thought that a mynah would magnetize new friends. My father's government job had caused us to move every two or three years throughout my childhood. I grew habituated to walking out of one circle and eventually entering another. Reserved by temperament, I didn't go out of my way to make friends but I reliably found some warm acquaintances and a close friendship or two wherever I lived. The move to Canada was different: we were leaving our country. I didn't know then, and didn't believe it when a friend told me so, that I was leaving India for good.

As I gazed at the San Marino birds feeding on berries, I might have been gazing at revenants from my past; forgotten yearnings ricocheted through me. The birds had clean white breasts and walnut-brown backs and were gaily decked up with a red half-moon on each ear and vermilion daubed on their undertail coverts. Their crests were dark, spiky, mohawk-like. I had chanced upon a rare flock of red-whiskered bulbuls, *Pycnonotus jocosus*, originally from eastern India, from the Old World family *Pycnonotidae*. The naturalist Kenn Kaufman writes that these birds escaped from an aviary in the Miami area in 1960, and that they subsequently settled in Florida. He doesn't mention a flock in San Marino, but here were the birds, flying demurely before my eyes. Evidently, the bulbuls appreciated the moderate climate here and the amply watered San Marino trees and scrub that produced berries and other small fruits. There was also abundant shrubbery here to host insects, which the bulbuls could fly-catch or glean from tree bark.

I would later learn that this tiny population of songbirds is not only gorgeous, but also heroic: they have survived California State and Los Angeles County agents hunting them down for years with pellet guns. In a 1985 article in the *Los Angeles Times*, state and county agents admitted that for some twenty years, they "had been shooting to kill [bulbuls] on government orders." Introduced species like bulbuls compete with native species and the consequences can be dire in sensitive areas such as in the Hawaiian Islands. Fruit eaters, bulbuls are also believed to be potential distributors of so-called noxious weed seeds, such as jujube and privet trees—so they're seen as a threat to agriculture. Incensed about the killing of bulbuls during the 1980s, Huntington director Robert Middlekauff asked the state to "produce evidence of the bulbuls' destructiveness" before allowing their eradication to continue. It turns out that bulbuls have not conclusively been shown to negatively impact the suburban environments they settle in, and even in Florida, the amount of fruit (papayas and mangoes) they eat is not significant. The *Los Angeles Times* quoted Middlekauff as saying, "They haven't provided evidence, and I certainly don't want people walking around with guns."

In the face of violent antagonism from Los Angeles County agents, I saw the bulbuls as an embodiment of the fifth *rasa, veera,* which, as Ravi Shankar writes, "expresses the sentiment of heroism, bravery, majesty and glory, grandeur and a dignified kind of excitement." The majestic bulbuls also carried within them a quality typical of fruit-eating birds—the languidness of summers in India.

The feeling of isolation that had nagged me in Santa Cruz had not left me in Pasadena. I might have been an albatross, albeit with a mate, flying over a cold, indifferent ocean. Life in the city, what I saw of it, felt dreary. Connections between people, as I lived through them, were fragile and brittle. While I had tasted friendship, and on occasion got together with other filmmakers, I experienced around me little in the way of a community and none of the satisfactions of a rich community life. I saw bone-dry, bone-white people, like skeletons rushing about, scarcely stopping even to exchange two words.

Strangely, the bulbuls reconnected me to a strain of life that I had been thirsting for. It struck me that at Sequoia National Park, it was the western tanager's *rasa*, its indefinable, melodious charm, that I had responded to. The encounter with the tanager may have been as gossamer and fleeting as a water strider's dance but it had also been as soulful as Ravi Shankar's music. As for the bulbuls, they hailed from the very birthplace of *rasa*. That *rasa* can be found in nature was something I had intuited early on, as a four-year-old gazing daily at snowy Himalayan peaks topped off with foamy-white clouds that quivered with life as I hiked up to my school in the hill station of Kasauli. Kālidāsa, the "Indian Shakespeare," wrote an epic poem, *Meghadūta*, about a cloud who acts as a messenger between a couple separated by unfortunate circumstances. Seeing an attractive cloud resting atop a mountain peak, the male protagonist reflects: "The heart of even a happily-situated man is perturbed at the sight of a cloud; what to say then when the person is longing for an embrace of his beloved!" Kālidāsa was invoking the first *rasa, shringara*. Ravi Shankar describes it as a "sentiment filled with longing for an absent lover. It contains both the physical and the mental aspects of love and is sometimes known as *adi* (original) *rasa,* because it represents the universal creative force."

The twelfth-century love poem Gītagovinda by Jayadeva has some of the most buoyant descriptions of the natural world that I have read: springtime forests hum with crying cuckoos mating on mango shoots, a backdrop for the earthly passion between Radha and Krishna, who loves to tease, all of which is a stand-in for our love of the divine.

The bulbuls animated what I had previously seen as a stodgy, affluent neighborhood and they also infused a strain of *rasa* in my life. The flock was a lighthouse; it suggested a spiritual embrace. A bird I had once only dreamed about had now abruptly materialized before my eyes, in what had otherwise felt like a burning desert. Could the bulbuls lead me back to the enchanting green I had traipsed through in my land of bamboos and to the intimacy with nature that I had since lost?

IV.

In the weeks to come, we strode yet farther through the San Marino neighborhood until one day we reached a park whose existence we hadn't known about. The first time we tried to enter Lacy Park, we were turned back. We had wandered out for a Sunday morning walk that went on lengthening, not thinking to carry money with us, but there was an admission fee to enter this public park. I expect this was a way to ensure that only the tony inhabitants of mansions strolled here, untroubled by unsightly outsiders. I telephoned the next day to lodge a protest about being charged a fee to walk through a public park, but I was told that the decision was made by the San Marino City Council and no exceptions would be made.

The next time, we took cash with us and were let into Lacy Park.

First we wandered among the local plants and were delighted to see red-crowned parrots, *Amazona viridigenalis*, perched on a bare tree. This vibrant bird, listed as being endangered on the IUCN (International Union for Conservation of Nature) Red List, is a native of Mexico and is imperiled due to the pet trade and habitat destruction. Soon we discovered that there were significant numbers of plants here from around the world. To my astonishment, I found myself walking under the arches of several deodar cedars, *Cedrus deodara*, from my birthplace in remote northeastern India. We might have been in a thicket in the Himalayas. Growing straight and tall, deodars have an exalted air, like heroes with arms outstretched but also slightly, humbly lowered. Their branches form distinct and well-separated layers, each silver-blue canopy reaching toward the arms of neighboring deodars.

These sacred trees, revered in Indian epics and traditionally a sanctuary for meditating sages, had surprisingly formed a community in emotionally frigid San Marino. The silver-blue needles from two deodars above us mingled in one another's vicinity and lifting our arms we took hold of a branch in order to peer at the needles, which were thin, long, and pointy, like the needles of a pine, though glaucous in color. We wondered why these trees are grouped as cedars. The foliage of North American cedars is utterly unlike the deodars'—it is braided, waxy, and flat.

IN THE MONTHS to come, I began to hike and bird voraciously. In wild areas such as the San Gabriel Mountains, Leo Carrillo State Park, Malibu Creek State Park, and Point

Mugu State Park, I discovered a constellation of trails where one could roam for hours and leave Los Angeles behind. On the Fourth of July, I had meant to watch a parade in Pacific Palisades, but instead I spent the afternoon in Malibu Creek State Park, utterly absorbed and heartbroken as I watched a snake slither into the nest of a Pacific-slope flycatcher, *Empidonax difficilis*, and consume a chick while its parent squawked futilely to save it.

It was here that I encountered other hidden populations of exotic birds. One evening, as I hiked in Malibu Creek State Park, a dozen monk parakeets, *Myiopsitta monachus*, flew past me like magical paper airplanes. Their chartreuse green recalled my bamboos. It felt as though I were not in Malibu but in their native South America. I was transfixed with awe while the parakeets cut through the air above me and sailed past a canopy of deciduous trees. Birds became a portal to a more vivid, enchanted world.

Birds allowed me once again to relish solitude in the way I had as a child. Since my Assam years, the wondrous embrace I had once experienced with nature had shriveled to an echo, a ghost of something lost. "You are a child of the universe," the poet Max Ehrmann tells us in "Desiderata," "no less than the trees and the stars; you have a right to be here." I had intuited this idea in my terraced garden in Assam, then lost this communion with nature in America. Seeing the transplanted bulbuls and the deodars seemingly at home in California was like seeing a dotted line that might one day lead me to a more living, breathing, wholly alive place.

V.

Early one morning, the phone rang shrilly. I sat up on my sleeping bag, covered with a white sheet embroidered with flowers. It was the co-director of the Telluride Film Festival. "We're doing a homage to the work of director Stan Brakhage this year," he said. "My wife and I simply loved your documentary. It's in keeping with Brakhage's experimental spirit."

Sitting on the hard floor of my bedroom, I gasped. I had sent the festival my film *The Song of the Little Road*, an exploration of how Ray's oeuvre is rooted in the Indian culture while also transcending culture and time so that his films are able to move us at the deepest levels. But I hadn't heard back from the festival for some months and I'd given up hope. My film would be screened at Telluride! I had toiled alone, and with a small crew of two editors, three cinematographers, and a sound designer for what felt like years. During sunbaked hikes in the nearby Eaton Canyon I had wondered whether I would ever be able to marshal together the resources needed to complete my film. And now it would premiere at an iconic festival.

In August I found myself in Telluride, Colorado, partying with birds of a different order: the actors Maggie Gyllenhaal and Mark Ruffalo. The latter told me that when one young woman exhorted him, "Come on, there's a party going on!" he responded, "There's always a party going on." The incessant socializing, introductions to famous filmmakers like Werner Herzog, and watching multiple films every day was all oddly unsatisfying. Snowcapped mountains with ribbons of trail gleamed enticingly, but I had meetings to attend with potential distributors, all of whom admired my documentary but were spooked by its originality and its daring experimental use of still photographs. I had poured myself into the dream of becoming a writer and a filmmaker, but even after Telluride, there was to be no clear path forward.

It was only when I returned home to the San Marino bulbuls that my face lit up and *rasa* once again dusted me with her golden wing.

I joined a local Audubon Society and began to go to as many birding expeditions as I could fit into our weekends. A trip to a remote state penitentiary to look for parrots? Sure. Drive a couple of hours to hike a mountain in the hope that we'll see a green-tailed towhee? Count me in.

In October, my documentary got a Los Angeles premiere at the American Cinemathèque, where it showed for three days to sizable crowds. But I was growing keenly aware that my artistic self was languishing here, that for each yes that I heard, a hundred noes reliably followed. My feature scripts had won numerous awards, but older white producers balked at letting me direct the stories I had written. When someone did take me on, they were either a novice or a retiree and were unable to secure the significant budget needed to make a feature. A master's degree from the so-called top film school didn't really matter if you weren't one of the boys. Graduating at the top of my class didn't matter either. Being an outsider and telling stories outside of the cultural norm were deal breakers. When I was birding, these muddled, twisted considerations dissolved along with the haze that hovered over trafficky roads. I saw only the birds and their *rasa*, the deodars and their welcoming arches, not the doors that were repeatedly shut on me.

AFTER A FEW weekends of birding continuously, often in fragmented bird habitats, I began to think about the challenges that birds faced. On the hour-long drives north of Los Angeles, while carpooling with other birders, I noticed sizable new developments mushrooming seemingly in the middle of nowhere. I pointed these out, hoping to draw my fellow birders into a discussion about how bird habitat was being decimated. I seldom drew more than inaudible murmurs, even when we went to see a burrowing owl, who peered at us anxiously from the sole undeveloped lot in a newly constructed suburb.

It felt obvious to me that bird habitats are key to maintaining healthy populations, which is only in the interest of birders. For instance, land that is overgrazed in Carrizo Plain National Monument does not magically convert back to grassland when the grazing stops. It turns instead to scrubland. Not just the long-billed curlew, but also the endangered aplomado falcon, *Falco femoralis*, relies on thriving grasslands. To my surprise, however, many of the birders around me, even Audubon board members, were so hungrily focused on their bird lists that I couldn't engage them in a conversation about the fate of Carrizo Plain, where they annually led bird-watching trips. While they were sympathetic to the problem of shrinking bird habitat, they avoided confronting the tragic situation and for the most part remained unresponsive when I brought it up. How is it that we can love birds and obsess over our bird lists, I sometimes wondered, and not be attentive to how bird habitats all around us are being fragmented or overgrazed or paved over with concrete?

THE PROBLEM OF habitat being paved over arrived unexpectedly at my doorstep. A pregnant opossum, *Didelphis marsupialis*, an animal with two (*di*) wombs (*delphus*) in ancient Greek and with a conical nose smudged pink at the tip, lived next door in the old tenantless house, and she regularly visited the apartment complex we lived in. The opossum's common name originates from a Proto-Algonquian word that means "white dog." One evening, a renter's dog spotted the opossum in our complex and chased her back aggressively. In her pregnant state, the dark-lipped opossum grew defensive and a vicious fight ensued, in which she mauled the dog. With my camera, I documented the aftermath of this bloody altercation. The dog was sent to a vet to get expensively stitched up and he returned with a cone, like a satellite dish, around his neck. The dog's owner complained about her three-thousand-dollar bill and about the apartment manager's bird feeder on the third floor, which spilled seeds onto the ground level outside her front door, attracting squirrels and opossums.

I interviewed Mickey Long, an ornithologist and director of the nearby Eaton Canyon Nature Center, who had a different take on the incident. He explained that opossums are wild animals who are with us to stay. It's usually they who are shaken up by dogs, not the other way around. Long pointed out why opossums are singular animals: they are marsupials with a prehensile tail and fifty teeth, and with more canines than we might expect to see; in the fossil record, the ancestor of the marsupials we admire today, such as kangaroos, wallabies, and koala bears, resembles the modern-day opossum. Like the bulbul, the opossum is an introduced animal in Los

Angeles—it does wander through wild areas, but its preferred habitat is the urban jungle.

One day I came home to see men with huge chain saws moving toward the bauhinia tree next door, where I'd had many memorable bird sightings. Were they going to cut down the ancient tree? I swiftly researched on the city's website and raced over to one of the men who had pulled out a chain saw.

"The bauhinia is a protected species," I told him.

He stared at me as though to ask, "What's your point?"

"You need a permit to cut it," I explained.

The men shrugged and strolled over to their boss who sat in the shade of a jeep. The man I had spoken to returned with a tattered old permit and handed it to me. I studied it. It was an expired permit to cut down a bay tree. I pointed this out, and soon all three men screeched away in the jeep.

Inevitably, they returned. Over the summer, Michael and I took a few days off to hike in British Columbia. When we returned home, I saw that both the maternal trees I had loved dearly—the bauhinia and the bay—were gone. Not only the trees, but the structures and the entire site had been razed. The opossum who was due to give birth any day had fled, never to be seen again.

The opossum had been thrust out of its sanctuary, now an ugly stretch of dirt with a bulldozer digging a vast trench in it, with no obvious place to retreat even while it was pregnant; its plight made a strong impression on me.

I edited the footage I had shot of the opossum and the dog into a short documentary—the film premiered at a festival in France, while no one seemed interested in it in

America—and the process made me think deeply about how bird and butterfly habitats were also daily being paved over. The black phoebe and the northern mockingbird had lost the towering bauhinia and bay trees and the surrounding shrubs, vines, and tall grasses (that shelter the insects the birds eat) as much as the opossum had. Whereas scientists had previously thought that declining bird populations in America were spurred by deforestation in Mexico and Central America, they now know that the dramatic declines we are witnessing in bird numbers have as much to do with the disruption of breeding sites right here at home. In addition to forestland, pockets of suburban habitat also provide critical rest stops for migrating songbirds and nesting sites for year-round residents. Conversely, razing down what trees remain in suburbia is like snatching away the last refuges of severely stressed birds: I observed this process unfold outside my window, where birds no longer came and their liquid song was replaced by the pounding of a sledgehammer.

4

A FLICKER OF LIGHT

I.

With its clean, freshly colored lines, the red-shafted flicker is a cartoon sprung to life. As if an endearing black bib and dark polka dots on a creamy underside weren't enough, the males also sport a rust-colored cap and a malar stripe or "mustache." In Arroyo Seco Canyon ("dry gulch" in Spanish), to the west of Pasadena, leafy deciduous boughs filter the harsh sun and give refuge to the red-shafted flicker—a subspecies of the northern flicker, *Colaptes auratus*. Here, as flickers drummed rhythmically on tree trunks, proclaiming their territory or calling out to kin, I might have been listening to the drumbeat of the Earth. In birding, there is a forgetting, a coming out of oneself, while paradoxically also a going deeper into oneself. Standing in a leafy canyon, waiting in green silence for a bird to appear, my mind hushes to a whisper.

I had first seen flickers flying high above in the desert section of the Huntington Library gardens in San Marino where we strolled regularly. I had been denied access to the research library, but no PhD was needed to walk on the grounds. At Huntington, the flock of red-whiskered bulbuls reappeared. In the hazy afternoon light, I watched the birds perch gracefully on palms and flutter through the desert garden. We stood among the barrel cacti, listening to their virtuoso cadenzas. One afternoon, two yellow-chevroned parakeets nearly collided with a clownish acorn woodpecker, who, shaken by the near miss, promptly dropped what it was holding in its mouth. I wasn't sure how I had missed all this activity before. I had strolled here a couple of times as a USC graduate student, but all I remembered from that time was a mass of agaves and barrel cacti and jumping out of the path of a lizard or two. Before I might have seen a palm tree, but now I noticed a mourning dove sheltered in its branches, and around the corner a mockingbird whistled from a flowering aloe, and from the tip of an agave shimmered the throat gorget of an Allen's hummingbird. One late October afternoon, a pair of red-shafted flickers flew repeatedly between two tall and distant pines and Michael noted that their reddish-orange wings glowed like flags in the afternoon sun.

The third largest woodpecker in North America, the flicker is a member of the Colaptini tribe of woodpeckers. The flicker isn't all outward, dressy flair; the real astonishment is the bird's courtship dance in which the male and female lavish each other with rhythmic, endearing head moves. The joie de vivre of these charming dandies and their laughing, *kiyi*-ing mews mingled in my dreams. One night I didn't sleep at all; uncharacteristically, I lay in the dark, thinking through the night until darkness began to lift. With the first light of morning, I sprang up and wrote a story that came out whole. I wrote *The Flicker's Dance* in a continuous fever; the screenplay tells the story of a terminally ill boy whose love for birds, especially for flickers, unexpectedly transforms the three adults in his life. When I finished writing, I realized with some shock that flickers had glided into my artistic life.

A few months later, the script won the Panavision New

Filmmaker Grant and I wondered if I might get this one made. A casting director sent the script to choice talent—the actor Julie Delpy read it on a flight from Paris to Los Angeles and, when the plane landed, she called her agent to say that she was interested. The actor Joe Mantegna wanted to play the father and invited me to a lovely meet and greet at his home. A stellar cast was put together, but it was a struggle to get a reliable producer who could get the film financed. In the meantime, I kept a watch for flickers in the mountains—though these charismatic birds inhabit the suburbs too, when some semblance of their preferred woodland habitat is left intact. I found them foraging on the ground for ants, pecking insects or larvae from bark crevices, or excavating a cavity in a snag.

One morning, Michael and I drove up to the San Gabriel Mountains in the Angeles National Forest and parked our Honda just off Highway 2. An exposed gravel path led to a canyon below; the sun was beating down on the south-facing pass, so we didn't want to linger. Nonetheless, I stopped abruptly. In a snag before us, a sizable cavity had been excavated, and a female flicker was perched beside it, feeding the three chicks huddled inside. All at once, I didn't care how hot I was. To be able to witness the domestic lives of flickers—the weak squeaks of the chicks and the mother trying to divide caterpillars among them—transcended any other consideration.

Eventually we hiked down to the canyon and to the white ribbon of stream running through it. I kept thinking about the flickers but when we hiked back up to the snag, the female was nowhere in sight and in the blinding light the chicks could no longer be seen in the cavity. It was as though earlier in the morning I had seen colors swirling in a kaleidoscope but now I saw only a black box.

WHETHER THEY KNOW it or not, flickers are generous birds. Later, other species of birds or reptiles nest in the cavities that flickers make. For this reason flickers are said to play a "central role in the ecology of woodland communities," with researchers such as K. Martin and colleagues now recognizing them as "keystone excavators that may influence the abundance of secondary cavity-nestering species in forest systems."

The North American Breeding Bird Survey notes, however, that flickers are declining in abundance across North America; a woodland species, they are sensitive to habitat loss. I began to admire flickers not only for their whimsical beauty, but also for the woodlands they drew me into. As the Cornell Lab of Ornithology notes, the flicker "is clearly a species of open woodlands, savannas, farmland with tree rows, and forest edges." While I observed flickers carving cavities in tree trunks or making music with staccato drumbeats, I came to recognize that I was also falling in love with trees.

THAT SUMMER WE drove up to Northern California where we hiked through some old-growth redwood forests. On the aptly named Revelation Trail in the Prairie Creek Redwoods State Park, we saw an unforgettable redwood. Two-thirds of the way up the immense, cinnamon-colored trunk, several branches were the size of whole redwood trees themselves. An entire forest existed palpably in the massive maternal redwood. With new trees that had branched out and grown from its womb, the parent redwood proudly wore a forest in its crown! Why don't we let our trees grow old enough to show us such heart-opening magic?

In this old-growth forest also grew tanbark oaks, identified by standing under them and looking up to see the veins on their leaves. Maple trees with gigantic leaves, larger than your outstretched hand. A western hemlock growing out of a fallen redwood, its roots wrapped around the log, giving the tree the appearance of an octopus, hence the name octopus hemlock. The tang of a California bay laurel, also called the California bay or *Umbellularia californica*, its leaves long and elliptical and familiar, used medicinally by Indigenous tribes and reminiscent of Mediterranean bay leaves used in Indian cooking. This was the leafy hardwood tree I had mourned at home, in addition to the bauhinia whose antioxidant-rich buds are stir-fried in India.

A couple of nights later, at Lassen Volcanic National Park, we cooked tomato soup for dinner on a propane burner; while chopping wood, Michael chipped our new hand ax on a stone but we lit a crackling fire anyway. As we were pitching our tent, some movement in an adjacent fir caught Michael's attention: a white-headed woodpecker, *Dryobates albolarvatus*, just above eye level. A member of the Campetherini tribe of small to midsize woodpeckers, this voracious eater of pine seeds frequents pine forests and rarely lives at higher elevations, among firs. "To eat large pine seeds, the woodpecker wedges them into a crevice in the bark of the tree," the Cornell Lab tells us, "where it hammers the seed to break it apart." I had never seen a white-headed woodpecker this close before. Dressed in a black cloak, its white-feathered head stood out. A prominent royal-red crown on the back of its head signaled that it was a male. It jabbed at the tree bark, then climbed and fluttered higher up the tree before disappearing into a grove of firs beyond.

Morning brought not the woodpeckers' drumming but the scolding calls of Steller's jays, *Cyanocitta stelleri*, and the tinny tooting of distant red-breasted nuthatches, *Sitta canadensis*. The eager toot of this little nuthatch is a joy to hear. Often one nuthatch is joined by another, then a few more, spurring a musical conversation. A brown creeper punctuated this conversation by adding *soo-Susie-soo*. Two white-headed woodpeckers inspected one of the young white firs that ringed our campsite. The birds' brilliant white heads stood out sharply against the burnt sienna bark; they reminded me of Trinity College deans in black flowing robes. We walked over to two almond-colored Jeffrey pines, bark fragmented like pieces of a jigsaw puzzle.

"They're like the plates of a stegosaurus," Michael said. He sniffed the bark and thought it smelled like sweet butterscotch.

I stepped closer, inched my nose to the bark, and inhaled. "Pineapple," I said. Curiously, the Jeffrey pines in Southern California smell like vanilla.

Seeing this commune of fragrant trees and the brilliant woodpeckers they supported, I reflected on how in the places where we live now there's almost no chance of getting lost in a grove of mature trees. Old-growth trees are like pages of an ancient manuscript; when they are sawed down, it's as though an earth-story is erased. The worn manuscript we have inherited is already riddled with lacunae. Must we go on ripping more pages out?

II.

My life was too modest and work-filled to travel exclusively to see birds. But when Michael was asked to visit Rutgers University, we flew there together and took an autumn weekend to revel in the Cape May Bird Observatory in New Jersey, a couple hours' drive away. Near the lighthouse, we walked into a grove of trees and each time we turned around we found ourselves staring at a yellow-shafted flicker. Something was going on. A subspecies of the red-shafted (they interbreed where ranges overlap), the yellow-shafted comprise the northern and eastern populations of flickers who are migratory, unlike the red-shafted in the western United States, who are year-round residents.

Very early the next morning, we drove to Higbee Beach. Getting out of the car, Michael said, "Oh, look, a flicker."

A yellow-shafted flicker was perched on the limb of a bare tree. Having seen several flickers during the previous day's visit to Cape May, we had been wondering if we would see more. At Higbee Beach, the air was fairly popping with yellow-shafted flickers. For almost an hour, flickers shot by, traveling in bursts of about fifty yards. At any given moment during this flicker-filled hour, there were approximately ten flickers in our field of view. This was the big flight—autumnal winds reliably funnel these migrating birds to the state's southern tip, and now we would witness their liftoff as they resumed their epic journeys.

At 7:20 in the morning, a skein of Canada geese, *Branta canadensis*, with graceful black necks and ivory chinstraps, struggled up into the sky. Large numbers of passerines—songbirds—were flying from bush to bush, and the flickers flew from tree to tree, while the Canada geese flew higher overhead. The wind was pelting all these birds, and the eddying gusts made it particularly challenging for the geese to take off. When the birds rose as individuals they became separated from one another and had great difficulty against the gusting wind. Coming together in groups of five or ten, they were still battered by the gales. After merging at last into groups of twenty, fifty, then over a hundred, the skein regained control. Over five skeins, each with over a hundred birds in a characteristic *V* formation, flew away into the violet-gray distance. The geese were migrating south, and the songbirds and the yellow-shafted flickers tailed the skein like colorful streamers. Our hikes seemed inconsequential compared to their grand adventure.

And yet, soon we, too, found ourselves migrating. Michael was offered a temporary position at Rutgers. In Manhattan, I met an experienced producer who took on *The Flicker's Dance* script. The trade newspaper *Variety* announced that a studio led by an Oscar-winning producer would finance the film.

Manhattan offered even more concrete than Pasadena, but daily excursions into the depths of Central Park kept me breathing. I wanted to bring to life experiences in the natural world that I'd left behind in California so I began to work on a new novel, set in the world of birding. I would take long walks through Central Park, where I was surprised to find a ficus tree with heart-shaped leaves, the same tree under which the Buddha is said to have achieved enlightenment. I pondered the relationships between the birders in my novel, many of whom raced about to see as many bird species as they could, leaving only one woman to think about conserving habitat, while I meandered into the wilder parts of the park, where I might spot a delightful common yellowthroat or a reclusive black-throated blue warbler or a trilling northern parula. Central Park became an indispensable part of my life in the city and it is linked in my mind with heart-opening ficus trees and jewel-like birds who helped me sort the threads of what it means to be a birder and what it can mean to love birds.

III.

A year later, in what we hoped would be a final move, we migrated to Santa Fe and, at the same time, I traveled to an international film market in South Korea where I was invited to showcase the script of *The Flicker's Dance*. In a hotel on the seashore of Busan, I met producers from all over the world and, after my return, the project became real: contracts were signed, lawyers engaged, the film was being cast, and a team of producers finalized plans to rent a production office on the East Coast.

Then the 2008 economic crash came, and the project fell apart, collapsing to the ground with astonishing speed. What had been something, what I had thrown myself into and seen unfurl into a sure thing, once again folded into nothing. These are the constant ups and downs of the material world that the Buddha saw through, and why he rejected the mind's "fermentations," its small and large sorrows, and why he sought instead the shade of a ficus tree. There wasn't much shade available in the Southwest desert I found myself in, but the flickers stuck by me anyway. Once I settled into Santa Fe, they never again left my side.

IN NEW MEXICO even the winters are sun-drenched and if you plant enough native grasses, yards turn a grassy gold in October with a few perennial sunflowers still blazing yellow before the cold November winds hush them into wintry sleep. One winter morning, I stood at my kitchen window and watched a red-shafted flicker atop a telephone pole, nodding its head with a bouncy move; its mate responded with a similar bouncing head move.

"This is the closest I'll come to seeing flickers dance," I thought.

The pair of flickers wasn't done. They slid down the pole and began to revolve around it in a fluid rhythmic motion while staying more or less on opposite sides. Were they playing or teasing? Their melodic mewing scented the air. No debutantes, these. They were enacting the dance of a married couple—and flickers are believed to mate for life. *Hasya*, the second *rasa*, is also known as the comic sentiment. "It can be shown through syncopated rhythmic patterns or an interplay of melody and rhythm between singer and accompanist, or between sitarist and tabla player," writes Ravi Shankar, "causing amusement and laughter."

As I watched the recital with the flickers mimicking each other's moves, I felt my heart lighten. With an irreverence fitting to the comic sentiment, one of the flickers abruptly flew off to a neighboring pine and the other flapped away in the opposite direction and landed on a wire—for a well-deserved rest. I munched another bite of granola and marveled at their comic performance.

From my back porch I would gaze at a flicker's streaked back while its bill probed between stones in the arroyo, so close that on its slate-gray head I could see rufous shadowing around its upper eyes. Flickers slurp up ants with their tongues and are capable of eating hundreds and thousands of ants, who otherwise love to trickle into the house in summertime. Their ant-eating prowess is a reason to salute flickers, if for some reason their arresting beauty or their rendition of the *hasya rasa* fails to move you.

ONE AFTERNOON, MICHAEL heard some fluttering in our chimney. Soon after, a flicker emerged, sooty as hell, into the fireplace; its red mustache was still clean and etched sharply, but the polka dots on its shirtfront were devilishly soiled, like a fine dandy with ash thrown on it. We opened the grate and the bird tentatively walked out.

First the flicker flew to the large rectangular west window, then, confused, it retreated to the fireplace, after which it flew determinedly to the right, into the round window, against which its bill thunked, sustaining a wound that began to bleed.

Dazed, it flew about the living room and perched at last atop a pistachio-green rocking chair. Michael spoke gently to the bird and he pointed out the door that led to the porch and garden. Amazingly, this strategy worked. With its beady black eyes, the confused, bleeding bird considered Michael, then pulled itself together and made its way out the door and to the porch before fluttering haltingly into the garden.

I wondered how it cleaned itself up after. From a northern New Mexico cabin, I once saw a flicker bathing in a puddle created in a gravel road by a summer storm. I didn't recognize the flicker at first; its clean lines and dainty polka dots were blurred in the muddy water. It was such a delicious, anomalous puddle in the bone-dry area that two other birds waited their turn: a juvenile western bluebird, petite, with a flash of blue along its tail, and a stolid common robin. The flicker graciously concluded its business and hopped over to a nearby boulder to dry itself. Later that day I saw the freshly bathed flicker, polka dots gleaming impeccably in the evening light, scaling the trunk of a massive ponderosa pine. Though my experience in Santa Fe had shown me that flickers have adapted to suburban areas, in pockets and patches and slim corridors of trees, seeing the flicker against a ponderosa at a forest's edge reminded me of its preference for woodlands; habitat loss has become such a crippling problem that even a relatively common species such as the flicker is declining in numbers.

In order to indulge my love of walking among trees, I parked my car as far as possible from the café I frequented in Santa Fe. Soon I began to see a downy woodpecker, *Dryobates pubescens*, tapping on a massive pine tree on Garcia Street. The most diminutive woodpecker in North America, the downy sports a vermilion hat that gleams in sunlight; a milky bar runs along its dark back. Its small size allows it to search for insects in places other woodpeckers can't get to. Unlike the skittish flickers, the downy woodpecker is scarcely daunted by gawkers. Its breast hazy white, the bird would go on diligently pecking and drumming at the pine while I stood underneath and fragrant wood chips sprinkled on me like benedictions.

The downy woodpecker and its larger cousin, the hairy woodpecker, on occasion visited the prairie crabapple tree in my backyard or the Siberian elm tree down the street but I relished seeing the red-shafted flickers the most. One September morning, waking early to a cacophony, I headed straight to the porch. My eyes roved. Near the distant poles and wires were the usual suspects—mourning doves, robins, and jays. But closer to where I stood, beyond a mature piñon pine, I discovered two flickers bickering like an old married couple. Theirs was a substantial, sustained argument, which they presented to each other in guttural, ululating notes. I got so enmeshed in the intricacies of their argument that the bracing air no longer stung my bare arms. The flickers stood beyond the piñon pine where they had some privacy and they sure acted like they did. The matter came nearly to blows and the one who'd been in danger of being struck stepped back and flicked its wing in disgust. It occurred to me that they're called flickers because of how they swiftly wave or flick their wings when defending their stance or territory. I hoped that come spring, the pair would make up and dance their enticing head moves again. The guilty party, speechless, moved away as though it would part and began to climb up the dirt hillside to walk off its steam but the nearly injured one couldn't resist following and letting loose a fresh string of complaints. Things were at a dismal impasse when the pair judiciously took the only way out—they heaved themselves into the air and dispersed into its blueness. The very act of flying together seemed to bring about a momentary truce.

AFTER A PERIPATETIC early life, I wanted to put down some roots. I hiked out to see a 150-year-old cottonwood in a rare wetland south of Santa Fe—the 35-acre Lenora Curtin Wetland Preserve where birds and mammals suckle at a natural ciénega or marsh. The cottonwood tree began its life at a tilted angle but then it branched into three trunks—one straight, the second counterweight, and the third along the original tilted axis. The last trunk hewed almost parallel to the ground, until it at last heaved down to the earth for support, or to give up the ghost, but then, incredibly, it went on growing upward. Humility and longevity are braided in this tree but when I climb it up and down and sideways, I am surprised by how abrasive the bark is. I don't think my childhood was tilted downward like this tree's, it was unpretentious and upright. But for some cosmic reason, beginning in my late teens and early twenties, certain tragedies began to occur; the spiral of deaths and the barrenness I experienced in the years after made my life itself kneel to the earth. Sitting with this tree, I thought about how life doesn't have to end when it crashes to the ground, that an upward curve, a way of growing back up into the blue air, remains plausible. I wondered if after the serious setbacks that had been hurled my way, I could live a life that was as resilient and rooted as this cottonwood's. On one hand, New Mexico is "halfway across the country," as the entertainment lawyer who had represented me in Manhattan sullenly reminded me. On the other hand, I was befriending familiar and new birds here and the iridescent air and vast skies had a way of soothing the soul.

Farther up the trail, among the green-gold cottonwoods, two flickers weaved, their rufous wings winking in the glimmering autumn light. The dashing songbirds I had seen here just two weeks back, the Townsend's warbler and the common yellowthroat, had already left. Migration is an astounding phenomenon but it's also a joy to have year-round residents like the flickers. Next week a snowstorm is expected and the gilded leaves will drift en masse to the ground, but the flickers will go on flashing their reddish-orange flags and lighting up our New Mexico winters.

Sometimes it is glorious simply to stay.

5

THE FRUIT ORCHARD

The first casita we rented in Santa Fe was stuccoed the color of cinnamon. Next door to our casita was a permaculture nonprofit and a woman named Teresa was mostly the sole employee there; we developed a friendship, born out of running into each other. Knowing that I sang for a local band, Teresa urged me to go to Camp Mabina. An instrumentalist and a dancer, Teresa was a veteran of the weeklong music camp held each summer in tiny Madrid, an hour's drive away. So it was that one June evening, I found myself standing in a circle of vibrant African and American musicians. I inhaled the sweet scent of wild fennel blown in by the wind and considered the faceless moon before me. It was as if I'd walked into a new life, another reincarnation.

In the tourmaline night, a bonfire the color of golden corn crackled and blazed in the dry New Mexico air. Some eighty campers held hands around the fire. Each year, a family traveled from Taos Pueblo to bless this music fiesta in a fruit orchard. New Mexico has nineteen active pueblos and Taos Pueblo has been continuously inhabited for the past one thousand years; scientists believe that some of its present structures were built around 1400 CE.

This summer, Coral V., a young woman from Taos Pueblo, led the cleansing ceremony. Her baby was crying and someone stepped outside the circle to comfort her. I didn't know anything about babies then; I vaguely wanted to have them but was naive about what it would entail. Two men, Coral's uncle and cousin, began to drum. The uncle's face was creased like the trunk of a ponderosa pine, while the cousin was dark and unreadable. They hit an enormous ocher drum with their mallets and they chanted as though they sought to give us a taste of heaven.

Coral and her uncle walked the circle, blowing sage smoke toward each person. She wore a long hyacinth-white skirt; a turquoise belt with embossed crosses clasped her slender waist. I was struck by her poise, the loveliness of her face, and the dark sleek river of hair flowing down her back. Coral began to tell a story.

"When I was eighteen, I lost my brother, who was then twenty-two." Her voice choked and she paused. "A few days after this, my brother came to me in a dream. He said, 'Do you want to see what heaven is like?'"

The night sky shimmered above. Holding hands and breathing in the sweet, bracing sage, we listened.

"I said, 'Of course I do.' And through him, I felt for a moment what it's like to be in heaven. There were no palm trees or a castle in the sky. . . . It was a feeling of connectedness to everything: earth, sky, tree, people. That love is all we have and the most important thing we have." Her voice smudged again, she wiped a tear.

A feeling of connectedness. That love is all we have. Something seemed to move inside me, as though her words had repositioned an inner glacier and some jagged edge inexplicably began to melt. A large tear fell from each eye. My hands were clasped to others' hands on both sides, so the tears rolled freely. I was thinking of my father. And my older brother. Why had neither of them visited me in an illuminating dream? I had dreamed only of fires, that my old family home was on fire and I was running and running, arms outstretched, tugging everyone to safety.

Coral smiled to apologize for her tears and her face shone like the moon. A spiritual light shone through her beauty. A redhead, face brightly made up, now peered from the kitchen door, deciding whether to join the circle.

The circle accrued energy and began to move in a dance; each person shuffled a step at a time, clockwise, in beat to the drumming. I, too, began to dance, holding hands with Papa Moise, a founding musician of the camp. A short, wiry Congolese man with a graying stubble and intense eyes, Papa was a maestro composer and singer. He would teach me unforgettable Congolese songs that I sing to this day. Before us, the fire hissed gold and yellow, then it roared. Compact bundles of sage sticks were offered to the flames, which then sputtered fragrant blessings. I inhaled the smoke and wondered how my neighbor Teresa had intuited that I would want to be here. Coral had suffered but she had seemingly transcended her tragedy. She exuded such grace! Embraced by her words, the sage smoke, and the dancers, I felt nearer to my father. I hadn't come here for this purpose. I had come for Emmanuel's advanced guitar class. I was the lead singer for a local band and I wanted to be able to play the guitar well enough to accompany myself.

Coral's cousin picked up the pace of the drumming, then his father outdid him—a mischievous smile crinkling his ancient face. We danced and danced, as though we were entering the drumbeat of the Earth; we echoed the rhythmic drumming of flickers and the sublime dance of cranes.

"Indian dance is not a dance in the sense in which we use that term," Erna Fergusson writes in her classic book *Dancing Gods*. "It is a ceremonial, a symbolic representation, a prayer."

Smoked with sage, the circle leapt to life. We moved until our thighs ached, our spirits ascended, sweaty palms clutched one another, hips swayed, and the circle fused into one organism.

The Puebloans drummed and chanted. They sang: "O, I love you. You may marry sixteen times. I'll get you yet."

Everyone laughed. And the chanting grew heavenly again.

Something cathartic happened that night. After tears rolled freely out during the dance, I felt clearer and wide-open and strangely closer to the Ortiz Mountains that loomed before me in the smoky blue air. Once again I felt like a child of the universe, dancing in the green folds of the earth. The possibility of catharsis in dance was not new to me. In the remote parts of India where I had spent my childhood, chanting and dancing weren't exotic acts—they were joyously performed during festivals. At the age of seven, I began learning how to sing in the Indian classical tradition and the next year I performed my first solo dance in the town hall. Now, the primal importance of ancient traditions rose to the forefront of my being. My blood throbbed with life.

In the East Indian tradition, the ecstatic dancer Lord Shiva, framed by flames, dances blissfully during the creation of the universe and its inevitable dissolution. Writing of Shiva's cosmic dance, the metaphysician Ananda K. Coomaraswamy quotes the poet Tirumular:

The dancing foot, the sound of the tinkling bells,
The songs that are sung, and the various steps,
The forms assumed by our Master as He dances,
Discover these in your own heart, so shall your bonds
   be broken.

And so it was. The ritual dance broke the bonds that still separated me from the natural world.

ON A SUNDAY morning, I had driven forty minutes south of Santa Fe to the tiny town of Madrid, population two hundred, and followed signs for a horse hospital to find a dirt road that curved into a ranch. A hand-scrawled sign, MABINA, suggested that I was entering the music camp. I parked in the dirt lot. To the left, a dusty fruit orchard was dotted with a few tents. To the right, a dirt path lined with olive and honey locust trees led to a plaza around which squatted some dun-colored stucco structures.

The orchard was brightly dreamlike, like a Van Gogh painting. It was only ten but the sun blazed overhead. In jeans and a turquoise cowgirl shirt, I walked into a grove of peach and apple trees and picked a campground. The dirt was dry and crunched under my sandals. I began to pitch my tent but the wind picked up, the dirt eddied, and the green-and-orange nylon tent walls flapped, tore, and fluttered out of my hands. After half an hour of fumbling, with dirt blowing into my eyes, I finally laid the footprint on the ground, pitched my tent, and tackled the fly. Whichever way I tried, the fly would pirouette in the wind rather than go over the tent. I ran an aluminum pole through the fly but it got badly bent in a violent gust. Abruptly, I felt as uprooted, as wobbly, as the fly. I tried to focus. I knew I must stake the tent in this wind, but the stakes wouldn't drive into the hard-packed dirt and my hands were raw with hammering. In the end, with dirt in my mouth, I impatiently flung a sleeping bag and chair into the tent to hold it down and then I hurried to the front office.

A trail of blooming Russian olive trees and New Mexico honey locusts, swooshing in the wind, led past a sizable white dome and a dance auditorium before spilling into the plaza. A line of dove-gray smoke arose from the Ortiz Mountains. Brushfire. As I crossed the plaza, to my right was the large North Tent where two stand-up marimbas were set up. I stopped in front of the dining hall and was about to walk up the porch to register when some movement diverted my eye. A black-chinned hummingbird, *Archilochus alexandri*, its back a soft emerald green. With an electric thrum, the hummingbird buzzed over to a glorious catalpa tree with wide leaves and white, conical flower heads.

It had a nest here. The black-chinned hummingbird paused momentarily, almost landing on the nest; instead it hovered, whirring, its wings spectral. The bird had ingeniously woven vegetal matter with insect and spider webbing, which is said to give the natal cup an elasticity that allows it to expand with the growing chicks. Two gray-brown heads poked out, smidgens of life, and two little bills opened. In this species only the female incubates the eggs and feeds the chicks. Using its long bill, the hummingbird fed its babies with the same frenetic energy with which it sips from flowers.

I stood less than ten feet away and marveled at how low the nest was, how exposed to danger from the accidental fling of an arm of a passing musician. I felt a wild desire to show the nest to someone—say, my father. I saw him smile as though he were looking at me. But then I noticed that a stranger was eyeing me with a bemused look.

"It sets up a nest here every year," the man said.

I nodded. A diligent migrant, the black-chinned hummingbird decamps for Mexico in the winter and this particular bird apparently returned to this area each spring. Musicians walked in and out of the porch to the dining hall, where registration was ongoing. After I had registered, I ran into a woman hawking the camp T-shirt—bloodred, with the silhouette of a female drummer. I bought it—it was a badge of belonging here. I felt vulnerable, like the hummingbird.

I walked back to the plaza and stood outside, watching women dance to live drumming in the auditorium. Wrapped in the pulse of music, I felt one with the hummingbird's thrumming. I saw it flit from one flower to the next, indulging full throttle its frenetic speed. The very air shimmered iridescent green; the bird could swing like a pendulum, hover and glide, whir and dart, or even fly backward. All this beauty of color, form, and spirit is concentrated in one of our tiniest birds. Hummingbirds famously have a high heartbeat, of more than five hundred beats per minute. As humans, we can't abide that pace; we also need to settle into our souls. That is what I would soon find myself doing in the evenings around the campfire.

IT WAS THE sort of windy day when one wonders how plants remain rooted. By the time I returned to my campsite in the early evening, my tent had vanished. Would someone actually steal a tent? After feeling puzzled and searching everywhere, I located the windblown contraption upside down in a corner of the orchard. I began to set up the tent again, feeling disoriented and tumbled about and emptied out in the way that I suppose one must be before the mind and body can receive a new insight. A woman passing by gave me a hand— she told me that she had no home and had all but lived her life in tents. Later, it rained so hard, another woman advised me to dig a trench around my tent. In the deepening dark, as the rain glistened like glass shards, everyone huddled in the dance auditorium to hear Papa Moise give his orientation speech. In a bracing manner, he spoke about what it means to be a community. I strained to listen. He wasn't always able to articulate his thoughts in the precise way he wanted to, and long pauses punctuated his sentences, until one or two of his advanced students nudged them into completion.

"We don't just bring this music to you from the street and give it to you," Papa said. "We live music, we eat music, we breathe music, we piss music."

It was Papa's habit to utter a few sentences and follow with a "say yeah, yeah!"

The crowd responded, "Yeah! Yeah!"

If he wasn't satisfied with the volume of the response, the cry was repeated.

The ritual of a nightly campfire got started on the second night. A few young people attended the camp without paying a fee and it was their lot to cart in the firewood. The sky was streaked with purple and slate gray and the last slivers of light vanished. "We take care of them," Papa said, referring to the young people doing chores. "We take care of each other."

I happened to be sitting across from Papa and I noted the striking look (haunted? distracted?) in his eyes. This was *mbongi* night and, as the campfire blazed, he spoke to us about traditions in African villages. I felt myself being pulled into the rhythm and mood of camp life. He explained that his "yeah, yeah" cry was in keeping with the call-and-response structure of Zimbabwean and Congolese songs. Papa told us that Africans could sing all night long, depending on the mood of the singer. Papa's philosophical treatises could also go on all night but in deference to his American audience, he had learned to clip his talks.

While describing all-night singing sessions, Papa said that mourning can be a three-week-long, all-night, joyous series of ceremonies in Congo. "Everyone comes, the entire village is there, we drink, we feast, we remember fondly the departed soul . . . and then we play music and we dance."

A three-week joyous ceremony? I had only experienced mourning as a somber, silent loss. In the days shortly after my father's death, I would abruptly burst into tears while driving. Perhaps there is some sense in scaffolding grief in a series of rituals or else it can be suppressed for years. I had involuntarily swallowed my pain and had tried to carry on—it was one way to keep breathing. As a graduate student, I'd had no choice; I knew my father wouldn't have wanted me to drop out. But had I mourned my father properly? I had quietly suffered his absence for years. Now my heart demurred. You rarely look at your own deepest sorrow.

In *Spirit in the Stone*, Mark Bahti writes that the hummingbird led the Apache into the upper worlds and was a messenger between the Apache and various supernatural beings. A whirring hummingbird is the epitome of an angelic, ethereal being, one adept at sundering the worldly veil. I rarely see a hummingbird sit still for extended periods. In those elusive moments, I have been able to appreciate the fanlike tail, rimmed with white, of a broad-tailed hummingbird, *Selasphorus platycercus*—the sun bird of the Acoma Puebloans—perched on brush while I hiked along the Jemez River, or the fragility of a gossamer Anna's hummingbird, *Calypte anna*, whom I held in my hand while researchers banded it at the Audubon Kern River Preserve in California.

In the buttery, flickering light of the fire, the bluish-purple lines of the Ortiz Mountains were faintly visible. Being at camp felt different from the life I had lived so far in North America, where I had experienced brittle connections, erratic friendships, and paper-thin communities. I thought of a Tewa prayer I'd heard quoted by the Native American anthropologist Alfonso Ortiz: "Within and around the earth, within and around the hills, within and around the mountains, your authority returns to you."

My father had spent a significant portion of his life in the natural world and he would have relished sitting by this campfire, among these mountains, in this orchard. It was a habit from his days in northeastern India, where fruit is abundant, that even after we moved to Delhi, whenever possible he liked to bring home whole crates of fruit. The most luscious find was a crate of ripe mangoes and my brothers and I would race up with it to our rooftop, where we would settle on a charpoy and suck the mangoes, not caring if the juice dribbled down our necks and arms.

I was twenty-three, a graduate student in Los Angeles, when my father was snatched away, as cruelly as though someone had hacked off your arm. He was fifty-four. A dedicated civil servant. After waiting years and years I still feel scalded when I approach his death. Much later, my younger brother would get a call from an Indian government official. On the prime minister's instructions, they planned to install a brass plaque in my father's name in a school he had attended. The official said that my father had made the highest sacrifice for his nation. A plaque in a school!

I think of him now, riding his bicycle, early in the mornings, or on his meandering evening strolls. When asked how he planned to get somewhere, he might say with a subtle smile, "Bus number 11." Meaning on two legs. After him, extended hikes through trees and up mountains have sustained me. Is it strange to think that the natural world can console us? That the universe can nourish us?

"The soul goes to join its ancestors, either at the directional shrines or on the flat-topped hills or mountains, depending on its status in life," Ortiz writes.

In the East Indian tradition, the best a person can hope for is to have their ashes submerged in the Ganges River, our goddess river. She will cleanse us, purify us, and bear us aloft from one world to another, perhaps to Shiva's mountaintop, from whose lofty heights Ganges flows down to the plains. India and Native America are entirely different civilizations but in the ways that they traditionally see the natural world as being sacred, they echo each other. Our souls recognize one another; the same sun comforts us, the same moon consoles us.

Under the starry night sky, surrounded by mountains, I listened to Papa, who was now talking freely, encouraged by the rapt eyes of a dozen musicians and the fragrant piñon logs burning feverishly. I recalled a time long past, when I had lived in India surrounded by family and encircled by community. But why did listening to Papa and Coral return me to those days? In the way that hummingbirds are nectar feeders, the music and the sense of community here was nectar for my soul. In Assam, in northeastern India, stories about mythology and animals were braided into my life, bamboos shimmered before me, and the everyday and the sacred were deliciously mingled. Could I achieve that state of grace while living in the West or would it forever remain a dream?

6

LE PETIT NUTHATCH

I.

The living room walls of the cinnamon casita were plastered an incandescent cream. I angled my wooden desk so it would face a grandmotherly apricot tree in the backyard. Michael and I had answered a rental ad for "a jewel at the end of a cul-de-sac." I had since discovered that the real jewel of our new home was the apricot tree, which stood with wide-open arms to embrace the crystalline sky. The casita was petite, but with glassy openings everywhere and chic French doors that showcased the tree. Our landlady had remodeled the garage of a house she had inherited into this independent unit and she was a businesswoman to the core, all leases, dollars, and granite countertops. After she had shown us around the place, I complimented the apricot tree.

All at once, her eyes softened. "When I built this place, I wanted to honor that tree," she said, folding her hands in namaste.

This part of the South Capitol neighborhood sits on a former fruit orchard. Our casita sidled against an open field where some straggly peach trees still grew, remnants of a once-vibrant orchard. While I completed the birding novel at my desk, I grew acquainted with a white-breasted nuthatch, *Sitta carolinensis*, who came punctually, at eleven in the morning, to visit the apricot tree in the backyard. From a distance, a nuthatch is a blur of bluish gray. But look closely at how the bird's sky-gray body contrasts with its milky breast and face. Its tooting call—*honk, honk, honk*—could be a sailor's horn. When I hear those honks, I anticipate the nuthatch's regal presence. It is staking its domain. With deft strokes, the bird navigated its way up and down the apricot tree, while its bill explored narrow crevices for insects. The nuthatch can glide headfirst down a tree or effortlessly deploy its sturdy feet to hang off a high branch. This bird gives Queen Elizabeth II a run for poise.

WHY DID I watch this nuthatch so keenly? I wasn't entirely sure until I reread *The Little Prince*. I had purchased the classic book when I was a graduate student at the University of Southern California: it was on the reading list of my still photography class. The professor was something of a legend and rumor had it the class was at the brink of being axed. In what was the final year the class would be offered, when I tried to enroll, it was full to capacity. Disappointed, I begged the professor to let me audit. It was true, he confirmed. This would be the last time. The university planned to convert the darkroom into an animation studio. The School of Cinematic Arts was endowed by the likes of George Lucas and Steven Spielberg and animation studios were becoming de rigueur, highways to the future, whereas darkrooms—the wombs of still photography—were passé.

Something moved the professor to let me audit his crowded classroom. On the first day of class, he handed out the required reading list. I was intrigued to see the name of a book I'd heard about, but had never read: *The Little*

Prince. I had precious little money to spend at the university bookstore but I walked right over and purchased *The Little Prince.* I read it breathlessly, wondering what insights I might stumble upon. Though I was charmed by Antoine de Saint-Exupéry's story and drawings, I couldn't make out what the book had to do with still photography. It was after the professor looked over our first assignments (he wasn't impressed) that he brought up *The Little Prince.* He asked us to consider that Saint-Exupéry's story has to do with a special way of seeing things. Could the concept of taming change how we approach our subjects with a camera? What he asked was seemingly obvious yet some deeper meaning remained unavailable to me. The book remained a koan, a paradoxical Zen riddle.

Once I befriended the nuthatch in my Santa Fe backyard, the koan's knots began to loosen. In the book, the fox explains to the little prince the proper rites of courtship: "It would have been better to come back at the same hour," says the fox. "If, for example, you come at four o'clock in the afternoon, then at three o'clock I shall begin to be happy. I shall feel happier and happier as the hour advances . . . One must observe the proper rites."

My nuthatch certainly took the fox's point to heart. It visited me at precisely the right time—when I was ready to take a break from writing and sit down with a cup of tea. The British have a habit they call elevenses. Even Paddington Bear (in *A Bear Called Paddington*) takes his elevenses—a bun with hot cocoa—together with Mr. Gruber in the latter's antique store. For my elevenses, I drank jasmine tea while the nuthatch gleaned insects from notches in the tree trunk or used the latter as a kitchen tool. The Cornell Lab of Ornithology tells us that the nuthatch gets its common name from its "habit of jamming large nuts and acorns into tree bark, then whacking them with their sharp bill to 'hatch' out the seed from the inside." This bird knew the gnarled, ridged trunk of the apricot tree like a map.

At different times of day, other birds stopped by: a ladder-backed woodpecker with a zebra back, a brown creeper who, true to its name, crept up and down the tree, and western bluebirds with chestnut breasts who favored the straggly fruit trees in the field beyond. Still, only the nuthatch visited in what could be called a ritualistic way. In return, I made a ritual of appreciating the bird. My elevenses bird was surprisingly salubrious. When the universe gives us a bird, we should accept it without too many questions. I sometimes return to books from my past in search of such unexpected clarity. It was only upon rereading *The Little Prince* in Santa Fe that I realized how crucial the concept of taming—to "establish ties"—is in the book, and possibly in our lives. It is a rare occurrence when one individual feels compelled to form ties to another. But all effort is wasted unless the one being tamed can recognize what is happening.

EN ROUTE TO a hike in Hyde Memorial State Park, I stopped at a picnic area and in the forest directly below me a pair of aspen trees glittered among the pines. A white-breasted nuthatch scuttled up and down a silvery aspen trunk barred with gray. It was my first nuthatch of the spring. Moments later, the bird entered a small round cavity in the tree trunk and vanished. I wondered when it would come out. Soon after, the nuthatch flew out and its mate entered the same hole. Was this their nest? The way the two nuthatches hovered about the cavity answered my question. Such a petite hole, scalloped in a tree trunk—and still, it was their world. I experienced a familiar delight. I would go on to hike this trail regularly, always pausing by the "nuthatch trees" to observe the birds flitting about a tree cavity, foraging on the ground, or caching food in tree bark. Even in the winter when the aspen trunks looked skeletal, and only the call of a chickadee could be reliably heard, sometimes a glaucous nuthatch would glide by and pause to check that the nest cavity was in tip-top condition; based on my sightings I suspected that the nuthatch is an year-round resident in our area and later I learned that these birds remain in their nesting territory throughout the winter.

The first nuthatch I had befriended in Santa Fe is long gone but the surprising way in which it unlocked the meaning of taming still lives on. Our old friendship nudges me to be present when I spot other epsilons (in math, an epsilon is used to denote an arbitrarily small value; the mathematician Paul Erdős, a flighty genius, used the term to refer to children and I find it does as well for small birds): a somber Say's phoebe foraging for its nest in my garden or spry bushtits scouring a piñon pine for insects or a heart-stopping swallowtail butterfly alighting on fresh lilac blooms. Each time I pause to appreciate a scuttling, tree-probing epsilon—a creeper, a chickadee, or a bushtit—the tie that the nuthatch and I established some years back is strengthened anew.

II.

I took to walking daily along a stretch of the Santa Fe River and the nuthatch, once it perceived my constancy, returned to me. On a late January morning, walking by the still-icy river, I saw a white-breasted nuthatch fly over from a large tree by a stuccoed house, cross the river, and hug a telephone pole before flying across the road on the other side, headed for a thin cluster of trees. All the while its brilliant white head with a gray cap gleamed as though it were a miniature bald eagle! I have since seen the nuthatch along other sections of the river in all seasons, which confirms that the nuthatch is a year-round resident here; it is generally believed not to migrate in any significant way. Its energy even in wintertime is frenetic, for this is the season when the monogamous bird begins its courtship. The male stashes seeds in bark crevices in preparation for its courtship ritual of feeding choice bits to the female. During the courtship display, as Kenn Kaufman writes in *Lives of North American Birds*, the male raises its head, spreads its tail, droops its wings, sways back and forth, and bows deeply.

One spring, I chanced upon a nuthatch nest and in the weeks to come I grew impressed by the devotion this bird has for its young. In mid-May, while looking for access to a different section of the river, we found ourselves on a private road and, a little later, we discovered a bird box nailed to a tree. Presently, I spotted a white-breasted nuthatch scuttle down and enter the hole in the center of the box. A little earlier, Michael had heard high-pitched squeaking from the box, which subdued once the nuthatch visited its chick. It was a brief visit; the nuthatch soon slid out and flew to a deciduous tree to its right and disappeared in the foliage.

It was meaningful to be able to *see* the nuthatch because once we found this hidden river trail and hiked alongside it, crossing single-plank bridges here and there, the leafy trees were often alive with morning arias but the canopy cover was too high above for us to glimpse the enthusiastic singers—we craned our necks but could only hear the other birds.

A week later, on our second visit, we saw the nuthatch chick at the entrance of the hole. It looked pensive, its bill inclined upward. It seemed a miracle when the tiny creature blinked. It had a soft chalk-white face with a dark patch on its head. A parent flew to the tree, scuttled down with a worm in its mouth, and fed it to the chick who, after the adult left, now faced us, seemingly more content with its fate. We left it to its musings and on our return from the hike, we saw both parents taking turns feeding their sole chick with the choicest insects or spiders they had found, and then swiftly flying away to avoid drawing attention to the nest. Inside the small circular opening, the chick again assumed a pensive expression—in profile with its bill tilted up, while it waited for its devoted parents to return with a fresh offering of insects.

At the very end of May when we returned to walk along the river, the nuthatch house was deserted. The chick was nowhere in sight, nor were its doting parents. We waited a while. Nothing. We wondered if a snake had gotten the chick. Last week, it had looked small and vulnerable, not yet ready to fledge. While it isn't known definitively how long nuthatch chicks take to fledge, it's estimated that they take anywhere from fourteen to twenty-eight days. And nuthatches raise only one brood each year. The chick we'd seen had looked nowhere near ready to leave the nest but perhaps we had underestimated it.

IN THE BEGINNING of July, as we began to hike what I now called the river trail, a security guard jumped out of his vehicle and barred our way. "Are you guys aware this is a private road?" he said.

We told him we were just accessing the river.

"There might be access off of Cerro Gordo," he said.

The car he had sprung out of was painted almost like a police car with black letters cautioning, Armed Private Security. Something was off-kilter about the man, though I couldn't pinpoint it. When I asked where exactly the other access point was that he was referring to, he confessed that he didn't know.

"I'll let you go this one time," he finally said.

Not five minutes later, as we were walking alongside the river, a man jumped out of his house and attempted to block our access. He had curly black hair and looked to be in his early fifties. He repeated the mantra that this was a private road. I had just seen the ugly red signs this same fellow had brutally nailed onto the trees that grew alongside the river, warning trespassers that they would be prosecuted. I looked him straight in the eye, challenging him to stop me from walking along the Santa Fe River. My two children were crouched alongside the water, poking twigs into it.

The man glanced at them as he assessed the situation, then he turned to look at me. "You can go this time. It's cool. You can go."

We kept on walking though I felt bruised by the experience of being unexpectedly pounced at by two big men. We came to a stretch of the river where we normally pause, among a sea of tall grasses, fuchsia lupines with fat yellow bumblebees, dandelion seeds drifting in the air. The river flowed swiftly, chattering with the rocks it lunged past. A saffron-yellow skipper paused on a leaf before flitting away. I took in the beauty but I continued to feel uneasy. Was this the last time I would be able to hike here? The men had acted as though they were doing me a favor, letting me pass this one time. I recalled a juvenile accipiter I'd seen here last month, its eyes glowing, sunbeams washing the bands on its tail. A magpie had attempted to chase the accipiter away; they'd faced off, pirouetting in midair, switched trees, then the juvenile picked up nerve and speed-bombed the magpie. They were still contesting when we left; we could hear their raucous cries. The week after this incident I had noticed that in a tree near where they'd been fighting, high up, was a magpie nest.

Neither the land nor the birds yield their stories all at once. You have to come back again and again, and somehow at the right time to be able to put together a picture of the lives of birds. But one irate, curly-haired man had just told me that henceforth he would block my access to the last strip of riparian land left in Santa Fe. Where else would I see tree swallows, their emerald bodies shining, slate-gray wings, smart blue-green-and-white faces, atop the snag of a fifty-foot-high elm tree? Where else would I listen to the fluty gossip of a yellow-breasted chat and feel exhilarated when I glimpsed its white spectacles and the mango sheen on its breast?

I had heard the chat's liquid, versatile series of calls on previous hikes and had wondered who was issuing them. A curve-billed thrasher's phrases would have been briefer, more rasping. One morning on a bone-white snag of a tall deciduous tree I spotted the fashionista soloist: it had a prominent white brow over its eye and a true mango-colored throat and breast that glistened in the morning light. With a soft olive-gray back, the bird was slightly smaller than a tanager and the lines of its body were more angular. Its whistling, popping calls were delightfully continuous. A shy bird, it soon flew away from the snag to dense shrubbery by the river's side. I also hear on this section of the trail the plaintive call of a wood pewee with a buzzing undertone. Near the river, swallowtail butterflies perch on masses of Austrian copper roses, *Rosa foetida*, shining saffron gold, while the children splash in the water.

On the way back when I saw a man reading a water gauge by an acequia, I asked if he was a city worker. No. He lived nearby. I related the encounter with the security guard and also with the house owner. He shook his head. "My name's BC," he said. "He has a few feet of property by the river that belong to him and I believe that yesterday, someone passing by, maybe a homeless person, was rude to a new tenant. They had an argument and the homeless person might have shouted out, 'I hope you get the virus,' as he walked away." Eyeing the children, BC cautioned, "I was told the guard has a gun."

Feeling stunned, I told BC about the nuthatch nest I had been monitoring all spring. I lamented that come next spring I wouldn't have access to it.

BC, who had lived in the neighborhood for decades,

didn't know about the nuthatch nest. Moved by my description of the nuthatches, he told me to use his name if anyone tried to block my access again.

I nodded gratefully. It had become a weekly ritual to hike this trail. It seems that we could still tiptoe over here, use BC's name, or just hope that no one would brandish a gun at my children because we are crossing ten feet of one man's property during the course of our hike. But there would be no joy in enacting a ritual this way.

At home, at dusk, the clouds were laden with mauve, capped with slate gray; a little later the mauve bled into the sky. I went on wondering at the travesty that access to a public river can be denied. How could the city have been so shortsighted as to not create a wider margin around the river? What does it say about who we are as a people when a gun-toting guard bars our access to an epsilon nuthatch? Is this what individuality run amok looks like? We, at any rate, have failed to tame one another. In *The Little Prince*, the fox confides in the little prince that whereas it takes time to make friends and to tame another person, people like to "buy things ready-made in stores. But since there are no stores where you can buy friends, people no longer have friends." I let out a long breath. We scarcely have neighbors anymore—we don't take the time to get to know them, and so we can't trust them. It wasn't good for the guard either to be standing all day long with a gun to bar neighbors from walking through. When we'd returned to our car, he was still pacing and this time I saw the gun in his holster. He looked like he was slipping out of his mind with ennui. I wish I could have told him about my nuthatch.

7

INTERLUDE: WESTERN TANAGER

Living in a petite casita, under the thumb of an overbearing landlord, I yearned to have a yard with more than a sole apricot tree. I dreamed about a piece of land with clusters of trees, where I might plant native sunflowers and penstemons and observe more birds. We were novices and, after months of searching for a place of our own, a place we could tame, we found only one affordable house with a tree-lined garden—and real potential as bird habitat—that looked straight out toward the Sandia Mountains. The day the sale was to go through, Michael was out of town and I got an abrupt call from the seller's real estate agent who apologetically told me that the homeowner had changed her mind.

"Her daughter was in town from L.A. over the weekend," the agent explained. "And she said to her mother, 'It's a beautiful house! Why are you selling it?'"

On the phone with the agent, I felt stunned. We had fallen in love with the round window in the living room that looked out on piñon pines with sprightly green needles and junipers with splintery, ash-colored bark in the backyard. I had never seen such a large, round window in a house. We'd walked out to the yard, toward a rose bed that edged wide-open land, like a canvas to plant native flowers in, and all at once were face-to-face with a long blue-green line of mountains in the distance. This was the place! We had strode back to the kitchen and told the agent that we were done looking.

"That's it?" she asked, surprised that we hadn't looked at the house longer.

But we didn't need to look longer. We knew this was the one.

In the weeks that followed, having spent considerable time and fees to complete all the inspections, paperwork, and signatures, we almost saw the place as ours. When the agent told us that the deal had gone through, we submitted a detailed loan application and were interviewed by the bank manager. Now I felt despondent. I knew I wouldn't be able to get a hold of Michael until the evening.

Just then, a western tanager flew over and hopped up to the grandmotherly apricot tree. It was the first time I had seen a tanager visit the casita. This bird, which can be mistaken for a summer popsicle, with its saturated yellow body, reddish-orange head, and striking black-and-white wings, was just the shot of light I needed. It dispelled my despair like sun lifting fog.

In that moment I began to wonder if I might be able to turn things around. I asked the agent to wait. I gazed at the tanager; the bird had created space for me to breathe and think. I collected myself and told the agent that we had our hearts set on this house and that we had put in significant time and fees into doing all the paperwork, the house inspection, and the radon test.

"She has offered to repay you the five hundred dollars for the home inspection," the agent said. "But I didn't realize this house meant so much to you!"

"It does," I said, standing almost against the French doors.

The tanager was perched on a nearby branch and I was drinking in the bird with my eyes. "We've looked for months and this was the only place we loved."

I added that our mortgage loan had been approved (a calculated guess on my part based on our meeting with the loan officer) and my understanding was that we would need to pay a few thousand dollars in fines if we backed out of the loan at this late stage. If that were to be the case, would the seller step up and pay the fine?

"Oh," said the agent. The finality of her call was suddenly shaken. She swiftly checked in with her real estate firm and then she called the seller; the news about the fine caused the latter to pause. Both the agent and the agency additionally impressed upon the seller that it wasn't kosher, it simply wasn't done, to back out at the last second.

The woman listened and she agreed to sell the house after all.

After I put the phone down, I was shaking. I knew our mortgage was due to be approved and I'd hated to stretch the truth. I opened my email and there was a message from the mortgage officer formally approving the loan—and the fine print said that we would be fined five thousand dollars if we withdrew at this point. I looked around for the tanager who had stayed for the duration of my phone call with the agent. But now that a way had been found out of my trouble, the bird had vanished.

A FEW DAYS after the agent's call, I drove up to our soon-to-be new home at the seller's request. She wanted me to look at some furniture and see if I wanted to buy anything before she tried to sell it off. As I drove up the incline that led to our new street, I saw the birds a few feet away on the dirt road. I slowed down my car to take them in. A pair of western tanagers on the dirt, glowing in the June sun, a whisper away from where I needed to pivot to get to my new street.

I took it as a sign. I was on a yellow brick road dotted with western tanagers.

Thoreau once compared the clear note of a rose-breasted grosbeak to that of a "tanager who has got rid of his hoarseness." This comparison may not reflect well on the tanager's call—a series of short, low-pitched notes—but the tanager had, in any case, called me and I had responded.

But what was going on? Had I achieved some miraculous communication with the western tanager? I don't think so.

The Indian spiritual master Sri Nisargadatta Maharaj once said, "I know nothing about miracles, and I wonder whether nature admits exceptions to her laws, unless we agree that everything is a miracle. To my mind, there is no such thing. There is consciousness in which everything happens. It is quite obvious and within the experience of everybody. You just do not look carefully enough. Look well, and see what I see."

I couldn't agree more.

When we allow ourselves to truly see the natural world we live in, we once again claim kinship with birds and other animals. We reforge our connection with nature, drink in the beauty of animals, and give up our cockamamie posture that we're the only inhabitants of the planet who count. When we listen to birds, we taste the joy this listening yields and we naturally refuse to despoil the earth, refuse to fragment and poison it. In nature, beauty springs from biodiversity; if we go on poisoning insects and clear-cutting forests, a day will come when the tanager will also be gone.

With each passing year I have observed fewer tanagers and when a summer goes by when not a single tanager visits my yard or the trails I frequent, I mourn this bird's absence. The tanager makes me pause and somehow transforms how I'm feeling. It reconnects me to the land and to myself and gratitude springs in my soul for this bird's beauty and its power over me. With gratitude comes a desire to protect—not only the tanager but also the insects it depends on.

"As in the cell so in the universe," say the Indian sages, suggesting that our inner cosmos unfailingly echoes the outer cosmos we live in. If we see our universe, and by extension our planet, as a "complex orderly self-inclusive system," which is how the Merriam Webster dictionary defines the word *cosmos*, we might think again about poisoning and disrupting its finely tuned systems. The absence of the tanager is but one indicator of the disruption we have inflicted and the root of this disruption is within us. We haven't been good neighbors on this planet. If we could see how our solipsism harms other animals, we might take more responsibility to remedy the harm we have done. When we heal the planet, it in turn heals us. It truly is a circle, like the glaucous Earth and the scuffed moon, like the round, round window that I was about to inherit.

8

THE BOBCAT IN MY ROSE BED

I.

New Mexico sounds like a remote hamlet to the rest of the country. Some even wonder if it is in the United States. "You're living in Mexico now?" a cousin once asked me. But we do have our moments. On a dull morning, there's nothing like a bobcat to bring the shine back in. I was newly pregnant with our first child when I saw a bobcat saunter past the round window. The stubby bobbed tail is what tipped me off.

That's no ordinary cat, I thought. The body was longer and bulkier, more muscular, than of any stray cat I'd seen out back. Michael walked into the room moments later and I wordlessly pointed out the animal. Reading the exclamation mark on my face, he saw the large cat ambling through the pines and his arm reached for the *Peterson Field Guide to Mammals of North America*.

The round hobbit window graces our living room; a wicker sofa across from this window is my reading haunt. From here, I observe the animals who pass by or those who gaze in. A chicken-wire fence used to surround our backyard but it was an ugly frame for the mature piñon pines and juniper trees that draw our periphery with a calligraphic brushstroke. We took the fence down. Now, wild animals can clamber up from the dry arroyo below us and wander around our property for reasons of their own. Over the years, I have come to appreciate the elegance of a bobcat, the mystery of a gray fox, the monkish silence of deer, and coyotes trotting in snow.

What gives a bobcat, *Lynx rufus*, away is its bobbed, six-inch tail with a black ink splotch on the tip. Michael handed me the mammals guide. I studied the bobcat drawing and checked it against the individual outside. The lines were similar and so was the coloring—a tawny back with faded spots and striking velvety black-and-white streaks on the face. More than double the size of an average housecat, the animal lay stretched out in the rose bed on the south side of the house. Here, the late-morning sun warmed its pale underbelly and luscious buff-colored coat while it retained the cover of a bare rosebush. It all felt surreal. Later I would read a *National Geographic* piece that said the bobcat "hunts by stealth, but delivers a deathblow by a leaping pounce that can cover 10 feet." Staring at the solitary, elusive wildcat outside my window, I wondered if I had fallen down a rabbit hole. "The eighth *rasa*, *adbhuta*," writes Ravi Shankar, "shows wonderment and amazement, exhilaration and even a little fear, as when one undergoes a strange new experience." That is just how I felt at the moment.

Michael didn't walk out to the porch; he took three photographs through the round window instead. We called our respective families—Michael's parents and my brother—in Toronto to report the bobcat sighting but by the ends of the calls, we felt dispirited. The Torontonians hadn't echoed our exhilaration. Instead, they were laser focused on the safety of the coming baby. This was to be a first grandchild on both sides of the family and they weren't eager to expose the baby to a bobcat. How would the child ever play in the backyard *after this?*

I understood their concern. Later, when I researched the bobcat, I learned about its "razor-sharp claws" and its powerful legs. "When within pouncing distance it hurls itself into its victim, generally on the head and neck," writes Stanley P. Young, a former lab director at the US Fish and Wildlife Service. "Whenever it can secure a hold on such a spot it quickly bites deeply into the victim's neck just below the back of the skull." The bobcat can take down antelope and mature deer, according to Young. It can hunt in the day or night, with a preference for the night—Young compares its eyesight to a crow's in the daytime and to an owl's at night. Like an echo of an owl's ear tufts, the hair on the bobcat's ears is speared to heighten its hearing. Its sharp eyesight and hearing are its true assets compared to, say, its sense of smell.

Although we appreciated the Torontonians' concern, we weren't ready to put up another fence. Michael had worked with someone to yank out the unsightly chain-link fence and we had paid a fee to the city to dispose of it. The kind of wooden fence that makes aesthetic sense in Santa Fe is called a coyote fence and it ain't cheap. There was another consideration. I saw myself as an enabler of community life by living in a house that neighbors could walk up to. Taking down our fence had opened up space for something to happen. We had brushstroked a wider circle of empathy and now a bobcat had entered this circle—our petite community. The animal had lit up our rose bed on a February morning when the bed wasn't otherwise a pretty sight. Yes, the baby's safety was critical. But the baby wasn't due for many months, not until October.

We floated the question of whether to call animal services and quickly decided against it. From the rose bed, the bobcat wandered over to the west slope of the house and napped under a large piñon pine. For half the day, its buff-colored body was visible, just a few feet from our living room windows. It liked our area enough to return to the piñon pine that night. The next morning, among fragrant pine needles were strewn remains of chicken feathers, a snapshot of struggle and death, where I'd last spotted the bobcat. The neighbors, two houses over, keep chickens and bees—today, they would have a missing bird.

IN TODAY'S FRENETIC world, how did our Santa Fe neighborhood remain a place where wildcats can freely roam? A few years back, an aggressive condominium developer had wanted to stack 230 units just up the hill and pave a wide road for the traffic that would inevitably zip by. This would be an unimaginable change from our sleepy dirt roads. Amy, who lives next door to the chicken and beekeepers, and another neighbor, Anne, stalked city hall meetings and whipped up a campaign about distinctive city landmarks that would be impacted. The condo developer fought back hard but in the end the neighborhood was granted historic designation, which means that the lots here cannot be subdivided. Mature piñon pines, olive-colored junipers, and sage-green chamisa still dot the land between the houses, forming a slender corridor not only for mammals like the bobcat, but also for migratory birds such as the Wilson's warbler, the western tanager, the Say's phoebe, and the green-tailed towhee.

Being fenceless does make us more approachable to our neighbors. After Anne passed away, her eighty-three-year-old widower, Bernie, developed a habit of walking up to our kitchen door unannounced. He always had a joke on his lips. "The Buddha ordered coffee and when he asked for his change back, the server said: 'Change comes from within.'"

AFTER READING MY literary novel set in the world of competitive birding, Pete Dunne, director of the Cape May Bird Observatory in New Jersey, called to tell me that the book had taken him back to his youth. Later, we spoke about what environmental issues will become critical in the coming years.

"Urban–wildlife interface is very high on the list," Pete said. "Maybe it is number one."

I nodded, recalling the short documentary I had made about the opossum in Pasadena. As human and climate change pressures shrink wild areas to a critical low point, more wild animals will begin to forage in our backyards. It's not uncommon today to hear news reports about pets and children having dangerous, even fatal, encounters with wildlife, including mountain lions and alligators. Dunne said that how we navigate urban–wildlife interface is not only going to be key for us, but it will also determine the welfare of animals and especially of birds.

SOON AFTER THE bobcat sighting, I checked in with a friend, Amy Fisher, a former ranger and now a wildlife consultant. She backed up our decision not to get the city's animal services section involved. "It's very tricky to inject the right dose of anesthetic," Amy said. This standard practice used to relocate wild animals can occasionally lead to an animal's death. Sometimes the animal is drugged to the extent that its survival in the wilderness is compromised.

As my pregnancy advanced, stray cats would wander through our backyard and remind me of the bobcat who had once visited. One late morning I watched through a window as an iridescent black-chinned hummingbird hovered over a sunset hyssop, droning in and out of the bell-shaped pink flowers. A little later when I walked out to the herb garden, I was astonished to see the hummingbird's sorry-looking corpse next to the flowering hyssop. I glimpsed the murderer, a gruff black cat, slinking away. It had scarcely bothered to eat the hummingbird. Stray domestic cats pose a significant danger to birds—scientists at the Smithsonian Conservation Biology Institute estimate that outdoor cats, *Felis catus*, kill a staggering 2.4 billion birds annually; cats make cuddly pets but keeping them indoors can help reduce the ecological threat they pose to birds. As a pregnant woman, I was also susceptible to contracting toxoplasmosis, a parasitic disease spread by exposure to infected cat feces. If infected, a woman can pass on a condition known as congenital toxoplasmosis to her child. I now wore gardening gloves when I simply had to mess about with plants.

IN JUNE, a few feet from the round window, next to a juniper tree, we discovered a desert cottontail's burrow ringed with gold-and-maroon tiger lilies. In the speckled light, I watched the mother rabbit, *Sylvilagus audubonii*, also known as Audubon's cottontail, use its paws to hurriedly cover up the hole with wood chips. One early morning, Michael saw her race up to the burrow to suckle her young. Three hungry mouths poked out of the hole for the feed and afterward darted back into the earth. Knowing that a mammal was suckling her babies right next to the round window, I felt a catch in my throat; my hand moved involuntarily to stroke the baby inside me.

II.

Our daughter was born in mid-October. The next day, a gray fox, *Urocyon cinereoargenteus,* visited us. The baby had just let out some loud cries and, moments later, the fox materialized. It stood by the chamisa, which was crowned with autumnal gold flowers. From the window, the fox stared at us, its silvery gray fur smudged with cinnamon around the ears and neck, the tip of its nose beaded black, its pointy ears taut. With such a penetrating, chocolaty gaze, it might be a messenger from the gods. Michael carried the baby to the window and pointed out the fox. With pensive scrutiny, the gray fox took in father and baby and then it swiftly vanished.

The animal made such an impression on Michael that he sketched it.

The next day, a mule deer came and he sketched it too. The first week with a first baby can be famously hectic but ours was transformed by the appearance of animals and birds— and the sketching—into a meditative retreat (the hectic part would come). My mother had sadly and unexpectedly passed away the previous winter and these animals became the first "family" to visit after our daughter's birth. Native Americans see animals as their relatives and that belief couldn't have felt truer to me than in this week when the visiting animals and the drumbeats of flickers and other woodpeckers serenaded us daily. We shared the animal sketches with friends who came to see the baby and they were as moved by the sketches as we had been by the animals. Maria, a friend who was returning to her native Peru, gave me a book, *Medicine Cards: The Discovery of Power Through the Ways of Animals*, inspired by Native American wisdom, to research the significance of the fox's visit.

In the chapter on the fox, I read: "Wiley Fox has many allies in the woodlands, including the foliage, which offers protection and much medicine. Fox is seemingly able to vanish amidst the lush undergrowth of the forest. This flora is Fox's ally. The ability to meld into one's surroundings and be unnoticed is a powerful gift when one is observing the activities of others. . . . Fox's ability to be unseen allows it to be the protector of the family unit."

In Assam, the fox was a vital part of our schoolgirl lore. If the sun was shining brightly and at the same time it unexpectedly began to rain, we grade-two girls would cry out: "A fox is getting married!" or "A fox is dancing at her wedding!"

At recess, we would reenact the fox's marriage ritual and offer the bride the choicest stones as wedding gifts. It fascinated me that the fox is also associated with the family unit in the Southwest. Now that I had my own family, I was grateful to receive the fox's blessing. To this day, my daughter tells me without prompting that her favorite animal is the fox.

I BEGAN TO wonder if it is the *shape* of the round window that attracts the animals. Once a greater roadrunner, *Geococcyx californianus*, hopped right up to the base of the window with a lizard in its mouth. I had wandered into the room while brushing my teeth and almost swallowed the toothpaste at the sight of a roadrunner with a splash of flame-blue orbital skin and a reptile hanging from its bill peering into my living room with its glowing yellow eyes. The circle is an elemental shape—our irises are circles, we tell each other stories while sitting in a circle, we often see our very lives as being circular. The window is what first attracted me to the house. In the Peter Jackson film *The Lord of the Rings: The Fellowship of the Ring*, the wizard Gandalf once goes to visit Bilbo Baggins. Gandalf enters through a round hobbit door and drinks tea with Bilbo at a long wooden table. I have since acquired a suspiciously similar wooden table and we drink prodigious quantities of tea, though not at that table.

The round window trembles on windy April days and lets in water when it rains hard. After one messy leak, we considered replacing the glass. The Andersen salesman, in a pressed white shirt and navy trousers, was appalled when he saw the window. "Such a large round window!" A plump man, he stepped up to the rim and pressed against the window, making it shake. "See, it's moving!"

He stoked fears of future leaks and advised that the glass "absolutely" needed to be replaced. But he didn't think he could find an exact replacement. "I would recommend that my crew replace this structure to a *square* window."

We gasped. To us the round window embodied the soul of the place.

But the Andersen man insisted he had no round windows with which to replace ours.

We said that a square window wouldn't do.

He perused his phone book–like catalog again. This time, on the very last page, he found the round glass of a window like ours. By now, he had injected such terror of apocalyptic scenarios involving major cracks and water seepage that we mutely signed the contract (for five thousand dollars) that he placed before us. Only after he left did we recover our wits. We read the contract over and discovered we had a twenty-four-hour "window" in which to make up our minds. The next morning, we called to cancel. No window salesperson has crossed our threshold since. But the bobcat and the fox remain members of our miniature community, sometimes extending us the courtesy of strolling by the round window and alerting us to their presence before exploring the yard or napping under the roses.

III.

A little over a year after the bobcat's visit, when our daughter was six months old, we woke up to find our ivory-white living room walls bare. The frames that used to hang there were gone. In the dark of the night, we'd had human visitors, more threatening than any animals who had visited so far. The deeper loss was the unsettling feeling that our home had been invaded, that two strangers (we saw muddy footprints) had pranced around in our living room a few feet away from where we'd been sleeping in our bedroom with the baby.

One evening an acquaintance, Jessica, was visiting us. My daughter—I'll call her Mia—was playing with Jessica when I saw the bobcat stroll by. We were in the living room. Jessica drew in a sharp breath but one-year-old Mia treated the sighting as a natural occurrence.

"Bobcat," she said, pointing at the animal crossing the porch.

The fear that thieves might waltz in again any night was fading. After a year, the house almost felt ours again. How is it that the bobcat elicits wonder in me more than fright? It is an elegant animal. Lithe, like many wildcats, but more so. It's the runway model of wildcats. The soft sheen on its coat doesn't hurt this image, nor does its insolent gaze. When it strides by our porch, the world slows down. Little else seems to matter. The bobcat walks by, almost in slow motion. Our coterie of resident birds is nowhere to be seen. Only the flickers, if they're around, see the bobcat out, one gliding behind it like a patrol plane and two others perched on a pole, bills moving in unison as they track the bobcat's movements with grim determination. As the scene unfurls, a mysterious stillness comes over the garden and seeps into me. I get the giddy feeling that I have stepped into a song. It's the kind of humming I need to hear in order to live.

9

THE MYSTERY DIMENSION

I.

After more than a decade of living in the Southwest, Native mythology has percolated into me, but our wild visitors also cracked open a way of experiencing this mythology. Depending on the tribe, a bobcat can be a divergent twin of a coyote or the rabbit's foe. A bobcat's visit could mean that "you are being stalked, physically or spiritually, by an enemy," as Native healer Bobby Lake-Thom writes. But the bobcat who called on us showed none of the aggressive signs of a bobcat who all but attacked Lake-Thom's toddler when they lived in a trailer in California. Lake-Thom concedes that the bobcat can also be a protector and its power and medicine can be used for good luck or for protection against other powers and people.

For clarity, I peered into the *Medicine Cards*. A relative of the lynx, and a member of the *Lynx* genus, the bobcat is also a keeper of secrets. "Lynx is not the *guardian* of secrets, but the *knower* of secrets. The problem lies in getting Lynx to instruct you." Mythological stories about the bobcat also feature other animals who visited my backyard, such as the coyote, who is thought to be a perfidious trickster, and the rabbit, who is ruled by fear. The bobcat, in any case, was fearlessly making its presence felt. A neighbor, some two blocks down, told me that he woke up one dawn to feed his chickens and discovered a bobcat standing atop the chicken coop.

In *Myths of Light*, Joseph Campbell writes about the four basic functions of a traditional mythology. "The first must be to open the mind of everybody in the society to that mystery dimension that cannot be analyzed, cannot be talked about but can only be experienced as out there and in here at once." As I excavated myths about the bobcat, I felt a surprising closeness to the animal. After some time, I began to feel that its presence around my house was not arbitrary. One autumn afternoon as I sat down to work at my desk, I found myself all at once looking into the bobcat's eyes. Less than ten feet away, it stared right at me, through the glass door. Its eyes were deeply knowing and we remained in an eye lock for some time. When it walked away, I noticed a limp in its step. I felt haunted by the limp; it felt somehow personal. It came to me in a flash—I yearned to introduce Mia to my parents. Losing them had in part driven me deeper into the natural world and it was in this mystery dimension that I experienced an echo of their presence.

II.

We can see a hilly mound from our west living room window, behind which is a national cemetery. One morning, around breakfast time, Michael saw a line of men, dressed in black, lined up along the mound. Through binoculars, we observed that they were carrying rifles. He called our local nonemergency dispatch line to find out what was going on.

"A mountain lion has been sighted in the area," a police-woman said. "They are trying to keep a watch and keep him at bay. They're waiting for animal services."

Shortly after, we saw a white animal services van parked behind where the men in black stood with pointed guns. I looked up animal services and was directed to their mission statement: "The City of Santa Fe Animal Services Division is comprised of one manager and six full-time Animal Services Officers who investigate and respond to vicious or stray animals, nuisance complaints, injured or ill animals, reports of cruelty or neglect, as well as other animal-related issues."

Apparently, this "vicious or stray" mountain lion got away. The *Santa Fe New Mexican* printed a warning asking people to keep small children inside the house.

One evening, a neighbor was walking down a dirt road with her grown daughter, scarcely more than a block from my house, when they ran into the mountain lion strolling in the opposite direction. Both parties eyed each other, pausing imperceptibly, before they continued on.

A few days later, the mountain lion was spotted around town, once under a cottonwood tree on Cordova Road. Toward the end of the week, animal services finally located the mountain lion in the south end of town. This time, they were able to shoot a tranquilizer into the animal. I wondered how they decided which forest to relocate it to. Or was the tranquilizer the wrong dose for the mountain lion, as my ranger friend Amy Fischer had once warned me about?

One January morning, Michael and I, along with our toddler, hiked the John P. Taylor Jr. Memorial Trail at the Bosque del Apache National Wildlife Refuge, two-and-a-half hours south of us. At the head of the trail, a sign warned that there were mountain lions in the area. There was an additional warning for parents of small children. This gave us pause but we had encountered mountain lion signs on the trails we'd hiked in California. This was going to be a short hike through a cottonwood savannah. After we had walked some distance, I let Mia stand on a bench so she could look at a gaggle of Ross's geese. She naturally wanted to jump from the bench. A little later, at an overlook at the end of the trail, Mia wanted to leap from another bench. There were significantly more Ross's and snow geese to look at here. A red-tailed hawk wheeled above us. But Michael didn't want us to linger. He was still anxious about that mountain lion sign. We turned around and began to hike back through the salt grass.

When we returned to the first bench, Mia raced to jump from it again. I scooted over to catch her because the ground was uneven and gnarled with thick protruding cottonwood roots. She was in her fierce and independent juvenile-eagle phase, however. Insulted that I had steadied her as she touched down, she began to wail.

Michael picked her up but she wanted down. He worried that her crying would attract a wild animal.

"We've been here a long time," he said.

The chill he'd been feeling abruptly infected me. I looked around. Shimmering cottonwoods with massive striated trunks surrounded us and beyond them loomed gloomy shadows. Was an animal watching us? We might not know until it was too late. We intuitively took turns carrying our cranky toddler the rest of the way. Michael kept glancing back because the grasses were tall enough to conceal a crouched mountain lion and the animal likes to pounce from behind. We speed walked to the head of the trail. When we at last reached our car, my sense of relief was profound.

At the visitor center, a wide-eyed ranger told us that last month, a mountain lion was sighted on the John P. Taylor Jr. Memorial Trail. A man hiking the trail had seen the mountain lion and had photographed it with his iPhone. "The lions in this area are collared. And this lion's radio collar was easily visible in the photograph." The ranger shuddered. "That was a little too close."

We eyed each other, stunned.

"When I go hiking alone, I attach some chimes on my knapsack so that with each step I take, I make some noise," she said.

All at once, we felt dispirited about how cavalierly we had gone on that hike. In our prebaby days, in California, if we'd hiked a trail with a mountain lion sign, we might ask a ranger or another hiker about the sign and would be assured that no one had seen a mountain lion here for years and the sign was to warn people to not linger, say, at dusk. Now that we had a toddler, the rules had changed. On the other hand, if we were to take Mia to only Disneyesque places, how would she grow a relationship with wild spaces? How would she learn to identify and care about a red-tailed hawk wheeling above her? How else would she encounter a silken white sheet of ten thousand geese instead of knowing the bird only by the game Duck, Duck, Goose that she likes to play?

III.

In the winter, a coyote raced past the round window as all three of us were standing nearby. The tan creature moving across shining, powdery snow was an unearthly sight. Mia jumped into her father's arms. They rushed to her bedroom's north-facing window and watched the coyote trot away on the dirt road. Since then, from our breakfast table I've seen pairs of coyotes go by, too thin in the winter. Early one morning, I was at a front window, expecting a visitor. Instead I saw a coyote cross the dirt road and move toward an open tract of land. The coyote hesitated, then it retraced its steps to a small arroyo, where it had stashed a half-eaten animal; it ate hungrily. I noted the rufous coloring along the coyote's head, the grayness of its body, the slight swing in its tail. In the middle of the night, we often hear coyotes howling from our driveway, from the piñon and juniper trees circling the backyard, or from the arroyo behind the property.

Unfenced houses aren't for everyone and we mostly keep our doors shut. In the backyard, our daughter trails us closely. Bobcats are known to eat small mammals and birds, not little children. A pack of coyotes once attacked a friend's medium-sized dog when she was hiking up in the hills with three dogs; her large dog tried to intervene and she picked up her small dog, but the coyotes had the middle dog surrounded. She gave up her middle one for lost and returned home with two dogs, only to have the middle one turn up at home, mangled and bedraggled, some five hours later. Coyotes usually stick to eating small rodents and rabbits. In a few months, we will have a second baby and the Toronto relatives will once again raise the question of a fence. Our position is that we are thinking about it.

OF ALL THE animals we have hosted here, our daughter has most enjoyed the mule deer, *Odocoileus hemionus*. Indigenous peoples believe that deer who hang around are bringing you a message from the spirit world. Still, we've not enjoyed seeing the deer eat our valerian buds, undeterred by the chicken-wire fence we put around the fuchsia flowers. "When the deer come," Mia likes to say, "Papa goes out with a broom and shoos them away." She has been trying to wake up early so that she can see the deer, for she has been dreaming about them.

When we took our annual trip to the Bosque del Apache National Wildlife Refuge, Mia was delighted to spot mule deer with their black-tipped tails. When we returned home, she asked, "Why didn't you shoo those deer away?"

"Because they live there. That's their home."

Humans have such a proprietary notion of home that we sometimes forget the obvious—where we live was once the former home of wild animals. From that perspective, even our neighborhood's historic designation is shortsighted. It may seem a radical idea but we collectively need to appreciate our *prehistoric* designation. Is it so surprising that the wild animals return when they are hungry and have the cover of trees? In ancient Greece, the word *oikos* referred to the basic unit in a society, the family unit, or a place of habitation. *Oikos* is the ancestor of the modern word *eco*, as in ecology or ecological consciousness. Once I settled into the idea that animals have as much right to inhabit the land as we do, my own ecological consciousness took flight. Without this insight, I would have remained like the chickens that author Annie Dillard once described—who attempt to lift off when they see a skein of geese migrating above but get exactly nowhere.

IV.

When I see a yearling deer munch our young Kansas hawthorn tree, I try to remember that it is hungry. But if this goes on, our three newly planted hawthorn trees won't get any taller; they will get munched to death. I care for my cosmos wildflowers, common though they are. This year, the flowers are disappearing as soon as they bloom. The desert cottontails are fattening themselves on the cosmos, shoots of Spanish broom, ice plants, black-eyed Susan, and just about any attractive flower or shrub we've planted. Flowering plants and grasses are said to form 80 percent of a cottontail's diet.

Bitten hard by mosquitoes, I sat on a garden bench, gazing at the headless cosmos stems. Mia noticed my silence. The round window, the moon of our domestic solar system, drew my gaze—it looked different from the outside, from the side the wild animals saw in.

A few feet away, mourning doves pecked at the clover seed we had just put in, cover crop to nourish our soil for next spring. The clover seedlings were coming out in the rose bed where the bobcat had once sat. But everywhere else, the seeds were stalling or birds were devouring them. I mustn't begrudge the birds the seeds. This is the give-and-take of community life. Seeds are like ideas; not all of them will sprout. It dawned on me why I no longer cared to keep bird lists. I felt certain that we need a new approach to birding, one that isn't divorced from cherishing and restoring the *oikos* we share with birds and other animals.

"Mama, how are your cosmos doing?" Mia asked.

I studied the doomed, beheaded plants: "Fine. They'll be just fine."

We got up from the bench. I walked and she skipped on the wood-chipped path back toward the porch. The round hobbit window took in our movements, the way it had done for the animals that had walked here before us. So long as the wind didn't crack the glass, it would go on being our "mystery dimension," as Campbell put it, something that "can only be experienced as out there and in here at once."

THE SECOND FUNCTION of mythology, Campbell noted, is to connect what is transcendent in the universe to the world of everyday experience. When our cosmic image reflects that mystery, "all the stars and little animals and trees and mountains are seen to express this unfathomable dimension." Mia and I watched from inside the round window as a surprise rainstorm gushed down. Its fury was spent in minutes. Afterward, spotted and canyon towhees returned for more seed eating. A cottontail scurried over to a firewheel plant, snipped off a flower, and vanished in a flash. Mia squealed that it was chasing its "brother rabbit." A curve-billed thrasher and a scrub jay fought over the crabapple tree, on top of which hung a cedar bird feeder. The way these two birds angled their heads is how Audubon portrays his birds.

This time, the thrasher subdued the jay and fluttered to

the top of the feeder to lord over its kingdom. Shortly, the crème de la crème returned: a black-chinned hummingbird sipped from a firecracker penstemon, while taking intermittent draughts from a Mojave sage. I fretted that not enough flowers had bloomed this year for the hummingbirds. They need what calories they can hoard for their imminent aerial march to Mexico or Central America. I lost myself in the hummingbird's electric thrumming and, when Mia tapped my arm, I started. It's a gift to be pulled out of oneself and wonder at the mystery of a bird, a plant, or even dry-caked earth (we have a lot of that in Santa Fe). Our backyard has ripened into a real community. For a storyteller, opening up to life is vital. The story-seeds that tend to flower are those that are nurtured by the soil of life.

10

MESSENGERS FROM THE PAST

I.

The crown jewel of our National Wildlife Refuge System, the Bosque del Apache, has been my annual pilgrimage site for a decade. The largest single population of sandhill cranes migrates to the Bosque late in the fall to overwinter along the Rio Grande. I have seen these cranes with crimson crowns in Southern California and at the Reifel Migratory Bird Sanctuary in British Columbia but they descend on the Bosque in staggering numbers. In the evenings, you stare at cranes with serpentine necks flying in over skies streaked rosy pink and clementine. New Mexico's skies can be striations of color approximating infinity but these numberless flocks of cranes and geese outdo the theatrics of the sky. When the cranes begin their fairylike descent onto milky-blue sheets of water, you find yourself in a place where humans are far outnumbered by birds. You let the primal orchestra of cranes and geese remind you of the place your ancestors came from.

The refuge is ninety miles south of Albuquerque, near the quaint town of San Antonio, New Mexico. Cradled between the Chupadera and Little San Pascual mountains, the core of the 57,000-acre refuge, some 13,000 acres, sits beside the Rio Grande, at the northern edge of the Chihuahuan Desert. One winter as I explored the arroyos, cornfields, and ponds in the refuge's North and South Loops, the cranes stood slate gray in the pale, rose-colored dusk. Their curved necks moved insistently against the grass as they foraged. There was ample food that year and they honked contentedly—a rich, rounded, baritone sound.

The cranes eat grasses such as millet that used to grow naturally and abundantly in this area. Over the last century, however, the free-spirited Rio Grande was aggressively drained and the valuable wetlands it supported, which in turn supported the cranes, were devastated. The rhizomes and roots of wetland plants are natural sources of protein and carbohydrates for cranes. The seeds of sedges and rushes offer healthy fats. Insects and crayfish, and the shells of snails and other invertebrates, as I learned at the Bosque, are a ready source of calcium. By ravaging our wetlands, we created a food desert for tens of thousands of sandhill cranes and now we're stuck growing crops for them. After whacking a whole ecosystem out of balance, we are scurrying to undo at least part of the damage we have inflicted, so as to avert the most visible cruelties that would otherwise ensue.

A ranger with a crinkled face said to me, "Last year, a ranger from a farming family in Montana changed everything here, crop-wise. . . . Before, we had an arrangement with neighboring farmers, who would supply us with crops to feed the birds. But there was never enough food." A crane eats a pound of corn a day, so seven thousand cranes need an impressive amount of corn. The Montana ranger assessed the food shortage and took the lead in planting the Bosque's fields. In addition to corn, he grew triticale, a cross between wheat and rye. They had a bumper crop.

"We'll never go back to the old way again," the ranger said.

THE CRANES NEED every calorie they can amass. In February, the greater sandhill cranes will embark on a spring flight to return to the northern Rocky Mountains in time for the breeding season. The lesser sandhill cranes, some 30 percent smaller than their greater cousins, will travel farther—to Alaska and as far as northeastern Siberia—to breed.

Sandhill cranes are monogamous birds; during courtship, the male valiantly tosses vegetation or mud into the air and fans its wings above the body, before dancing with abandon and letting out a unison call. Then the pair throw their heads back— the male at a deeper angle—and the female lets out two calls for each call the male emits. Lifelong pairs rely on this short, sharp unison call for relationship maintenance—it's a pair's shorthand to stay connected, or to alert a mate to a threat in their breeding area. Dancing, too, is used not only in courtship rituals, which are said to be infrequent in lifelong pairs, but also as a communal activity. These cranes have at least ten different types of dances and as many calls; their dances are so lively, with leaps, bows, and head pumps that I wonder whether this is why a group of cranes is also referred to as a dance or swoop of cranes.

Before nesting, the cranes paint themselves with mud and vegetation in order to blend into their landscape. They subscribe to the philosophy of slow parenting, incubating a clutch of two eggs for roughly a month and allowing their chicks up to a generous five months to fledge. One study showed that young siblings frequently grow aggressive with one another but the parents use food to mediate such conflicts. I find them to be very relatable birds.

By the time groups of cranes arrive in New Mexico in late autumn, they have molted and I see them in fresh dove-gray-and-maroon plumage. Standing with heads erect in the winter sunshine, their gleaming gray bodies and crimson crowns are painterly, with the velvety sheen of a medieval tapestry. Their aloof stance adds to their allure. In flight the very lines of a crane and its wingspan of seven feet are reminiscent of a time before ours. They are as ancient as can be, hearkening back to the Pleistocene. A ten-million-year-old crane fossil found in Ashfall Fossil Beds State Historical Park in Nebraska is said to belong to a crowned crane, a relative of the sandhills. The oldest sandhill crane fossil, unearthed in what is today Florida, is some 2.5 million years old. Some years back, I saw an exhibit at the San Diego Natural History Museum that explored how birds evolved from dinosaurs. "A bird didn't just evolve from a *T. rex* overnight," says Stephen Brusatte, a paleontologist at the University of Edinburgh in Scotland, "but rather the classic features of birds evolved one by one; first bipedal locomotion, then feathers, then a wishbone, then more complex feathers that look like quill-pen feathers, then wings. The end result is a relatively seamless transition between dinosaurs and birds, so much so that you can't just draw an easy line between these two groups."

Aldo Leopold wrote about the sound of cranes: "We hear the trumpet in the orchestra of evolution."

THAT EVENING AT the Bosque, we saw a gathering of sandhill cranes and snow geese unlike any other we had observed here. The water was powder blue and rose pink and multitudes of cranes and geese flew in and congregated upon the painted water to roost. Some estimates have it that at its peak, there are forty thousand geese in the refuge and half as many cranes. When I looked up, geese streaked the sky everywhere, punctuated only by the cranes flying in like robotic fairies. I drank in the ambrosial dusk as I reflected on the *rasa* of cranes.

The painted sky, reflected in the water, lent the scene a supernatural setting—here, one could tune in with what is transcendent in the universe, as Campbell would have said. The sun, an enormous ball of reddish mauve, flashed unabashedly into my face. Apollo the sun god is believed to have disguised himself as a crane when he visited mortals to signal that spring was coming. Two silhouetted cranes cavorted against the regal sun disk. The leggy birds now stood in the ponds where they like to roost in four to eight inches of shallow water. As twilight set in, a corresponding stillness enveloped the cranes and my heart. My arms ached from holding my toddler but I went on watching until the birds' velvet-gray plumage at last fused with the darkening sky and the misty gray of the water.

The cranes would begin to leave next month. Most would fly north to their next major migratory stop: Nebraska's Platte River valley, a threatened habitat in North America's Central Flyway. Like us, they are transient visitors here. But for the sight of cranes performing their elusive dance, I may have seen all there is to see at the Bosque yet I keep returning each year. It's as though I, too, migrate to the Bosque.

II.

On the June day when our second baby was born, two midwives measured her head to toe, head circumference, weight, heartbeat, and the frequency with which she drank milk. It was enough to make me recall the hummingbird banding station we had volunteered at at the Audubon Kern River Preserve in our California days. Six hours later, the baby was released from the birth center. On day seven, I decided to skip her optional hearing exam; I couldn't imagine taking my fledgling to some hearing clinic in the maze of a hospital complex.

One evening, the two-month-old baby lay on our bed, near an open window. The fall migration season was beginning. Mustached red-shafted flickers are year-round residents but they were more active now. Yellow-rumped warblers flitted from one tree to the next. A ruby-crowned kinglet hopped secretively in a juniper tree, there was a flash of yellow and black as a Scott's oriole took cover in the crabapple, and the streaky orange of a pair of evening grosbeaks, altitudinal migrants, was visible in a mature piñon pine, the one that had to be rescued from a scale infestation. A spotted towhee trilled and I saw the baby register the sound. She turned her head to the window, then she looked back up at me, wanting an explanation.

"That's a bird," I said. "You just heard a bird."

I couldn't help but smile. Now I knew for sure that she could hear. Since then, I have seen her watch as a crow flies by or when a robin hops over to the herb bed, fishing for worms. If birds are messengers from the past, the descendants of dinosaurs, then the baby is getting acquainted with our planet's past. At breakfast time, nary a bird flies across the backyard without eliciting an "ah" from her. At the age of one, she pointed at the birds, especially at the mourning doves that perch regularly on the telephone wires. Theodore Roosevelt wrote about this dove: "There can be no more mournful sound of unending grief than the sound of a mourning dove." I see this bird differently. The curved shape and flutter of a mourning dove's wings as it takes off never fail to brighten me. It's the best shorthand reminder I have in my backyard of the otherworldly flight of cranes. In November, the cranes will return to the Bosque. In the winter, we will take our infant to the Bosque to look for dancing cranes and to listen to "the orchestra of evolution."

III.

"What was that?" Michael put the car in reverse.

One January, we were on the Bosque's North Loop and I wondered if Michael had just seen an accipiter at the edge of the cottonwood grove. Instead, in a clearing between the grove and a dry ditch, stood a herd of a dozen or so javelinas, *Pecari tajacu*. Bristly charcoal gray, with pink snouts, and across their shoulders the cream stripe that lends them the common name, collared peccary. Two juveniles broke into a run, kicking up a shower of dust, after which the portly, tailless creatures raced up a storm. They recalled the wild boars in *Princess Mononoke*, the Japanese animation film that pits the natural world against our brutal industrial realities. Unlike in life, in the film it is the boars who have been corrupted by greed.

I took in their feral, speckled-gray bodies. Their scent glands, under the eyes and on the back, earn them the name musk hog and the scent is used to establish a herd's territory. A couple of babies in the herd shuffled in the dirt while some javelinas stared right at us. Our single pair of binoculars were in hot demand and exchanged hands fast, though the herd was only some thirty feet away. One javelina used its back hoof to scratch its ear. Then I made a mistake. I rarely photograph animals, believing instead in the primacy of the experience. But this time, the photographer in me was aroused and I asked Michael to get our camera from the trunk. A javelina was spooked by the sound of the trunk being shut and it ran like a streak of lightning. The others stirred and vanished into the cottonwood grove. Only two javelinas lingered, as did we, until they also left.

In the peccary family, javelinas are found as far down as South America. They are the color of stone and seem just as ancient and enigmatic. The Spanish word *bosque*, which means "forest" or "woodlands," has a suggestion of the unknown. Forests are among the few places whose allure has not been stripped by the frenetic merry-go-round of civilization. That which is wild may have its fury but it also has grace. While observing the javelinas, I had sensed the tenderness within their wild coat of armor. They were curious about us, they seemed to inch toward us. Their children went on playing as the adults gazed at us, while also rightly being wary of us. I felt stirred by the sighting, but also astonished that after so many years of living in the Southwest, it was only now that I had seen a herd of javelinas.

THE NEXT MORNING at the Bosque, a fresh sight awaited. A cloud of snow geese in the sky, so many that our necks craned up and our mouths parted in silent awe.

"They look like glitter . . . so tiny and beautiful," Mia said.

"You mean like confetti?"

"Like fish flying in the sky."

There were hundreds, yet somehow there is no chaos when the skein flies together; the geese don't collide into one another, instead they coexist in harmonious formations. Is the seeming chaos of nature an illusion? When the veil is drawn, we begin to see patterns and even an order that is comforting.

IT WAS PAST 5:00 p.m. and we still hadn't left. The water was like glass, as the bright orb of the sun slipped behind the chocolate mountains. A skunk, its tail erect like a black-and-white question mark, scuttled forward along the side of a dry arroyo. Three baby-boomer photographers raced after it with the gusto of paparazzi chasing a new starlet. The skunk showed them its rear and disappeared in some brush. Pied-billed grebes floated unmolested on the placid water as the sky blushed pink. Abruptly, among the numberless cranes at the edge of a cornfield, one group opened its wings in a dance formation. At last! Oh, what an ingenious, spirited dance! One pair of dusky wings splashed open, then in a choreographed sequence, the next crane flashed its wings, and the next, in slow motion. Their movements recalled the traditional African dances I have watched over the years in Camp Mabina and later I wasn't surprised to learn, as Paul A. Johnsgard writes, that cranes "have served as models for human tribal dances in places as remote as the Aegean, Australia, and Siberia." Among cranes, dancing can be connected to courtship but it is also a kind of ritualized socializing that includes even aggressive behaviors, an ironing out of family and flock relationships, a reforging of community.

Just then, the snow geese, a wide band of glittering white on the cerulean water, took off. The sky sprang to life with dazzling wings tinged with black. The birds hovered above us and drifted in a cloud formation, dense and massive like Kālidāsa's cloud messenger—who carried messages of love between two separated lovers—showering us with cosmic blessings as we left our refuge.

11

DAMSELS FLOATING IN AIR

On the day after Thanksgiving, after appreciating favorite dishes such as Japanese yams glazed with coconut butter, I like to give thanks to the land and its rivers. But as we approached the Rio Grande, I experienced a familiar regret: the once-wild river was denatured to a stream. A US Fish and Wildlife publication notes that there was once a time when melting spring snows from the mountains filled the Rio Grande with water "until it overflowed its banks, flooding the land around it." Heavy summer monsoons "swelled the river even more. At times, the overflowing water was so powerful that the entire path of the river changed, forming new ponds and marshes in the old riverbed." A cacophony of vegetation grew in these fertile floodplains, providing crucial food for wildlife such as sandhill cranes who migrated here "to spend the winter feasting on nutritious grasses like chufa and millet while other animals thrived amid the cottonwood forests and shrublands." Over time, however, the Rio Grande has been so plagued by diversions, dams, drought, and other forms of fragmentation that the river began to shrink, its wetlands began to vanish, and even the cranes began to disappear; the actor and social commentator Will Rogers once described the Rio Grande as "the only river I know of that is in need of irrigating."

When we got to the Bosque, the sandhill cranes seemed scarcely to be around. In one pond I observed northern pintails, ducks with distinctive white throats and chests and a bluish-white stripe behind the ear. Some seventy-five pintails, tails spiked, floated in the water; one American wigeon, with green eye shadow and a white stripe on the head, sailed among them. The water was choppy and the charcoal-brown heads of the pintails, with their black-and-white rears, bobbed in it. I watched these ducks coolly, as I do acquaintances. I was looking for old friends.

We abruptly came upon twenty sandhill cranes feeding in buff-colored grass in the south fields and they raised their elegant velvet-gray necks to honk. They *crane* their heads upward just so before letting out gusty music. I observed their rust-speckled gray bodies from the Coyote Deck, an aptly named lookout, for I have seen coyotes, who prey on these birds, skulking nearby. Mountain ranges flanked the Rio Grande to its east and west; I was surrounded by water, rock, and gusts. It was so windy, I felt like I would blow away.

We drove on, Ravi Shankar's sitar wafting out of our car stereo as we watched a kestrel kiting above, against ragged, mud-colored mountains. At ten thousand feet, the mountains loomed over us, a counterpoint to the glaucous ponds we were circling. We reached a field where I could get a better view of the sandhill cranes: the striking bloody-maroon patch that extends behind the eye is part red skin and part tiny feathers. Their tenacious bills, probing the unyielding wintry ground, were muddy from feeding.

The hulking spines of the Chupadera Mountains to the west and Little San Pascual to the east loomed over us, as they had over Juan de Oñate in the summer of 1598 when the Spanish conquistador rode on horseback with his men up the Rio Grande Valley to New Mexico, purportedly to spread Catholicism in the area. Back then the Spanish referred to the Rio Grande as El Rio Bravo del Norte or the Fierce River of the North. Today, the river is anything but fierce. In the North Loop an entire village of snow geese and cranes were mixed in together, the geese gleaming when the sun peeked out of the clouds. Flocks of red-winged blackbirds flew in their midst, black feathers shining like silk. This crowded field of densely packed birds, feeding, standing, and sleeping—over a thousand, easily—at first glance seemed to be higgledy-piggledy. However, fresh groups of honking, bellowing sandhill cranes flew in and landed neatly in their midst, without ruffling a single neighbor's feathers. These birds get along better than a thousand humans packed into a wintry field might. The gaggle of geese maintained their family units in the crowded arena and yielded space so that other families might also demarcate themselves. It was remarkable how many cranes alighted into place like ballerinas, without bumping into any of the geese.

MY EYE WAS on the cranes but I was thinking about the land that held them. Both the Bosque and the neighboring

Sevilleta National Wildlife Refuge are also home to endangered species such as the silvery minnow, which is said to be "the final survivor of a suite of small native minnow species" once found throughout the Rio Grande, and the jumping mouse, a small creature hidden from sight, but no less vital to the biome or the regional ecosystem. Sevilleta, the 230,000-acre refuge where we headed next, is rich land; four biomes intersect here—the piñon-juniper woodland that I know from my backyard, the Great Plains short-grass prairie, the Chihuahuan Desert, and the Colorado Plateau shrublands. The Rio Grande flows through the soul of the refuge, flanked by sprawling cottonwood trees, salt grass, and rust-colored native coyote willow. Aldo Leopold was an early believer in the importance of willows to stabilize streambeds and minimize erosion. If erosion continues unchecked, he warned, the Southwest would one day simply blow away.

Like many ranches and forests in the Southwest, Sevilleta was once overgrazed and a ripe candidate for extreme soil erosion. But here's what makes Sevilleta different: the landowner, General Thomas Campbell, after grazing cattle and sheep here for thirty years, acknowledged that the land was badly eroded and established a foundation with a desire to restore the integrity of the land and with a stipulation that the restoration process be studied. Some years later, the foundation donated the land to the nature conservancy, who eventually turned it over to the state. Today, scientists from all over the world come here to study how Sevilleta's four unique biomes have healed.

The land has sprung back to the degree that even mountain lions freely roam here. General Campbell sowed seeds that decades later flowered and mended the land. That cougars still roam in New Mexico is an occasion for giving thanks, for the eastern cougar is now believed to be extinct. In the visitor center, a stuffed cougar—one of the largest ever seen in New Mexico—and a standing black bear made a deep impression on my younger daughter, Pika. She was overwhelmed by the bigness of these mammals but her eyes shone with wonder.

A volunteer told us that there were more cranes in the fields in Bernardo because it was so wet at the Bosque. The fields in Bernardo? We'd never heard of them before. Each year, up to thirty thousand cranes winter not only at the Bosque but also in the surrounding Rio Grande Valley. Grateful for the tip, we took down the volunteer's directions to the Bernardo Wildlife Management Area.

Outside, the morning was frigid and windy. A flock of canyon towhees pecked at some seeds. As I had learned at the visitor center, the short-grass prairie is rich in insects and seeds; pronghorns graze these nutritious grasses. Beyond where the eye can see, the Chihuahuan Desert features magical trees like honey mesquite, *Prosopis glandulosa*, and the screwbean mesquite, *Prosopis pubescens*, whose talon-like seedpods I keep on my desk. Desert yucca punctuates the landscape. A jackrabbit's long ears remain alert for predators while a roadrunner is quick to dart behind its allies: sagebrush, saltbush, and rabbitbrush.

At the Bernardo Wildlife Management Area, hundreds of

cranes were on the dirt road and they moved away in swaths as our car approached. They signaled to one another and moved in small groups. When we stopped at an observation deck, the cranes flew over us: flapping, coasting, repeat. Behind them, a turkey vulture drifted. The cranes filled the sky with throaty, gurgling honks, punctuated with sharper notes from a crane at the back. These social birds are said to maintain conversational contact with one another even while flying.

"The Romans referred to the cranes as *grues*, apparently from the sound of their calls," writes Paul A. Johnsgard in *Crane Music*. "The related Latin word *congruere*, meaning to agree, is the basis for the modern English word 'congruence,' and both derive from the highly coordinated and cooperative behavior typical of cranes." In *Sandhill Crane Display Dictionary*, you can learn about how they purr before they intend to fly or how a couple rubs necks against each other and lets out short, high calls—an antiphonal duet.

After climbing two flights of stairs to a deck, I saw more cranes feeding in the cornfields nearby, a few thousand cranes. The fields were dry and golden and the cranes were feasting. This was a more intimate experience than what I get at the Bosque. It wasn't until now that I felt like I was among the cranes and their ancient calls permeated me as I spent a wintry morning *with* them. After ambling along the edge of the fields, we drove slowly. Clearly no one had been here all morning—a flock was congregated *on* the dirt road along an irrigation ditch. They scattered as we approached, clumps of mud and grass still in their toes as they flew away.

Several hundred cranes, perhaps a thousand, were congregated in the cornfields to our right. As I went on watching, a pair abruptly opened its wings as though in laughter and others engaged delightfully in banter or a half dance before briskly returning to forage. I felt sure that this dance expressed levity more than courtship. Meanwhile, a few cranes at the edge of the flock looked around like sentries, wary of unwanted visitors. A threatening or "tall alert" posture might be called for, accompanied by a rattling call.

As I watched the S-shaped ashen necks of the cranes move, sometimes in unison, I wondered what they were eating with such deep focus. In addition to grains such as corn, milo (or sorghum), and millet, I learned that they eat insects, rodents, and frogs. Their sharp, sturdy bills, useful for penetrating frozen soil, have serrated edges to grasp slippery food such as tubers, worms, and snakes.

One bird held a clump of dirt in one foot and with a swift turn of head, snacked on it. The nearby irrigation ditches were bordered with salt grass, bulrush, and coyote willow. Some cranes sat in the tawny field, others were still feeding. The ones who grew satiated fell asleep while standing on one leg with neck turned back like a rope and head tucked into the back feathers. It's a yoga posture, for sure.

Corn with golden leaves still on it wavered stiffly in the wind. A crane's head peeking out from this tan vegetation was like a bird-of-paradise flower. In golden midday light, the flowerlike head moved mischievously through the corn; a prettier head with a red-velvet crown would be hard to find.

The bird moved with the buoyancy of a child at play but the movements were also measured, with a staccato step. The attractive head abruptly ducked out of sight. It had found a russet ear of corn to snack on.

The field was pale gold, gleaming white and pearl gray, with splashes of velvety bloodred crowns. How fitting that these imperial birds should wear a crown. How purposefully yet daintily they walked, their poise unshaken even in moments of anxiety. Their spindly legs moved in tandem with the Earth's rhythm; I felt myself slowing down, body and soul, this was the only way to observe them.

Each bird is a sentient being worthy of our respect but cranes have the added advantage of having a size similarity to us. At almost four feet tall, a greater sandhill crane is taller than four-year-old Pika (the greater sandhill crane is some eight inches taller than the lesser). The cranes moved in unison. When the children, in butterfly dresses, unwittingly took a step or two forward, to satiate their curiosity about this unusual spectacle, the birds shifted away as a group, a few steps farther back into the field. Watching them through binoculars, I saw them all but whisper into one another's ears, with a dart of mustard-yellow eyes and a quickened step.

The wind picked up; one of the children asked why the birds were flying so fast. They seemed to be flying faster than usual: Was the wind blowing them about? They took off as if by magic: How can such a tall creature be all at once airborne? They intelligently ride the air currents and the thermal winds that buoy them during migration. Johnsgard cites radiotelemetry studies which show that "greater sandhill cranes can fly nonstop as far as 360 miles during a 9.5 hour period, averaging some thirty eight miles per hour," with other studies suggesting that they can fly up to 500 miles in a day. They descend daintily on their spindly legs, using their large wings to slow down before they touch down. Seeing a crane slow down like a parachute before it lands, you wonder what inventions it has inspired. You might think that such a large creature would be awkward and unwieldy in the air but it's quite the opposite. This bird with impressive dimensions, though otherwise spindly, is graceful in flight like a damsel floating in enchanted skies.

So striking is the beauty of cranes, so stunning their ancient history, that how we react to these birds says something about us. I was standing in the Bernardo Wildlife Management Area where water-intensive crops are grown for the cranes—but this is an anomaly. The Bosque and half a dozen refuges like it are something of an underfunded, overmanaged anomaly where seven-foot-high corn plants have to be shucked down each season so that the cranes can feed from them, and where precious water has to be temporarily diverted from the Rio Grande and an amalgam of sources so the cranes can roost in it.

You might think that cranes have an occasion to give thanks to us. I wish that were the case. These refuges exist, however, because the rest of our world is inhospitable to these magical creatures. We have fragmented our rivers and drained our wetlands and built malls over them. Sandhill cranes might thrive better if we at least restored the wetlands in their staging and wintering areas.

Then there is the fact that crane hunting has been legal in Canada since 1959 and in the United States since 1961. Johnsgard writes that between the late 1970s and the early 1980s alone, an estimated 17,000 birds were shot, many of which were juveniles. Juvenile cranes are twice as vulnerable when hunters use decoys. Sandhill cranes are among fifty-eight bird species, out of over a thousand migratory bird species, who are *not* protected by the Migratory Bird Treaty Act.

BACK IN SANTA Fe on a Monday morning in early December, I told everyone I ran into about the sandhill cranes that were stopping at the Bosque. Acquaintances I spoke to nodded as though they were vaguely aware that such a place existed.

An eminent toxicologist, an expert in poisons, said, "I have a cousin at the mining school there [in Socorro]. She teaches how to blow things up. . . . There's also a world-famous burger near there."

"Socorro is not much of a town," I interrupted, "but the Bosque is beautiful."

"Oh, yes!"

Freddie, a server at the local bakery, said, "I've wanted to go. But it's very expensive, right?"

"It's five dollars a day to be at the refuge."

Freddie laughed out loud. We both did.

"I thought it was very expensive; that's why I didn't go," he said.

Walking out with a loaf of olive bread, I thought that it's

very expensive *not* to go to places like the Bosque and never to become acquainted with sandhill cranes. How can we afford to lose out on such joy? I give thanks for the cranes, for their fidelity to one another, and for their astonishing fidelity to the ravaged Rio Grande.

12

CREPUSCULAR ACTIVITIES

*O*wling is a verb, so says Debbie Pike, a ranger at the Las Vegas National Wildlife Refuge in New Mexico. It's not quite mid-July and the air is capricious and steamy—the monsoons are looming. I have made impromptu plans to join Debbie's annual owling hike: we will search for owls in the twilight and then stargaze until 10:00 p.m. I book an overnight stay at the El Fidel, a historic hotel in Las Vegas, New Mexico. The hour long drive from Santa Fe to Las Vegas is remarkably green—it was a wet spring—and the latter town's name, which means "the meadows" in Spanish, feels relevant again. The name Las Vegas may now be synonymous with gambling and nightlife, but tonight we are going to explore nightlife of a different order; even the children approve of this trip.

Our first neighbor in our Santa Fe house was a great horned owl, *Bubo virginianus*. The year we moved in, I would drift off to sleep with the owl's hooting lullaby in my ear or wake up to rosy-aubergine skies with the call, "*Whoo-who, whoo, whoo?* Who's awake, me too," cradling my first disoriented instants. In time the owl's midfrequency calls and its shadowy presence on our telephone pole, or in a cluster of junipers and piñon pines, blended into the symphony of our high-desert land. The owl migrated to more suitable elevations for the breeding season and would reappear when

I least expected it; when I wanted to see it, it was nowhere to be found. Over eleven years our resident great horned owl has accrued the status of a sphinx and I yearned to reach out and decode this stealthy bird.

Some Native American tribes believe that owls embody voices from beyond the grave. In the country of my childhood, India, owls are seen as ill omens and associated with death. My grandmother is said to have seen an owl on a tree outside her window in Chandigarh, Punjab, the evening before she passed away. I was only a small child then but this image of her communing with an owl was something I held on to and wondered about. Was the owl at her window a signal that her time on Earth was up? Did she intuit this before she slipped into eternal sleep?

Not all cultures see the owl as an ominous creature. In the Indian state of Bengal, the sight of a white owl signifies great luck—the film director Satyajit Ray reported seeing this owl out his bedroom window shortly before his long-suffering debut film at last found a financier. This owl, Uluka, is a vehicle of goddess Lakshmi, who ladles out wealth and prosperity to her devotees. I have experienced both good and ill luck with owls, all in the same night. Over a decade back, when I was owling in the San Gabriel Mountains in Southern California, we had the stellar luck of getting close looks at most of the owls we had set out to find but just as we began to drive down the mountain in the tourmaline night, we came within a hairbreadth of a head-on collision with a race car driver. My throat constricted in the instant of the near collision, my body stopped breathing, acta est fabula, and I felt like an utter fool for chasing owls at midnight, knowing full well that an owl had signaled death to my grandmother.

In downtown Las Vegas, the historic El Fidel is a red-brick structure that will turn a hundred in 2023. The lobby is spacious and light-filled but our room is bare-bones with hospital-blue sheets. No matter. We don't plan to spend much time here. I am eager to get to the wildlife refuge (it's been ten years) but first we will try out the new sushi bar in the hotel. At 6:00 p.m. on a Friday evening, the train-compartment-like sushi bar is packed to capacity and our hostess seats us instead at a round table in the corridor. A German shepherd and a cat roam in the lobby and our children's eyes are roving.

"There's the cat!" says Mia

"Where?" Pika swings around and her elbow tips her double-decker glass, which cracks into two, spilling ice-cold water on my lap, and as my left hand reflexively reaches to catch the bottom of the jagged glass to stem the flow of water, a triangular shard sinks into my forefinger. Soaked through, and with a blood-smeared hand, I jump up. Our young waitress had asked if she should bring to-go cups for the kids but I hate to add more plastic (or worse, Styrofoam) to the landfill, and I said, "Regular glasses are fine." These, however, are not regular glasses—each double-decker consists of a long fluted glass fused onto a second fluted glass—but fragile, foot-long contraptions.

Not one to solicit attention in public, I pad over to the other end of the corridor, near the kitchen, where workers in black T-shirts busily walk past me to access the adjoining walk-in supply closet.

I whisper to a middle-aged worker: "Would you have a Band-Aid?"

One look at my bloody left hand, cupped in the right, and he says, "Oh, yes."

I shuffle to a corner, to be out of the way as I wait for a Band-Aid. By now my children have trailed me and as I lower my glance to meet their eyes, I see, to my horror, a hundred drops of crimson blood dotting a spiraling circumference around me on the white-tiled floor. Just half an hour earlier when I had walked into the hotel, I had read on a plaque that shortly after the hotel was inaugurated in 1923, shots were fired inside during a bar fight and an onlooker was accidentally killed. An odd detail to frame, I had thought.

A co-owner of the hotel is saying to my children, "Let's sit down on a bench now so we don't track this . . . everywhere."

"I'm a former pediatric nurse," she tells me. Eyeing the gash on my forefinger, she says, "You might need stitches." She tightens one Band-Aid over the finger. "Please apply pressure on it." She presses on another Band-Aid, then a megabandage over the first two. A second hotel owner stops by to survey the bloodstained floor. By this time, my finger is transformed into a Corinthian pillar.

"I might have to take you to the hospital," says Michael, who has sustained his own minor wound and now also sports a Band-Aid.

"I won't miss the owl hike," I say. There is no time to go upstairs to change my sopping dress. Luckily it is a maroon color, so the bloodstains blend in.

AT 7:15 P.M. we are at the refuge headquarters, just in time to hear Debbie Pike's talk on the crepuscular birds we will look for: the Western screech-owl, *Megascops kennicottii*, who nests in ponderosa pine cavities, and the great horned owl, along with the master of camouflage, the common poor-will, *Phalaenoptilus nuttallii*, whose onomatopoeic name is a nod to its song (*poor-willip, poor-willip*), and the fast-diving common nighthawk, *Chordeiles minor*. After the talk, we spray on the citronella-based mosquito repellent that Debbie has provided. In an olive-gray ranger uniform, she is middle-aged, smooth-skinned, and cheerful. We all drive in a caravan toward the Gallinas Nature Trail. To access the trailhead, our party of some two dozen people walks through a cattle gate, next to which a red-lettered sign warns: Caution: Hazardous Wildlife Out and About. Michael wonders if *hazardous wildlife* is code for rattlesnakes but Debbie is already some distance ahead, leading the hike.

The mile-long trail begins with an open short-grass prairie: a narrow dirt path is flanked by native grasses such as blue grama and buffalo grass, and spiked with buttery-and-claret upright prairie coneflowers, floppy mullein leaves, and sparkling-white morning glory. Along the horizon squat olive-green mesas, layered against the Sangre de Cristo (Blood of Christ) Mountains, with Mora Rock to the far right. It is dreamlike to walk in the chartreuse prairie in the twilight and going by the children's springy steps, they find it agreeable to be between earth and sky at a time when they're normally indoors and brushing their teeth. Our lives today shrink away from crepuscular activities but twilight is a fecund, in-between time that can yield reflections or ancestral stories on a rooftop charpoy in India or around a roaring Pueblo campfire. The prairie is greenly expansive; the light is tinged with honey gold and the sky striated with colors from blush pink to dove gray. The scene makes me wonder: Why have we spent so many luminous dusks inside? How could I bear to be shut away while *all this* was unfolding outside?

A superstructure of rocks—salmon pink, ocher, and terra-cotta—devours the trail and we toggle over smooth and broken stones, ruins from settler homes, which our four-year-old calls "a bumpy path!" We hike up to Box Canyon's sheer walls of stone and some of the hikers brazenly perch on the precipitous edge of the steel-gray canyon. We settle a few feet back on a rock formation, where mosquitoes at once descend upon us.

Debbie fiddles with her iPhone to play the Western screech-owl's bouncing-ball call. She warns us not to try this at home and to leave this method of owling to the rangers, so as to not unduly stress the birds. I nod, agreeing. The recording she plays is a string of accelerating notes. We wait for the squat, pale-gray owl to respond. All at once, a pair of slate-gray nighthawks flies over the canyon rim and, before we can blink, the birds, with the speed and suddenness of bomber planes, dive directly over our heads, eliciting gasps from the children. The sleek nighthawks retreat to the lip of the canyon; the tallow flash in their wings giving them away and their serrated wings give off a distinct *phruuu* sound as they pick up speed. The lively pair explores the alcoves in the canyon, which merges ahead into the deeper Gallinas Canyon.

The sky turns a sullen blue-gray as Debbie duly plays

another screech-owl recording. Mistaking the recording for the actual bird, Pika stands up and strides closer to the edge of the 150-foot canyon—"to see the owls"—while I nervously jump up and try to coax her back.

"That's only a recording," I whisper, "to get the owl to come here." I have to be careful: if a hard note were to enter my voice, she might be tempted to giddily run around. Pika is keen to see an owl tonight and I attempt to gently steer her away from the dangerously steep rim. Perhaps she remembers her delight last fall when we were in our backyard with a telescope to look at the Super Blood Moon of 2018. The hit of that evening were two great horned owls who hooted incessantly at us from a high snag in our neighbor's tree. In the brilliant moonlight we got surprisingly clear looks at the marbled ash-brown owls who stared at us with immense eyes, which are 3 percent of their body weight. None among us was more delighted than Pika, who was then all of three, and who treasures her lunch box with a large owl stitched on top. She couldn't take her eyes off the massive owls with their devilish tufts and she executed *petit jetés* in the air while watching them. With their cinnamon-colored facial disks turned to us—the circular faceplate funnels the softest sounds to their ears—the owls let out plangent hoots; they couldn't have failed to notice her. Their calls and presence filled our yard, and our hearts, with an archaic wildness.

Within a week, another incident occurred involving Pika and one of the owls. The great horned owl is a formidable top predator with deathly talons and an average wingspan of four feet. The Cornell Lab of Ornithology notes, "This powerful predator can take down birds and mammals even larger than itself, but it also dines on daintier fare such as tiny scorpions, mice, and frogs." The owl also dines on pricklier fare such as the common porcupine (whose nesting sites I've encountered north of us at the Alamosa National Wildlife Refuge) and it has been known to give its chicks a glossy snake that it has decapitated.

In the twilight, Pika was following Michael to the compost pile in the back, as she sometimes likes to do. She was near a cluster of piñon and juniper trees, following some ten feet behind Michael, when she made an unintelligible sound. Some intuition caused Michael to turn around and walk back to her. Just then, he experienced a substantial swooshing right over his head, before a creature vanished into the darkness. The incident nagged him until he wondered the next day if a great horned owl, perched on a nearby piñon tree, had swooped down to inspect Pika, who was toddler-esque then, but when Michael turned around to check on her, the owl's plans were disrupted.

When we related this incident to Jay Gatlin, a wildlife biologist and owl specialist at Carson National Forest, her eyes lit up and she wasn't surprised. "That sounds like owl behavior," she said. "Owls are ambush predators—they come from above and pounce. . . . It could also be a defense mechanism if a fledgling was nearby." Jay added that the single owl-related human fatality she knows of involved a man who was wearing a "raccoon hat," when a great horned owl pounced on his neck. "Their crushing power is twenty-eight pounds—that's how strong their toes are." Early naturalists referred to this owl as "the tiger of the air."

Perhaps the foiled attempt at inspecting my toddler

gnawed at our great horned owl. One late evening, it sat perched on the long stucco wall that runs along our front brick staircase. We were away at a restaurant. On the drive back home, Mia was scowling over something. As she sulkily climbed up the front steps in the darkness, she saw the great horned owl perched on the stucco wall. Mia gasped. She was face-to-face with the twenty-inch-tall, three-pound bird, ear tufts bristling, custard eyes gleaming, dark barring across its breast and underside; the owl was just a whisper away. As it alighted, its wings all but brushed past her, giving a supernatural embrace before it flew silently into the night. All at once, Mia's temper shifted. Her face shone like the moon. "It flew over my head!" she gushed.

Seeing her experience of pure awe, the *adbhuta rasa*, something melted inside me. The susurration of the owl's wings, my daughter's wide-eyed face illuminating the night, her amazement at the encounter . . . I saw the owl through her eyes. I experienced afresh the lustrous embrace the natural world had given me when I was her age—seven. Silently, we walked up the brick steps and entered our home, the owl's embrace connecting us with a silvery yarn whose one end my daughter held around her finger and the other end was wound around mine.

My neighborhood's historic designation has inadvertently conferred protection to the great horned owl. Three years back, the city purchased St. Catherine's School, which is now used on occasion as a film set—for months the grounds were dressed up to look like the Middle East. On the top floor of the former school lives a great horned owl. I can't enter the grounds because a private security guard is posted at the gate but a friend who knows this guard was allowed a peek, and she confirmed the presence of owl pellets directly below the belfry.

DEBBIE HAD TOLD us at the headquarters that she would play the great horned owl recording last. The largest owl in New Mexico, the great horned preys on smaller owls. So when she plays the familiar call, "Who's awake, me too," it confirms that we aren't having much luck tonight; the Western screech-owl, a mottled lesson in camouflage, did not care to appear. To sprinkle salt over our disappointment, even the great horned owl does not respond. All we hear is the cavernous silence of the night, the lusty buzzing of mosquitoes, and the slapping of thighs and arms to swat them away. The sky has darkened and the night is riddled with concealed hollows: the canyon floor, rock pits, and the seemingly silent arms of ghostly ponderosa pines. For the Zuni peoples of the Southwest, the owl is "the keeper of the night," a fierce bird who can control "the dark side of nature." The owl has the wisdom and the patience "to see what others cannot see." Tonight, both the Western screech and the great horned owls have chosen to remain unseen.

In the end Debbie says, "If you don't want to go on being mosquito food, we can go now."

Flashlights turn on and we beeline to begin the rocky half of our mile-long hike, with the children jumping to avoid stepping on dung beetles. Hiking in near darkness, I think about how, over the course of eleven years, the great horned owl has deepened the mystery of my nights and revealed that the night can at once stir and cleanse me.

The Hopi people of the Southwest have acknowledged

this owl's potency with a great horned *katsina*, a spiritual doll named Mongwu, who is beneficial to agriculture and keeps their fields free of rodents. It's well-known that at night the owl takes over the red-tailed hawk's shift, though it can also hunt during the day. It fascinates me that the formidable Mongwu, the owl *katsina*, also performs a cathartic role: It makes a dramatic appearance in Hopi summer dances in order to knock sense into the *katsina* clowns. Hopi author Alph H. Secakuku notes that Mongwu plays the role of a sorcerer and secretly plans with the chief clown how the offending clowns might be punished. Tonight, we have tried to achieve a certain degree of owlishness by sitting at a canyon's edge at night but now I suspect we are the clowns whom Mongwu is silently laughing at.

IN THE BLACK of night, we return to the trailhead, which spills out into a dirt square—a cattle corral—where two rangers from Fort Union National Monument await us with telescopes. I have been thinking absorbedly about owls and have forgotten about this segment of our hike. Through one telescope, I see the translucent, almost-full moon; my eyes linger over its luminous three-dimensional craters and its pearl-gray edge against the blackness of deep space.

A gaunt old lady approaches me and whispers that she's glad I brought my children along. "They need this," she says, gesturing toward the wide-open prairie.

Just then, Debbie bursts out of the trailhead. "They're troopers!" she tells me, eyeing the children. "They can hike!" This is a relief. I had been anxious that they wouldn't stay quiet enough while we waited for the owls.

Through the second telescope, I see our largest, stormiest planet, Jupiter, and its three moons (out of seventy-five known moons). One ranger talks about how looking at stars has been an activity we have long indulged in to ponder our place in the universe. Have we been pondering owls for almost as long? "Among the Sioux, Hin-Han the owl guards the entrance to the Milky Way over which the souls of the dead must pass to reach the spirit land," Richard Erdoes and Alfonso Ortiz note in *American Indian Myths and Legends*. "Those who fail the owl's inspection because they do not have the proper tattoo on their wrists or elsewhere are thrown into the bottomless abyss." The Sioux belief brings to the fore human ambivalence about owls: Are they wise creatures who guard the entrance to the Milky Way or do they embody blood-seeking, screeching voices from the bottomless abyss?

In the refuge, the night is growing cool but the luminous moon above has a magnetic pull, and I linger and commune with my fellow owlers. My heart wells with gratitude for this ample prairie where I can wrestle with the enigma of owls, and for the rangers with whom I have savored the contours of the moon and Jupiter. All this is nearly enough to overlook the fact that my forefinger is throbbing with pain.

AT THE HOTEL desk, we run into the co-owners just before they leave work past 10:00 p.m. They inquire about my finger and on hearing about the throbbing the man suggests I rebandage my wound before going to bed. Back in my room, I take his advice. I unravel the bandages and discover that my finger was tied up so tightly that the tip is now purplish gray. "Ugh!" we exclaim, taking in the sickly color.

No sooner is the last Band-Aid off than dark-red blood begins to seep out of the gash. I swiftly press fresh Band-Aids into service to staunch the blood flow. I hope I won't need stitches tomorrow. Tonight, owling has been a peephole into the cryptic labyrinth of the night but luck has remained as elusive as the owls themselves.

WE ARE BACK at the refuge by 7:45 but it's already too bright to see much more than shadowy silhouettes of the shorebirds in the pond near the refuge headquarters. Two days before, I had spoken to the Las Vegas National Wildlife Refuge biologist and he had confirmed that in past years, long-billed curlews have been spotted in the ponds in the summer; this refuge is one of the last remaining sizable wetlands in New Mexico. I am keeping an eye out for the enchanting curlew whom I first encountered in Northern California. We hike on a marked trail, surrounded by prairie grasses such as little bluestem and side oats grama, whose narrow leaves minimize evaporation. The otherwise-stark tree chollas are lit with surprisingly fuchsia flowers. Cliff swallows dart about against the pale sky. A blue heron, tuft atop its head, studies the edge of the water. Canada geese with their young, along with a motley of ducks, float around and sun themselves, while an American coot vigorously ducks in and out of the silvery water. We hit a watery arroyo sans a bridge and are forced to turn around. Our trail is redolent with wasps, ants, dung beetles, and crickets, including a translucent orange-red Jerusalem cricket. Mia doesn't want to step on any of these small creatures and she gets bothered that so many of them are in our way. The children brighten when they see a juvenile jackrabbit running errands around its square house, assembled out of broken flagstones.

After the hike, we drive around the 8,600-acre refuge, stopping to see sunny-yellow meadowlarks flashing their black bibs from a wire. A few yards ahead, perched on a road sign is a finch-like bird, dark bluish with chestnut markings, but with a more pronounced beak than a finch. A blue bunting! Fortified by this wink from Lady Luck, we walk up to an overlook to search for shorebirds, but the July sun is blazing now and the birds are hopelessly silhouetted. Mia is feeling restless and terribly queasy. The stabbing pain in my forefinger has dulled only slightly and last night's mosquito bites are begging to be itched—I have more than a dozen puffy bites on each leg. I'm beginning to think that we had better leave.

We are in the car, looping toward the refuge exit, when a small owl flies past. Michael reverses the car and we find ourselves face-to-face with two burrowing owls on metal posts, the third having flown off from its perch on a Do Not Pass sign and alerted us to the presence of the other two. The two remaining owls are slightly farther back from the road, but still easily visible. The children breathe in sharply. The burrowing owl, one of the more diminutive owl species, is reputed to be shy but these round-headed owls calmly glare at us for an eternity. The first part of the owl's scientific name is a nod to Athena, the virgin goddess of wisdom in Greek mythology, who, like the Indian goddess Lakshmi, is generally accompanied by an owl.

The long whitish legs of the burrowing owls have the appearance of leggings and when one owl bobs its head up and down, sometimes accompanied by a cluck, it gives the impression of a short gentleman bowing. I see now why the settlers called this owl the howdy bird. There's something Victorian about their stiff posture, though the owls mean for it to signify a menacing and strident defense of their territory. Standing erect, they're watching us as much as we're gazing at them. I leisurely take in their speckled, tawny-and-cream bodies, and the arched buffy supercilliaries—brows—under which are housed brilliant yellow-and-black eyes.

Pika opens her car window and holds up her lunch box to show these birds the owl embroidered boldly on top. Perhaps she has internalized the call-and-response technique that Debbie was using last night. To our surprise, the burrowing owls consider the owl on Pika's lunch box with curiosity. The next week, Michael mentions this incident to a biologist friend, who delightedly comments about Pika's strategy: "It might elicit a response."

"What are you doing here?" the children murmur to the owls. "You are supposed to be sleeping now."

Most owls are active in the night or at the crepuscular hours of dawn and dusk but a handful of owls, including the burrowing owl, hunt during the day. The western burrowing owl generally uses burrows made by other animals, including badgers, rock squirrels, prairie dogs, and desert tortoises, but Debbie had told us that in the Las Vegas National Wildlife Refuge, these owls make their own burrows.

One gets the feeling that these owls are studying us, albeit with an indifferent air. While humans are not technically a predator—among the burrowing owls' main predators are badgers, coyotes, foxes, and raptors such as Swainson's hawks and great horned owls—the primary threat to burrowing owl populations is believed to be from habitat loss, fragmentation, and "human-related mortality on wintering grounds and during migration." The latter means roadkill, power-line electrocutions, and shootings. But who would want to shoot these owls with rounded heads sans tufts, which makes them look rather like *matryoshka* dolls? What kind of human would want to point a gun at a petite chocolaty owl with streaks of vanilla on its breast and sprinkles on its head and back?

After luxuriating in the presence of the doll-like owls on the Las Vegas signposts, we contentedly drive on past magenta musk thistles. A mountain chickadee, more delicate looking than its more common cousin, the black-capped chickadee, flies off a tree snag. The sight of the owls has elevated our spirits and we are feeling luminously awake. Mia insists that she is no longer queasy and we exit the refuge in search of lunch.

BACK AT HOME, I brood over the owl outside my maternal grandmother's window and I call my aunt in New Delhi to ask about the incident. My aunt is the sole surviving elder who had lived with my grandmother at the time, in Chandigarh, Punjab, and perhaps she can tell me what species of owl had appeared in an oracular capacity to my grandmother on her very last night.

"It wasn't an owl; it was a rat," my aunt says.

I feel dumbstruck, as though someone has slapped me and cruelly erased a cherished image and the meaning I had attached to it.

"A rat?"

"It was rattling in the almirah in her bedroom. So she told Tiklu [my aunt's son] about it and asked if he could get the rat out of the room."

I gulp. I don't want to believe this. I want to pin down this distortion of family lore to my aunt's dotage. What if there was an owl on the tree *in addition* to the rat in the almirah? Whoever told me about the owl? It must have been my mother. And she is no longer alive to field my inane questions.

TWO WEEKS AFTER the owling hike, I plan a five-day field trip, which will include the still more remote Maxwell National Wildlife Refuge, over an hour north of Las Vegas. I call up Chris Lohrengel, refuge manager and sole ranger at Maxwell, whom I've spoken with before. "We'll drive up there this Friday," I tell him, knowing that unless I give fair warning, I will find the visitor center closed. I also call the nearby Cimarron Canyon State Park to inquire about the owls found in the park.

"I had one on my deck yesterday," the ranger says. "A great horned."

The Cimarron trail I am planning to hike on weaves through riparian habitat and it has just opened: it is kept closed from mid-May until the first of August for elk calving.

"It's a bit silly," the ranger says over the phone. "The elk have calved long back." He goes on to tell me that the owl is his favorite animal. When I ask why, he adds: "Because of their stealth hunting ability . . . and their remarkable vision. . . . They can see a rat a hundred and fifty feet away, in the dark."

I mull over the remarkable vision of owls and I think that of course they also have remarkable hearing, with their facial disks channeling even the faintest sound to their ear tufts. Perhaps an owl was on the tree *because* it heard a rat rattling in the almirah?

13

PRAIRIE DOG TOWN

On the two-hour drive north to Maxwell, we stop first at the Las Vegas National Wildlife Refuge—to check up on the burrowing owls there. As we drive up to the visitor center, I spot Debbie on a noisy John Deere tractor, mowing a patch of wild grass. I open my car window to say hi and breathe in air thick with gasoline. In an olive-gray uniform, which she perhaps lives in, Debbie smiles back but she goes on mowing. The visitor center is locked and we decide to walk an adjacent trail first. No sooner have we started than we find a snakeskin, dead center on the trail. It's translucent white, feels like dry corn husk. The touch of snakeskin takes me back to the shimmering skins I encountered in my old garden in Assam, India, where I used to roam perpetually when I was seven, and how I daydreamed about the mysterious creatures who had left the skins behind.

A local painter arrives at the visitor center with a framed painting that Debbie had commissioned—of Princess Fiona, her pet pig. Debbie is still on her John Deere and we wave her over. She unlocks the door and, a minute later, a dark-gray pig wanders out into the lobby from her inner office. Unlike in the portrait, the pig isn't wearing a crown or a tutu. "She's naked today," Debbie says.

I pet the animal's coarse hair and the pig nuzzles lovingly against my ankle. The children giggle. They adore most dogs but it takes some mental gymnastics to warm up to a charcoal-gray pig. Pika puts her hand out to pet Princess Fiona but when the pig snorts roughly, she steps back, stunned.

Debbie confirms that the snakeskin we saw belonged to a bull snake. I ask her about the Hazardous Wildlife sign we'd walked past on the night of the owling hike at the Gallinas trailhead.

"That means snakes," she says. "I just didn't want to come out and say it."

"When I was seven," I say, "I used to collect the snakeskins I'd find in my garden."

"What did you do with them?"

"Oh, I stashed them in a little cave."

Debbie's face lights up. "When I was a kid, my dad gave me a taco box in which I stashed random things I'd find outside: animal hair, scat. . . . These were my treasures!"

We do a loop of the Las Vegas refuge before leaving. Instead of burrowing owls, we see their predator, a flotilla of Swainson's hawks posted on successive telephone poles, as though they've taken charge of the refuge's communication system. As in the morning after the owling hike, we are the lone visitors at the refuge.

WE ARRIVE LATE at the 3,700-acre Maxwell National Wildlife Refuge and are lucky that the refuge manager, Chris Lohrengel's pickup is still parked in front of the modest headquarters. Four wild turkeys skirt around the silent headquarters before skittering away. Chris is a middle-aged man with an anxious air.

"Debbie says hi," I tell him.

He receives the greeting warily and he sighs when we mention our encounter with Debbie's pig.

"I guess she's there all alone," I say, echoing a sentiment I had heard Debbie express to the painter.

Chris nods knowingly. "It's just me here . . . and a maintenance man, who has a doctor's appointment today.

"We're understaffed," he adds, a refrain that we will hear again over the next four days in as many refuges and also at the Great Sand Dunes National Park. "It was the recession in 2008 that set back the wildlife refuges. . . . In the Southwest region alone, there are forty-five unfilled positions. At Maxwell, we've fared a bit better than some other refuges. The regional manager has been fair. . . . He told me to focus only on what I think is important."

The talk turns, inevitably, to owls. Chris offers to show us a great horned owl nest in a stand of elm trees behind his workshop. "A pair has been using it for a few years," he says.

The wind is picking up. The elm trees tower over us and I crane my neck to search for the nest—it's a massive bowl of twigs, which, from below at least, looks more ruffled than neat. While this is a typical nest site for the great horned in New Mexico, the owls have also been known to nest in yucca, in cavities along cliff walls, and even in a high niche in the depths of Carlsbad Caverns.

"They've raised two sets of young this year. I would be working here and I would see two owlets." Chris gestures to the lower branches where the brood of owlets would perch and stare at him. "This was in May. They're fledged now. They've all left."

I nod. The roughly monthlong incubation would have

occurred in March or April and the young fledge by the first week of May. It's August now. In a couple of months, great horned owls will once again croon hooting songs to establish pair bonds and begin their seasonal, altitudinal migration, often within the state, to higher elevations in time for a fresh nesting season.

After we return to the headquarters, Chris tells us about a prairie dog colony at the edge of the refuge where we might see some burrowing owls. I grin. I'm here to see these leggy, ground-dwelling owls but we decide to save them for last. We thank Chris and leave the headquarters.

In another stand of tall trees that line the dirt road, on a high snag, I spot a ravishing Swainson's hawk with a chocolate-colored bib. We linger under the tree and Mia mimics the hawk's *pweee, preee, kree* call. Three trees over, on another high snag is perched a prairie falcon with a telltale malar—mustache—stripe. This falcon fiercely defends its nesting sites against the great horned owl, who is a predator. What I love about prairie falcons is that they are among birds who've been known to play—according to the Cornell Lab, they throw cow dung in the air and then dive to catch it.

DRAGONFLIES AND DAMSELFLIES head alongside us toward Lake 13. An American avocet, with its distinctive rusty-orange head, feeds at the water's shallow edge. The slight curve at the end of its bill recalls a sickle. In the late afternoon, the water in the center of the lake is jade green and edged with blue-gray. Some ring-billed gulls with black wing tips are also feeding here. The avocet bobs its head and a second avocet, its back to us, flaps its wings in the water. A steady rain begins and the water turns gray.

On our way to the prairie dog colony, we spot a pair of now-familiar Swainson's hawks, with chocolate-brown backs, and their cacao bibs prominent against their milky bellies. We're surrounded by open, scrubby grassland. A little ahead, a black-tailed prairie dog, *Cynomys ludovicianus*, squeaks in alarm and ducks into its mound. Then I see a few more prairie dogs atop their mud houses. And, at last, I spot a pair of burrowing owls standing on their mud mounds. The first owl flies due east from its mound near a prairie dog to a spot directly in front of the second burrowing owl. It pauses there before flying away. The second owl registers our presence, but stays put in a way that make me wonder if juveniles are nearby in satellite burrows, which are generally located near the nest borrow.

In the web of high-desert life, the burrowing owl needs allies. These owls often use burrows excavated by prairie dogs or ground squirrels; the population of burrowing owls has plummeted, in part because their symbiosis with prairie dogs is largely ignored and the latter animal continues to be persecuted. Prairie dogs are a keystone species in the short-grass prairie; according to Defenders of Wildlife, their colonies create islands of habitat that benefit some 150 other species. The tragedy is that prairie dogs are very unpopular with farmers and developers—they are brutally poisoned and their habitats are paved over. In the periphery of the Santa Fe airport, prairie dog burrows are systematically sealed and what was believed to be a population of sixty pairs of burrowing owls in 2007, when I first moved to Santa Fe, is today down to just one pair. The North American Breeding Bird Survey found that burrowing owl populations have declined by 33 percent between 1966 and 2015.

The Zuni tribe considers the burrowing owl to be the priest of the prairie dogs. I am thinking that these owls also look the part of a priest: shaggy cream brows and a pale mustache lend them an air of somber authority and they do not have the satanic ear tufts of the great horned owl. The congregation of prairie dogs presumably pays its dues by excavating the tunnels this priestly owl inhabits.

One owl ducks under the lip of its burrow. Why do they live in such close quarters with the prairie dogs? The Prairie Wildlife Research Center notes that burrowing owls "thrive on healthy prairie dog colonies because of the insect abundance. . . . Often burrowing owls will use dung to disguise the scent of their burrows from predators and attract food such as dung beetles."

A few days later, Jay Gatlin, the Carson National Forest wildlife biologist, affirms that these owls "put scat around their burrows to attract insects."

"Their own scat, or prairie dog scat?"

"Probably any scat they can find, including coyote scat."

Burrowing owls winter in the southern United States and in Mexico and as far south as Central America. They arrive here, in their northern New Mexico breeding grounds, after mid-March. In April pairs establish bonds, with nesting following in May. Out of a large egg clutch, after some forty days of incubation, two or three chicks hatch in mid- to late June. I need to keep searching to find a raptor who's not a devoted parent; burrowing owls go as far as to lose weight while feeding their nestlings. They also remain together with their young for at least a month after fledging. So it's likely that in early August, a juvenile is nearby, using a satellite burrow. The juvenile's distress call is said to be a "rattlesnake rasp" but I hear only the disapproving chatter of prairie dogs.

The lemony-yellow irises of the burrowing owl have the alertness of a mother guarding her young; the posture is erect and the buffy supercilliaries above the eye and the malar stripe are showing as they do when the owl is on the defensive. These owls use the sentry system to defend nest burrows and perhaps this one is the designated sentry. After the owl has taken us in, it warily rotates its head to one side and then to the other. It stares us down again before it rotates its head all the way back so that its eyes vanish.

Owls have a barrel-shaped eye socket, which doesn't let them roll their eyes, but the disadvantage is more than compensated for by their ability to rotate their heads 270 degrees. This burrowing owl is purposefully alert; its head turns again to the front and, after a flash of lemony eye, it turns fluidly to the side. It is almost 4:30 now and the light is gray. It is still raining and the owl, tawny in this light, stays on duty until we move on.

ON THE DRIVE back to our inn, we spot a pronghorn antelope. I rest my eyes on this lovely animal, a comeback kid of conservation, with its autumn-gold-and-white body and a black painterly streak on its face. Just minutes later, a pair of bison come into view.

"I've never seen buffalo," Mia says. "And I've wanted to."

We slow down. It's a black pair with a caramel-colored

calf. The adults are imposing with their bulk and horns. The calf shadows the mother, nudging her for milk, but she keeps slipping away from the calf's grasp. The male follows at a distance of some ten feet.

That night, our innkeeper tells us that the bison are from Ted Turner's ranch, a 560,000-acre property.

Scientists now believe that bison are keystone herbivores in North American grasslands. The manner in which they graze, wandering far and wide, trimming the grass and fertilizing the soil, unlike domesticated cows who graze predominantly in localized areas, actually promotes grassland biodiversity.

THE PRONGHORN ANTELOPE lingers in my mind—its fragility and splendor suggest African wildlife (its closest living relatives are the giraffe and the okapi). A hundred years ago, the pronghorn was headed toward extinction but this exquisite antelope has since recovered, largely due to its protected status in refuge lands. The next morning we return to the Maxwell refuge and, to my astonishment, I spot a flock of some thirty pronghorns, including young ones, on a large grassy mound a half mile or so east of the refuge entrance. I get a superb look with my binoculars. That life thrives in this refuge suggests that Chris, single-handedly, is taking care of what is important. On a sign I read that the Maxwell refuge was established in 1963, and some four hundred acres of corn, alfalfa, and other crops are grown here annually for migrating birds. Surely the numbers are outdated? I can't imagine Chris doing all that farming to boot. By the time we finish another loop of Lake 13, it's a sweltering noon and cicadas are chirping.

This time, on our way out of the refuge, I see two dozen

prairie dogs atop their mud mounds, skittering, doing sun salutations, and eating with humanlike gestures; others are undertaking their ancient work of keeping tunnels in order and aerating the earth. Several grasshoppers settle on our windshield. There are easily a dozen burrowing owls scattered among the prairie dogs. The owls are quick to register our presence and fly back a few feet. They are dotted throughout the prairie dog colony, a diagonal line here, a horizontal there, as though sketching an owl constellation.

A couple of days later, when I tell wildlife biologist Jay Gatlin that I am interested in researching Native American attitudes toward owls, she introduces me to her colleague, forester Erica Enjady, from the Mescalero Apache Tribe. Over the phone, Erica acknowledges that her work to protect owl habitats has in the past conflicted with prevailing attitudes in her tribe. "When I was mitigating endangered species habitat for the New Mexico spotted owl, and trying to implement NEPA [National Environmental Policy Act] guidelines, I would get asked the question [by tribal members]: 'Why are we doing this?'"

Many Native tribes see the owl as an omen of death and a bird to be eschewed. "There's this conflict with the white man's attitude, about whether we want them [owls] to flourish," Erica says. Over the years, she has thought about the symbolism of owls in Native cultures, including among the Navajo, who share beliefs about owls with the Mescalero Apache. Once a nomadic tribe, the Mescalero Apache now have some five thousand members in south-central New Mexico. Erica tells me that the beliefs of her tribe haven't been well-documented. "I don't know if that's because of a lack of interest from anthropologists or because there was a strong pushback from my tribe early on.

"For my tribe, an owl represents a messenger," she says. "People assume that the message is bad but for my family, it is not necessarily bad—it's just that something big is going to happen."

Now she offers her take: "When something good happens, we like to take responsibility. But when it's negative, we don't want that attributed to us. We don't want to acknowledge it's our doing—and it gets put on the owl!

"The people in my tribe don't say the names of owls and snakes; they might call them 'those birds that come out at night,'" Erica says and I note that she herself avoids using the species names of owls. I ask her why she became a forester.

"Because I believe in the ethic of caring for watersheds and . . . restoring the land. I wanted to have a career working in natural environments. . . . The New Mexico spotted owl was in the news when I was entering college in the late nineties. It was a hot topic when I graduated."

The New Mexico spotted owl is still in the news, this time because the WildEarth Guardians has sued the Forest Service for failing to protect its habitat; contrary to Forest Service claims, it turns out that logging is not beneficial for this owl. When I ask Erica about which owls she has encountered in the wild, she answers vaguely. I ask her to describe what she feels when, during her fieldwork, she comes upon an owl.

"For me, it's recognizing that there's an owl here and that it means something. And I'm going to leave it alone and walk the other way."

ON OUR WAY to Great Sand Dunes National Park we stop in Taos and at the Millicent Rogers Museum, I admire an owl pot, circa 1150–1450, from Paquimé in northern Chihuahua, Mexico. Painted dove gray, with terra-cotta-and-black stripes, this ancient owl is a study in how opposing geometrical lines can harmonize in a circle. I wonder if opposing cultural and ecological views about the place of owls in our world can meet somewhere so that we can begin restoring the habitat we stripped away by plugging their burrows or logging the mature trees where they nest. The great horned owl looks off pensively into the distance but paradoxically draws the viewer in. I sketch the owl with my pen to try to comprehend its hypnotic power.

In *Cuentos: Tales from the Hispanic Southwest*, owls are associated with witchcraft or sorcery. In one tale, "The Dance of the Owls," a traveler feigns sleep while he watches an astonishing metamorphosis: his two hostesses rub magic powder on their bodies and invoke Satan to transform themselves into owls and then they leave the house through the chimney. It's not enough for the traveler to watch this indelible scene; he must try out the magic powder for himself and, after flinging off his Christian medallion, he invokes Satan and takes on the body of an owl. When he flies off the rooftop to a nearby cluster of juniper trees, he discovers two owls dancing wildly around the trees in the blackness of the night. When I retell this story over the phone to Erica, who is part Hispanic and part Mescalero Apache, she listens with rapt attention and she laughs when I tell her that in the morning, the two women rib the traveler about their nocturnal adventure—and he lives to tell the tale, albeit with a permanent scratch from a wildcat on his arm. Erica is impressed by the ending of the story, in which the two women reveal that they knew about the traveler's antics but instead of cursing him as he had feared, they good-humoredly send him on his way.

"In northern New Mexico Hispanic culture, owls are symbolic of medicine that sometimes gets interpreted to mean sorcery or magic," Erica says. "But peel back the layers and the original meaning is closer to natural medicine with herbs, not magic or evil."

In my own culture, the owl offers a different kind of medicine. Its unwavering gaze burnishes its reputation for intelligence and wisdom and as the chosen bird who accompanies the goddess of wealth, Lakshmi, the owl's gaze exhorts us to use wealth wisely. Its presence is a reminder not to become trapped in material wealth, but to seek true wealth from Lakshmi's sister, Saraswati, the goddess of learning. It is perhaps with a nod to Saraswati that I have spent these last days of the summer chasing owls.

OVER THE NEXT four days, I observe birds in the Alamosa and Monte Vista National Wildlife Refuges in Colorado and I am passively looking for owls, but while I see a few spectacular birds, such as the white-faced ibis near the water's edge, in these otherwise forlorn, drought-stricken refuges, I do not as much as hear an owl. Instead I see clouds, like puffy owls in the sky. On our first evening at Great Sand Dunes National Park, around dusk, we hike the Montville Nature Trail, which skirts a gurgling stream and is reputed to be rich in birds, but we see nary a crepuscular bird and instead I get devoured by a devilish swarm of mosquitoes.

BACK AT HOME, after dinner we play a newly minted game: "I'm thinking of a bird whose name begins with the letter *P* and it lives in India." After everyone has had a turn asking a question, Pika says: "I'm thinking of a bird that comes out in the winter." When no one can guess the bird she has in mind, she spills out the answer: "Snowy owl."

I look at her, astonished. I've never spoken to her about this owl, a native of arctic regions, certainly not of the arid Southwest. Neither has Michael ever discussed this owl with her. "Who told you about the snowy owl?" I ask with curiosity.

In lieu of an answer, Pika gives me a *Mona Lisa* smile, as though she simply knows. Her enigmatic look suggests that my query is unanswerable or, if an answer exists, it has already flown to a nether-realm and is now as unknowable as whether or not an owl perched outside my grandmother's window before her death. The snowy owl is a large white owl, like Uluka, the owl who is a vehicle of the goddess Lakshmi, and I have always thought of my younger daughter as a petite Lakshmi—for Pika disperses wealth in the form of smiles and hugs. All this means little in rational terms but braiding nature and mythology into my life can be surprisingly meaningful. Just as burrowing owls prefer to live close to prairie dogs, I prefer to live close to birds— they align me nearer to the source. Still more contiguous to the source are small children and the elderly and I suspect that they comprehend a flash of yellow eye and the vocabulary of talons, mottled wings, and clandestine signals far better than the rest of us.

14

CERRO PEDERNAL

O n the morning of January 2, 2020, we walk into the Rio Grande Gorge visitor center in the village of Pilar in northern New Mexico. A stout blonde woman at the desk swings her head in surprise: "Are you crazy?"

"We're here looking for bald eagles," I say.

Outside, a blustery snowstorm is picking up speed. It would have been awkward, however, to change our plans. A week before, when we returned home from a snowy Christmas Day hike, Pika had noticed water dripping next to her indoor play table. Today, roofers are coming to finish installing a partial new roof. The smell of burning tar, I've learned, snuffs out holiday cheer. Having already postponed our search for eagles in the Taos area to get the leak fixed, we have run out of elbow room: it's the last weekend before schools and work start up again.

Bald eagles winter in New Mexico and in February they begin to leave the state for nesting grounds as far north as Canada and Alaska. In the early 1980s surveys showed that over 200 bald eagles wintered in the state; as the species continued to benefit from its endangered status, that number rose to 512 birds in 1990. The bald eagle was delisted from the endangered species list in 2007 and few population counts have been done since then. Based on field observations I did in the Rio Mora and Las Vegas National Wildlife Refuges this past December, I am beginning to wonder if their numbers have lately dipped.

At the mention of bald eagles, the sixtysomething woman at the desk nods and warms up some. "We have one that hangs around near the gauge station, not far from the junction bridge."

"Just one?" I ask.

"Just one this year. I think I bring bad luck to this place. . . . Last year my husband and I went to Alaska and I thought the place would be swarming with bald eagles, with all those fish hatcheries nearby. But we saw only two eagles."

"Or maybe our world is getting less hospitable for them."

"A couple of years back we had two here. But one didn't make it. He died."

"Died?"

"It was a nightmare that year. We had so little water in the river, there were hardly any fish. This one, he didn't migrate away; we found him under the bridge," she says, referring to the bridge that skirts the village of Pilar.

In the winter of 2017–18, we had very little precipitation, a drought was ongoing, and the oldest water gauge in the state, at the Embudo station along the Rio Grande, was at its lowest recorded level ever. Many scientists believe that in the Southwest we are in a megadrought that began in the early 2000s.

"We called Game and Fish and, before they came, all the people around here went over and had a look at him. When Game and Fish took him away, he was still alive but not for long. They said he was dehydrated. And I wondered, how could that be, couldn't he get water from the river? But they mostly get their water from the fish, I'm told."

I stare at a topographical map of the area spread out on the counter. The bald eagle was too weak to migrate! I feel sick thinking about the fate of the bird.

She hammers in the final nail: "It died of starvation."

Telling the story has moved her as well. Her name is Laurie. For some time we speak of other misadventures (of hikers, climbers, and treasure hunters) before we return to eagles. "The one we have now is the village pet," she says with a wan smile, before she gives us directions to drive some seven miles toward the John Dunn Bridge and a stern warning not to go beyond the bridge where the road grows steep. A tragic incident occurred near there last fall when a kayaker got separated from his kayak. He attempted to scale a cliff to get back to his campground but fell to his death in a treacherous section of the river called the Taos Box.

As WE WALK out of the visitor center, an old man is snapping ice off his windshield wipers. My eyelashes are wet with snow; the storm is mounting. The man asks us about road conditions south of here, toward Albuquerque. When I tell him that we are headed to the 157 detour to look for a bald eagle, he winces.

The village of Pilar is about the size of a postcard. We drive past the bridge under which the ailing eagle had retreated. The road ahead has not been plowed and is soon covered in several inches of snow. Fog ominously creeps up our car's windows. I clean off the condensation with the back of my hand and peer out. We are driving along the edge of the Rio Grande and if the car were to skid we would land neatly in the frigid water below. I scan the bare, snow-dusted trees along the far side of the river and the ginger-colored coyote willow along the side adjacent to us. The sugar-white morning yields no sign of birdlife. I recall how the people of Pilar had bonded with the two eagles, now down to one. Last winter was different: Michael was shoveling up a snow mountain for the children to slide down. Laurie had told us that this past summer, the river had abundant rainbow trout. Still, could it be that only one eagle has returned here?

The river gurgles fiercely—I dart an anxious look. While driving toward Pilar I had noted the river's jade color but up close the water seems perilous. A jarring image flashes through my mind: we skid over the ice, and . . . A couple miles later we reach a section of the narrow road that is milky white. No other tracks. Are we the first ones to foolishly drive through this morning? We don't have iPhones. I occasionally carry a flip phone for emergencies but a few days back, when the car got stuck in snow, I discovered that my rickety old monthly plan had been phased out. In any case, there is no reception here. The kayaker who fell to his death in this area had been trying to text a friend to rescue him and his texts grew increasingly abusive because his friend wasn't receiving them and didn't respond. So Laurie had told us.

I abruptly say, "I think we should turn back."

Michael was starting to think the same thing. I scan the snowy snags along the river once again. Nothing. After we have turned around, I spot the glistening white back of a duck in the water—a redhead—and, near the bridge, a few mallards.

"Sometimes the search is enough," I say out loud. And I mean it.

WE REACH THE junction where we turn left, and north, onto the narrow highway to Taos and we turn into the heart of the snowstorm. Soon, the harrowing icy road, the frenzied drivers, the hairpin turns along the winding canyon, and the driving blizzard of snow have me silently awash in a wave of anxiety while the children play unaware in the back seat with their old puppy stuffies. When we at last reach Taos, we head straight to an old haunt, the Hanuman Temple, but we cannot drive down to the parking lot until a minivan stuck in the snow is able to screech its way out.

THE ROAD TO the Red River Fish Hatchery, where we are headed the next morning, is rich with tall ponderosa pines, their trunks lined like the palm of an elderly man. The lofty ponderosas, profoundly green, stand out like royalty among the courtier-like piñon pines with their slightly bent canopies. A little later, I stand on a wooden bridge bordering the hatchery and listen to the river warbling below. Along the icy riverbank, trees and shrubs are laden with powdery snow and the lowest branches genuflect to the water. A pair of noisy, crackling-gray Clark's nutcrackers flies past. A man in waders and an orange worker's vest shoves through some shrubbery and flings his fishing line into the river. Radiant cliffs, their terra-cotta and chocolate-brown boulders dotted with snow, tower above; a bald eagle might be camouflaged among these boulders.

I meticulously scan the cliffs. Nada.

We walk around the fish hatchery. The bald eagle is a fish eagle—its feeding and nesting behavior is believed to be closer to ospreys and kites than, for instance, the golden eagle. The bald eagle also steals fish from ospreys, *Pandion haliaetus*, a habit that Benjamin Franklin vigorously objected to. "For my own part, I wish the bald eagle had not been chosen the representative of our country," Franklin wrote.

He is a bird of bad moral character. He does not get his living honestly. You may have seen him perched on some dead tree near the river, where, too lazy to fish for himself, he watches the labour of the fishing hawk; and when that diligent bird has at length taken a fish, and is bearing it to his nest for the support of his mate and young ones, the bald eagle pursues him, and takes it from him.

So. The bald eagle is an opportunist. Isn't that supposedly an American characteristic? In Franklin's time, it is believed that there were some hundred thousand pairs of bald eagles in the country. We Americans have since poisoned our land and our water and even the US Fish and Wildlife Service acknowledges that bald eagles were poisoned when they ate fish contaminated with DDT. In 1963, there were fewer than five hundred pairs of bald eagles remaining in the country. What does this story say about our moral character?

The hatchery naturally stinks of fish. As I walk around, a pewter-colored dipper tests the dark water in a pond before it slips underneath. Charcoal-colored fish move sluggishly in the murky pond. On land, flocks of juncos, or snowbirds, flit about. From a wooden post a buff-colored Townsend's solitaire surveys the frigid, sparkling morning.

AROUND TAOS, WHEN I tell a handful of people why I am here, eyes light up and hot tips come my way. A music teacher at a play space, Twirl, used to work for a hot-air balloon company. "When I glided into the Rio Grande Gorge with the owner of the company, he would point out a couple of bald eagle nests built neatly on sheer cliff faces," she tells me, her eyes widening. "He knew about such things. . . . He would ask us to hush when we went past those nests."

A waitress at El Gamal, a Mediterranean restaurant, says that when she drove her niece down to Santa Fe recently, she asked her to look out for a bald eagle, south of Pilar, near a coffee shop named Sugar's. The niece did in fact spot the eagle flying in the canyon to her right. The waitress mimics how her niece's jaw dropped and she rasped: "It's over there!"

"When I first saw it, I gasped at the bigness of the bird," the waitress confesses. "'What *is* that?' I thought. I first saw it on a tree near Sugar's. And I've looked for it there ever since."

The people I talk to would not call themselves birders but they speak of the bald eagle with reverence; they keep an eye out for *the bird*.

HAVING FOUND ONLY stories in Taos, the next morning, on a chilly Saturday, we wake early and head south and west to the Midwinter Bald Eagle Survey at Abiquiu Lake. For now this is my last hope. Started some forty years back by the National Wildlife Federation, the count has been conducted jointly by the US Geological Survey and the Army Corps of Engineers since 2007. In 2019, volunteers counted seven eagles—three adults and four juveniles. From the narrow, winding road that leaves Taos, I point out to Mia the imposing mesa we are headed toward. Cerro Pedernal means "flint hill," an unprepossessing name. But the sloping lines of Pedernal Mountain, as it is known in English, fuse dramatically into a flat mesa top. Georgia O'Keeffe could see Pedernal Mountain from her glassy studio in Abiquiu and she adored painting it.

"God told me if I painted it enough, I could have it," she liked to say.

AT THE ARMY Corps of Engineers' project office, we wait for an officer to brief the volunteers gathered here. A man seated behind me is telling a story: "My cousin is a lawyer in Iowa. . . . A Native American client of his was incarcerated for a drug offence; he asked the lawyer [my cousin] to keep his bald eagle carcass in his freezer while he was in prison. My cousin had him sign off on it, to sign a document verifying that he was holding the carcass for him. On Thanksgiving, my cousin would say to the extended family, 'Excuse my bald eagle carcass.'"

I am relieved when Tom Mueller, an ACE officer, begins to talk. He gives us some statistics about the Army Corps of Engineers—they manage twelve million acres nationally—and about the count. "In the last decade the highest number of birds counted was in 2015 when eighteen birds were seen." Mueller acknowledges that the number has since dipped down to seven birds.

"But the important thing is that we are here to count today," he says. "Consistency is important in counts."

So the numbers *have* dipped. Why?

WE ARE FORTUNATE to get a spot on the patrol boat, which
has a capacity of seven people in addition to the captain. For
an hour and a half, we will search the coves around Abiquiu
Lake, a 5,200-acre reservoir that drinks from the Rio Chama,
and which gleams steely gray before us.

Captain Kuhlman, a redhead with a pale tapered face and
ginger goatee, is a reticent man, perhaps in his thirties, all
but unapproachable; once the boat leaves the dock, however,
his mood shifts. "We're the bird dogs of the hunt," he jokes.
"We'll flush out those eagles for the folks counting up on the
cliff."

At the project office we had been forewarned that it can
get very windy and cold on the boat but this is the only way
to get close views of eagles. The volunteers on the sheer cliffs
(where I didn't want my children to be standing) will have to
rely on their scopes.

The sun peeps marginally out of the dense clouds.

"It will only get warmer from here on," First Mate Mueller
predicts.

The cliffs here are even more dramatic than those in Red
River. This striking red rock has stood here since the time of
the dinosaurs; two-hundred-million-year-old reptile fossils
have been discovered in its folds. No less than a thousand
specimens of the theropod dinosaur *Coelophysis* have been
found in the quarry of the neighboring Ghost Ranch. Frosty
gusts stir the bluish-green water, which is open in the center of the lake, but edged all around with glassy ice. As we
motor toward the coves, word comes on Mueller's two-way
radio that an eagle has been spotted near some brush along
the waterfront.

At the head of the boat, I look out through my binoculars. For an instant I think I've found the eagle. "I see it," I say, only to retract: I have seen a remarkable eagle-shaped boulder capped with snow. The cliffsides here, dotted with snow, couldn't be a more felicitous camouflage for the eagles. It is exceedingly cold out on the lake and the wind picks up so that my hair is flapping about. The mood is sober. We haven't seen anything so far, scarcely even a duck!

Mueller comes across as a serious man until you notice the hint of a smile on his full lips. His prediction that it will only get warmer has not borne out. Now he requests that Captain Kuhlman steer the boat into the mouth of a scalloped cove. "The observers on the cliff tops won't be able to see in there," he adds.

Kuhlman agrees to give it a shot. At the approach to this cove, the water is a stiff unbuckling sheet of ice. The boat makes a worrying drone as it cuts through the ice, splintering it here and there, until an ugly grating sound prevails—this could only mean that the boat has hit an obdurate slab. Presently, the boat stalls almost exactly at the moment when we glimpse the mouth of the cove. Nothing here.

"You might want to back up," Michael says.

Which is what Captain Kuhlman does, muttering under his breath. He weaves the shaky boat off the ice and floats her along the farthest cliffs that border the lake. Here, unknown to us, a coveted sight awaits. The water is a patchwork of jade green and slate blue with a ubiquitous glassy sheen. The sun teases, not coming out forcefully enough to warm the air, nevertheless lighting up the antediluvian red rocks until the snow on the cliffsides gleams. We are nearing the other end of the lake and, all at once, on a tree snag against the cliffs, there it is. As close as I could wish for.

Mueller gasps. He has been doing this count for eight years. "This is the closest I've gotten," he says. "Ever."

Pika points excitedly at the bird.

The bald eagle is looking off to its left; it's in profile. It turns its head so that for a long instant it looks directly at us and then it fluidly turns its head to the right. It has taken note of us. I swallow. The eagle moved its head with utter control, there was no wavering; it paused and leveled eyes with us long enough to see and let us know that we had been seen, before it turned to its right.

"It will take off soon," the captain quietly predicts.

But the eagle stays. For the moment, our presence does not deter its watch. Adjectives fall short: stately, imperious, but most of all, magnetic. Its beak, a splash of egg-yolk yellow, projects out of a brilliant white head, mounted on a dark chocolate body. The bird glows in the soft winter sun, its beak and feet seemingly spun of gold, its white feathery head luminous. I soak in its piercing, yet serene gaze, its sibylline presence. It no longer matters that it is a glacial January morning.

The eagle shifts position so that its body is now horizontal and its tail lifts up long enough for me to see its white trousers and bare lower legs, an adaptation that helps it to hunt in the water. It retracts to vertical position. Will it stay? No.

The eagle rises into the sky, its massive chocolaty wings effortlessly slicing the air. All at once I see it soar past the mountain O'Keeffe loved. Both Pedernal and the bald eagle are titans and I feel as though I am listening to a strain of a sacred song. I shake my head, incredulous, but the eagle *is* gliding against the backdrop of Cerro Pedernal; my heart is molten like when I once sang an eighth-century ode to the Ganges River, onstage. As I follow the eagle's stirring flight through my binoculars, I see *another* eagle in the sky flying in from the opposite direction and crossing paths with the first. On the heels of the unsuccessful Taos trip to find a bald eagle, it is overwhelming to see two at once, bisecting each other's paths in the shimmering air. I track the second bird's flight until it vanishes behind some cliffs. Now I have lost sight of the first eagle, too, and I frantically scan the landscape until a boy on our boat, in a blue puffer jacket, calls out: "Bald eagle."

The first eagle is perched right on the tawny waterfront and we're fortuitously headed in that direction. Beyond the dull-blond beach, the land rises into an incline dotted with juniper trees and brush. This time we don't get a close look. Its immense wings on full display, the eagle flies farther back, toward a juniper, and it perches on a post next to the tree. Here it holds its ground with an air of wariness. It knows we haven't left but it refuses to let our presence alter the course of its morning.

"Somehow I think it's a male," Mueller says.

"Because of its bravado?" Kuhlman quips.

They laugh.

Our boat is far enough away now that the bird is probably right to be undeterred. The eagle has grown small to the eye but it is still a focal point, a flag in the landscape, an exclamation point! The boat turns slightly and now we face the wind; it grows increasingly frosty.

Captain Kuhlman tells us that the bald eagles in Abiquiu Lake come from British Columbia. "These are solid birds," he says with a trace of pride. He contrasts these sizable eagles with the ones that summer north of us in Colorado and who fly down to Mexico for the winter. "The eagles from Colorado are a bit smaller," he says.

Kuhlman is onto something. Within a species, there is an empirical rule, a biological law that animals living at higher altitudes and in colder regions are bigger. Bald eagles show reverse sexual dimorphism, which means that a female can be 25 percent bigger than a male. A 1988 study showed that in New Mexico, a southern male can weigh as little as six and a half pounds to a northern female's fourteen pounds.

Musing over the differing winter trajectories of this species, Kuhlman adds, "So what is cold is a relative thing."

The air is now cuttingly icy. Pika is growing alarmingly cold and though she had snuggled up to me several minutes back, she has now quieted in a way that has me concerned. She had acted similarly two years back when after a fresh snowstorm on a December morning at the Grand Canyon, we had walked out onto an icy trial; she was two and a half then and I had been carrying her. She buried her face into my chest and fell asleep abruptly in a way that I found frightening. I turned around and briskly walked her to a small visitor center and stayed there until she returned to her familiar self. Now, with the wind slapping against our faces, her cheeks are wan and cold. I bite my lip. There is no way to quit the boat. I murmur to her and when I get little in the way of a response, I ask if she would like hot chocolate after.

"Yes," she says at last, in a way that makes me think that hot chocolate would be just the thing. I ask Mueller what our plan is.

"We're turning around soon," he assures.

"She's only four and a half," I say, by way of explanation. "*I'm* getting cold," he adds sympathetically.

I nod, eyeing Mueller's solid frame. Pika is petite and a small body can lose heat rapidly. I cuddle her into my winter coat insofar as it's possible; Michael is anxious about hypothermia. A little later, a woman from the rear of the boat comes over and offers our children hand warmers, which they tuck into their gloves.

ON OCCASION, THE Army Corps officers heading the other teams of volunteers (we saw two small groups, looking like stick figures, standing atop gusty, vertical cliffsides) radio Kuhlman or Mueller to report a sighting. After all is tallied, however, in accordance with the numbered, gridded maps the officers are carrying, we are at a total of only three sightings. All are adult bald eagles. Does this historically low number signify a dip that we should be concerned about? Are population numbers declining? Or have warmer winters caused a distribution shift? 2019 was the second warmest year on record since 1850. Later I discover a long-term study published in 2015 in the *Journal of Raptor Research* that acknowledges that the number of eagles counted in New Mexico has decreased by 1.7 percent per year between 1990 and 2010, with a "significant decrease" also noted in eagle populations in Arizona, Colorado, Nebraska, and Texas. This startling finding flies in the face of the accepted theory about the robust recovery of this very American bird. The eagle populations in the northern states seem stable, however, which suggests that in the era of climate change, fewer eagles might be migrating this far south because the Southwest is only getting hotter and drier.

Mueller is telling me that 51 percent of the water in Abiquiu Lake is being stored here for the city of Albuquerque. I wonder aloud about the unchecked development going on in our water-starved state. Not only in Albuquerque, but also in Santa Fe, where sustainability does get talked about, construction is booming. Where will we find water for thousands of new residents? "Does the Army Corps of Engineers have any say in the matter?"

"No," he bluntly says.

I stare in surprise.

"The City of Albuquerque could drain their portion of the lake dry if they wanted to," he adds. "There's nothing to prevent it. Not unless Congress was to pass some legislation."

I must be listening grimly, for to ease the darkness of his statement, he mentions that two progressive senators, Tom Udall and Martin Heinrich, "get it . . . and they're trying to initiate some legislation."

Water rights in New Mexico are very complicated. Still, I wonder: Are there truly no checks to prevent shortsighted cities from draining our reservoirs? Bald eagles hew close to water sources such as rivers and reservoirs and as the marrow of our land is sucked dry, there will be fewer areas for the eagles from British Columbia to winter in.

My eyes turn to the striking red rock cliffs before me, anointed with snow, the glassy blue-green water, the undulating tan waterfront. When I saw that eagle fly against O'Keeffe's mountain—the one about which she'd said that if she painted it enough times, God would give it to her—the eagle had rippled through this stillness and into my heart. I struggle not to let Mueller's honest pronouncements about the forces that stand against the eagles and the land snuff out the way in which my heart had felt luminous. But the gloomy statistics persist: we found only three birds this year.

We are headed straight back to the dock now. "Normally I take pride in parking the boat like a Cadillac," Kuhlman is saying. "But today . . ."

Only now does Mueller reveal that the motor steering of our boat gave out sometime during our voyage and even the manual steering is barely working now.

Kuhlman laments that he will have to jam the boat into the dock, and just when his wife and child are watching from the waterfront!

"The boat is acting like it knows it's being replaced this spring," Mueller says.

Despite the constraints, Kuhlman docks the boat with relative grace. His face lightens with palpable relief and he offers Pika a hand as she hops back to land. Her figure, huddled in a charcoal jacket, is tiny against the gleaming lakefront and the massive snow-speckled cliffs. Her generation will inherit this land one day; sometimes I wonder if these journeys will spark in her a love of wild places and a desire to keep the land from degrading more.

The way Kuhlman shakes hands with me, and the gleam in his eyes, is an acknowledgement that this was no ordinary trip. The icy barrier he had kept up before we got onto the boat has melted. The Earth exhales a whiff of sunshine.

Soon, Michael and I are wandering up a steep incline in search of our car. The children follow, while asking us something. We nod reassuringly: a search for hot chocolate is now on.

15

LA JORNADA DEL MUERTO

Two weeks after the Abiquiu Lake bald eagle count, I am still troubled about the low numbers of eagles I have observed this winter in northern New Mexico. Are things any different in the southern part of the state? I call the visitor center at the Bosque.

"I saw two this morning," a volunteer tells me.

Good. I am eager to count the eagles there. I would also like to search farther south, in the fabled Elephant Butte Lake State Park, where I haven't been yet, to understand if the low bald eagle numbers this winter in northern New Mexico are an anomaly.

On the Friday afternoon of Martin Luther King Jr. weekend, driving south, we stop by the Bosque, in Socorro. After finding no eagles there, early the next morning, we head down the I-25. At a wildlife refuge I had recently bought a book (a fat binder, really) on county-by-county birding in New Mexico. The book's twenty-year-old directions lead us to Exit 89, off Interstate 25, to enter the northern end of Elephant Butte Lake State Park—North Monticello Point. Based also on a birding trip a Texan birding group undertook here three years back, which I read about online, I imagine that we'll see hundreds of shorebirds here, perhaps with eagles flying overhead.

At first glance the landscape of North Monticello Point is

utterly bare. Mountains squat sullenly some distance ahead but everywhere the prehistoric terrain is dotted with straggly, desert-hardened brush: creosote bush, four-wing saltbush, and snakeweed. In the dry, bracing air, we drive past a steep sandstone cliff. Abruptly we see water below—in this arid land, the sweeping sight of vibrant, turquoise water comes as a shock. Michael is surprised that we are so close to the water. Our book's directions suggest that we are to drive past a cove and scan nearby cliffs for eagles. Instead we are oddly all but level with the water.

Elephant Butte Lake is New Mexico's largest state park, a 40,000-acre lake on the Rio Grande. The offspring of a dam dating back to 1916, the lake is said to have hundreds of miles of shoreline with a depth of some 165 feet. We drive on and encounter an old sign with a faded, rudimentary map, which does very little to orient us.

We stay on the desolate gravel road, absorbing the landscape, which seems untouched, even abandoned. A handful of cows materialize next to our car—two are black, one is black with a white head, and two others are copper brown; they gaze at us meditatively. The gravel road curves and now turquoise water appears all along our right flank. Strangely, some trees ahead are partially submerged in the water.

The children grow fascinated with the cows. The black cow with a white head peers forward and all but sticks its head into Mia's window. She briskly shuts her window and giggles, cowering under her jacket. Pika stretches up from her seat and curves an arm around me. "A hug," she croons with a smile. Mia cannot stop giggling about the cow who almost jutted in through her window.

"Why am I the only one that doesn't seem to be happy here?" Michael says.

The uncharacteristic statement yanks me out of the children's jesting. I note that we're on a small gravel mound. Abruptly, water has crept up to our left as well. Michael is alarmed to see water closing in on our left flank in addition to the right. In an artificial reservoir, the shoreline can vary from year to year. The road ahead (if tire tracks on gravel can be called a road) plunges down and we can't see where it ends.

Michael notes that some of the submerged trees are directly ahead. This final piece of information suggests that we are advancing headfirst into the lake.

Something about the mound makes Michael think that he shouldn't turn the car around here. The mound feels as small as the Little Prince's asteroid. Michael intuits that the surface isn't stable. If the gravel ahead is wet, it could be loose and cause the car to skid or it might buckle and the car could get stuck. He gingerly reverses all the way back onto a slightly wider gravel road.

For the moment, we cannot bring ourselves to think about how close we came to plunging into the lake. The straggly trees growing out of the water give the place a ghostly air. The trees, two-thirds submerged, are still green, so it seems that water levels might have shifted recently but the green looks like mossy growth on dead trees. A few juncos flit about in the brush. This is a long, risky road to take to see a few juncos.

WE LOOP AROUND a gravel circle. In a landscape where cows are the only mammals in sight, all at once, a man in a jeep waves fleetingly but he drives away before I can open my dry mouth. Now we are at the isolated edge of a vast expanse of the lake. Two gulls with black wing tips glide away in the distance. We take another gravel road to get away from the water but we're barely clearing the road. Two caramel-colored cows materialize in addition to some others. A black mother, #9837, and her calf stand to the side and, as we gratingly inch forward, they step in front of the car and block our path. We halt and reason with the cows.

"Please clear off the road," we ask politely.

After they've had their fill of staring, the pair moves on.

The car makes odd, shattering noises as it drives over the gravel and we worry about what would happen were we to get a flat tire. The only thing my flip phone can do now is tell the time. Will mutinous cows encircle us? To my right, a calf suckles its mother's udder. We pause. The path splits into a gulley strewn with stones and we stick to the one that scarcely resembles a road. Snakeweed abounds. At last we spot a sign and inch toward it but the sign is blank and riddled with bullet holes. If ever there was a melancholy, Daliesque stretch of land!

Earlier in the day, Michael and I had been talking about how crossing this part of southern New Mexico was known to Spanish colonialists as La Jornada del Muerto, the journey of death. This was a barren, waterless, and forage-less section for the Spanish settlers traveling on horseback, wagon, and foot, along the 1,600-mile-long route from Mexico City to Santa Fe. Ninety miles of arid scrub without a drop of water must have given the Spanish a grim dose of reality about this region and undercut their dreams of finding Cíbola, the imagined Seven Cities of Gold. Three hundred years later, we confront the possibility of getting stuck here.

Along the gravel path, four deer scatter upon our approach, leaping out of sight. Now we face reality: perhaps this area has altered since the birding binder was put together and water levels have shifted significantly. Far from being a birding paradise, this landscape is not without a sunbaked, stark beauty. An old nest is perched precariously in a disheveled snag; what eggs it might have once contained have since rolled off.

Sometimes you return from a place bone-dry.

We weave our way out of the forsaken landscape and I feel unspeakably grateful when we make it back to an actual road. As we drive toward the town of Truth or Consequences ("Truth or Dare," as Mia calls it), we see a sign for the Jornada del Muerto Historic Site. A hawk flies high over us. I feel that I have knelt at the crust of the earth, that I have touched her rough and bony surface and have come away with skinned knees and an admonition. Humbled and rattled, I also know I was in the presence of something harshly exquisite and true. Now that I have escaped, I know that what I encountered there was somehow essential. There are scarcely any words to map the inner experience but everything trivial has dropped away, and my heart feels like it has been stretched open.

AFTER A SIMPLE lunch of pumpkin soup at the Passion Pie Cafe, we get on the road to Percha Dam State Park, reputed to be one of the state's hidden birding treasures. A roadrunner scuttles across in front of us and takes cover in nearby brush. Since no other cars are behind us and we are in a fairly deserted area, we stop. Seen from our car, the roadrunner seems diminutive and vulnerable. Its streaky-gray-and-tan colors blend remarkably into the brush alongside the road. As it darts in and out of the brush, the leggy bird holds my gaze. The beauty of the desert is stripped back, scuffed; it asks for close observation and true patience before it reveals itself.

In Percha Dam State Park, the soles of our shoes grow riddled with spiky goat's heads—the "horned" seeds of weedy *Acanthospermum hispidum*—but we see more campgrounds than birds. The sun glowers with a white-hot face. I hike a trail that flanks the Rio Grande: a pair of white-winged doves and an equal number of yellow-rumped warblers, nothing more. Perhaps it's the time of day (early afternoon) or the low water level—the river here lies listless and brackish-green with algae. The air feels unconscionably warm. "We're having T-shirt weather," a local woman tells me. Later I learn that this January was the Earth's hottest January on record. Ever. Climate change is no longer a future threat: scientists believe that about a quarter of threatened bird species have already been impacted, in part because their breeding seasons are sensitive to temperature changes. I suspect now that bald eagles are also in the ranks of birds who have been impacted.

Closer to the dam, the river is a greenish trickle, throttled everywhere by bleached rocks. All the dams I have seen are tremendously ugly, like concrete bridges turned inside out. Percha is no exception—it has taken a sledgehammer to the river's native beauty.

WHEN WE APPROACH our last stop in the area, Caballo Lake State Park, we have to choose between two entrances. The first takes us to a parking lot for a boat ramp. A diamond-shaped sign warns, ROAD ENDS IN WATER. Both

Michael and I stare at the spot where the ramp meets the lake. Something hits us: at North Monticello Point, we had been driving on a disused boat ramp! We will only know for sure after we get home and can dig online for maps.

We opt for Caballo Lake's river entrance, which is supposedly good for birds. Eight gulls fly over. This could be a good omen. However, at this man-made reservoir, the birding outlook turns out to be unabashedly drab. I stand at the riverbank, tobacco stinging my nose. Two men smoke nearby. Despite the low water level, two people are sunk in camping chairs, fishing. Spanish songs playing on a portable radio might have introduced cheer if they weren't braided with static. Our children sit on a boulder and simply gaze at the stagnant river, after which they busy themselves searching for snail shells. The ocher hillsides flanking the river are peppered with thorny beavertail cacti and swordlike yucca. Pity the soul who takes a tumble down these barbed hillsides!

A medium-sized bird flies up to a dry, slim cottonwood. I keep watch though it is hidden behind mustard-brown leaves. It flies to a nearby snag and quickly drops to the ground. I give chase. My inkling is borne out. A curve-billed thrasher! Its long, sharp, slightly curved bill probes the ground under the dry leaves, causing a scrunching sound. Its alert, translucent amber eyes look up; it shifts back to a beavertail cactus that has turned purplish magenta. Soon the thrasher climbs up a thorny mesquite. Lanky and with a spiked bill, it's the perfect bird for this austere, elegiac landscape.

"There couldn't be a more ideal bird," I think as the thrasher relentlessly prods the membrane of the earth.

IN THE LAST couple of days, we have driven some three hundred miles to look for bald eagles. After our arid day, as we enter the Bosque I am in need of some comfort. This time around I appreciate better the Bosque's bounty, its watery beauty, and its diverse bouquet of birds. As we enter the North Loop, the hostess-like killdeer with a striped necklace wades at the edge of some mudflats.

At the Coyote Deck at sundown, snow geese honk as they splash-land in the water for the night. The plangent, splattering sounds fill my heart. In the gloaming, the birds are incandescent. The only other people on the deck are a middle-aged couple. Watching the geese, the woman says, "They're coming in by the boatloads."

The mountains are edged in clean lines against the pallid sky and the loftiest among them, the Magdalenas, are dark cerulean and highlighted with snow. In a darkening field, the snow geese gleam like pearls. Soon, squash blossom petals brushstroke the sky and light turns to shadow, but the geese keep flying in, their silhouettes like pictograms in the sky. I sniff a skunk in the air as an accipiter, also called a true hawk, glides above me with its short, rounded wings and slender tail. A mule deer ducks behind some trees. The water is greenish gray, but flanged with light. Where the shining geese have descended on it en masse, it is rose pink. The sky is redolent with honking and hooting. May we forever have such symphonic skies!

After we leave the geese behind, the air soon turns eerie. I see dark raptor-like birds concealed in cottonwoods but there's not enough light to identify them. A pond turns pale blue and then the water and the sky fuse, separated only by a tawny strip of cornfield.

Each visit to the Bosque has been a singular experience. I don't keep count but I've come to this refuge some two dozen times in the last decade. The experience of abundance here supersedes any one incident or sighting. The luminous, blissful shades of water and sky enter my heart, a counterweight to the mundane, steely, overly industrialized world outside.

"Mom, look!" Mia points out the last pond as we exit the refuge. Here, the cranes are like Victorian children, wading daintily in the shallow water. Or they are still, their handsome silhouettes in profile like fine sculptures in the twilight. My heart is full with seeing.

THE NEXT MORNING, when we return to the Bosque before leaving for home, our close call at North Monticello Point still haunts us. Michael estimates that "if we had continued to drive for another half minute," we would have run into watery danger. At North Monticello Point when we were precariously perched on that shape-shifting mound, no diamond-shaped sign warned, ROAD ENDS IN WATER.

When the safe boundaries that we take for granted in everyday life disappear, we are exposed to startling risks but the experience can also crack the heart open. It strips away what is unnecessary. That is how I still feel after yesterday's expedition: raw and ajar. At any moment, while absorbed in transient joy or sorrow, we are only dimly aware that we stand on a precipitous mound. The road ahead plunges down—we can't see the end point, yet it patiently and inexorably awaits us.

AS SOON AS we drive into the loops, the signs are promising. In the first pond, a showy hooded merganser and a black-and-white bufflehead swim side by side in the azure morning. An accipiter flaps swiftly before gliding above me while a Swainson's hawk squats at the side of the pond—this is an unusually close sighting of the latter bird. In almost the same instant, we spot a bald eagle atop a tree snag in the water.

Excitedly, we stop at the Flight Deck and stride out to the ramp. The water is milky blue and the snag, stripped bare, is gilded in the soft light. The eagle looks around with an effortless air of being a lord of the skies. Naturally it has picked the highest point on the snag to perch.

I am focused on this bird but Mia sees another snag in the distance, across the lake, and borrows my binoculars to inspect the bird atop it. "A bald eagle!" she cries.

Soon we drive around the lake and to the other side, near the aptly named Eagle Scout Deck. When I walk toward the eagle, I gasp. The bird is little more than a hundred feet away, as radiant as the wintry morning.

A juvenile eagle, brownish all over with nascent white markings, flies above us and the mature eagle on the snag raises its head and calls out distinctly, "Kree, kree, kree."

This is the prelude. Now the eagle adds to its insistent message, with similar notes, but lower in pitch. The juvenile obediently heads across the pond. Conscientious parents, bald eagles watch over their young not only during the twelve weeks it takes on average for the chicks to fledge, but for several weeks after. The chicks fledge in mid-June and the juvenile that just flew overhead could be seven months old.

I have been standing here so long that my hands are frozen but I am too excited to put on my gloves. I don't want to look away because for the last several moments, the adult eagle has been looking directly at me. I gaze at its sleek, impressively hooked beak and into its limpid eyes. Are we communing with each other? Its white head feathers stand up stiffly in the wind and the winter sun causes its head to gleam. Its body is the color of the burnt toast I had for breakfast. To save time, I didn't make a new toast and now the precious few minutes I hoarded are spent profitably with the eagle.

A man stops next to me and begins to photograph the bird. At the sound of the clicks, so incongruent with this landscape, the eagle gets into its familiar liftoff posture and swiftly rises into the sky. The man mutters, lamenting the eagle's departure. I go on gazing at the flying eagle—unlike the crane, the eagle is lithe and seemingly weightless when airborne.

WE HAVE A rough idea of where the juvenile eagle was headed and now we drive in that direction. A little farther along the road, Michael spots where the juvenile has landed in a cluster of trees, to our left and across from the pond we are now skirting. We halt. An elderly man has just set up a spotting scope to see the bird and he graciously offers us views. Michael lifts up the children, who are eager to look through the scope. The perched juvenile is characteristically dark with burgeoning white markings.

As we drive on, to our right a colony of gulls sails over an arroyo. Abruptly it strikes me that those nondescript birds we saw yesterday evening, perched guardedly in a cluster of cottonwood trees, were juvenile eagles. The evening light wasn't right to make a clear identification and the birds were behind dry cottonwood leaves, but the juvenile I have just seen through the scope is imprinted in my consciousness and it's of the same mold as the ones I saw yesterday. Juveniles can be fairly dark in body and beak. They are chocolate brown when they fledge but they molt in successive years, emerging with splashes of white. Only after the age of five do they acquire the distinctive white head and tail of an adult.

Pairs of buffleheads dive playfully, looking like curved chess sets and occasionally a hooded merganser brightens the water. Alongside a canal rests a group of American wigeons, with iridescent green stripes behind their eyes and white *tilaks* or forehead markings anointing their heads. Along the North Loop, in the shallow waters of a pond to our left, we see the outstretched wings of a juvenile eagle. Strewn across the surface of the water near the juvenile are small white feathers with specks of red. It soon grows clear that the youngster is standing atop a snow goose carcass, picking methodically at it. On a tree behind the eagle, on a branch almost directly overhead, sits another juvenile, riveted by the devouring of the goose. To our right is a wider pond in which a snow-white tundra swan, *Cygnus columbianus*, a rarity in this region, probes the water with its black beak. Like the sandhill cranes, the tundra swan eats grains from open, harvested fields in the winter. We reluctantly drive on, but not before seeing another tree to the right of the feasting scene, where a *third* juvenile eagle sits patiently. Is it waiting its turn?

As we leave the grove of cottonwoods and move out into an open expanse, in a mushroom-shaped tree ahead, a mature bald eagle is perched and chattering with two juveniles. When the parent stretches its wing and scratches its chest with its beak, its head is folded over and it looks strangely headless.

We must have hit the bald eagle bonanza.

Slightly farther ahead, in the sky, two ravens playfully heckle a juvenile eagle. The game goes on for some time. Michael watches in surprise when instead of being defensive, the juvenile eagle begins to play with the ravens, executing swooping turns in the air like an amateur pilot.

We pause at the desert garden to inspect their coterie of birds; Gambel's quails skitter away and white-winged doves flutter up to the trees along the rim. Pika runs her fingers along the chicken-claw-like seedpods of screwbean mesquite trees. A little later, we walk over to the visitor center, where we tell a ranger about our jarring experience at North Monticello Point. She looks the place up but can tell us absolutely nothing about it. At last she gives us the phone number of Elephant Butte Lake State Park. "I would give them a call," she says.

We are about to leave the Bosque, to return home, but eagles beckon us back. On the snag where we had seen the morning's first eagle are now perched a pair of mature eagles. It would be rude to leave without a farewell. The larger eagle, to our right, is the female. Mindful of not double counting, today we have seen at least two or three mature eagles and between six to seven juveniles. We head home reminiscing about the juvenile eagle who refused to be heckled by the two ravens and instead began to play with them.

AT HOME, MICHAEL googles North Monticello Point and almost nothing comes up, except that it was once listed as a birding hot spot in a National Geographic book. He searches deeper and discovers that a couple of years back, water levels in the area were at 5 percent (we were in a serious drought) but now the levels are at 30 percent. So back then trees grew on land that is now submerged. We doubt that the trees we saw there were alive; most likely we saw moss on the spectral trees.

Did sections of the state park get decommissioned and are no longer maintained? The roads looked as though they had been let go a decade back.

We cast a wider search for maps. This time, we pull up a map of Elephant Butte Lake State Park. One section on the map is labeled as North Monticello Point. I zoom in. The location we were just about in is marked a gravel ramp for boats; it is shown with parallel dotted lines, signaling that it's no longer in use. I find it chilling to stare at the dotted lines and realize that we were driving straight ahead on that very ramp. Our fear is borne out. If Michael had not been vigilant, things might have turned out very differently.

Later in the week, Michael calls the Elephant Butte Lake State Park and tells a receptionist about our experience. He wants to alert the authorities there about the danger of having an unmarked boat ramp.

The receptionist doesn't seem to know what he is talking about. "I'll ask a ranger to look into it and get back to you," she says at last. She duly takes down our phone number.

But we never hear back from anyone at Elephant Butte, which is perhaps a fitting ending to our surreal odyssey. Late in the spring, a friend introduces me to a naturalist whose mother does emergency rescue in the Elephant Butte area.

"For some reason, they have a high number of drownings there," he says with a grimace.

16

LIFTING THE VEIL

In a few days, the bald eagles will begin to migrate away. New Mexico is recognized as an important wintering area for bald eagles who go on to nest in Canada. The birds begin to leave in February and, before it's too late, I would like to get a clearer idea of how many eagles wintered this year in the Taos area. I still don't have clear answers about why I didn't see any eagles there in early January. Based on field observations, I suspect that bald eagle populations are not stable in New Mexico. But it's not until I get a response from Kirsten McDonnell, an eagle biologist at the US Fish and Wildlife Service, that my hunch is confirmed. Kirsten tells me that a 2016 analysis done by the USFWS "estimated a median bald eagle population size of approximately 650 bald eagles in the Southwest (AZ, NM, TX, OK)." In 1990, there were 512 bald eagles in New Mexico alone.

"We who live this plodding life here below never know how many eagles fly over us," Thoreau once wrote in his journal. "They are concealed in the empyrean." On the morning of January 25, we drive up to Taos to nudge open the empyrean veil. We stop at Sugar's but the trees around the café are bare, with no sign of activity. The cafe is closed. A rickety, faded Ice Cream sign nonetheless attracts the children's attention: "Ice cream? Are we stopping here for ice cream?"

Michael runs across the narrow highway; from the dirt embankment above the riverside, he sees only an orange-beaked common merganser in the rushing water below.

We continue north on the highway, along the part where the river rushes past the Embudo gauge. I'm feeling anxious; two random people I've met (the El Gamal waitress and a businesswoman in a café last week) have glimpsed a bald eagle flying in the canyon here, whereas three weeks back, I devoted the better part of a weekend to the effort and still missed the bird. Michael is driving faster than he would like to—the drivers here tailgate, cut ahead, and seem to be in a terrific hurry to get to the laid-back town of Taos. As we whiz by, I scan the ghostly cottonwood trees to my right. To enter the empyrean realm of eagles feels like a hopeless quest.

"I see it!" I cry out.

This is a minor miracle, for the bird is perched on the side of a tall cottonwood that faces the water, so I only glimpse its dark-brown back and a portion of its distinctive white head. At the next opportunity, we make a left onto a dirt turnout. We can see nothing from here. The line of cottonwoods has been left too far behind. By some good fortune, a dirt path that begins here continues down to the riverbank, with a few scattered picnic tables below. We park at the end of the dirt road, jump out of the car, and peer around the line of trees that stretches ahead. Abruptly I see large wings, dark gray in the shadowy light, dive down into the water. It's our bird! And it is hunting. It vanishes like the mist. The eagle has a formidable eight-foot wingspan and when you encounter it at such close range, some primal

memory flutters through your soul. This is a different experience from observing an eagle at a refuge; this feels more
authentic, a sight merited.

A trail begins a few feet away and we hop and skip over
the rocks blocking the trailhead. The trail runs alongside
the chattering river, skirting the very line of cottonwoods in
whose canopy I had originally seen the bird. In our drought-
stricken state, bald eagles steer close to artificial lakes and
rivers. On this chilly morning, the trail is frozen white but we
hike on, breathless with anticipation.

As we approach the end of one section of the trail, I grow
nervous that we've lost the bird. Michael gets off the trail and
weaves his way up to a tree.

"It's here," he whispers.

I follow. Two trees down, I see the bird perched above.
So close, its white head incandescent. Each time I see a bald
eagle, it seems to be the first time. On a higher branch of the
same tree is an enormous, shaggy nest. Only a handful of
pairs of bald eagles stay on in New Mexico to breed and the
number of breeding pairs hasn't improved in years. Could
this be a rare breeding site?

Bald eagles are more conscientious than Benjamin
Franklin believed them to be. Not only are these eagles monogamous but they also return to the same nesting site year
after year, stacking a fresh layer of twigs on the old, stick-
lined nest. The female lays a clutch of two to four eggs and
the male loyally feeds her during the thirty-five-day incubation period.

I lift the binoculars to my eyes and, in that moment, the
skittish eagle takes off. Through my binoculars, I follow its

flight across the galloping river and past terra-cotta cliffs until the lustrous bird vanishes from sight.

DURING A QUICK stop at the Rio Grande Gorge visitor center, we miss Laurie. The person behind the desk is gray-faced and borderline rude. No matter. In a hoarse voice the elderly woman mutters something about an eagle who died last year because of a trachea problem: "It couldn't get anything down."

Is this a different bird from the eagle Laurie had told us about? Perhaps, since the eagle Laurie had spoken of had died of starvation two winters back. Later I read in the raptor bible, *Raptors of New Mexico*, that while it is not known what suppresses the bald eagle population in New Mexico, "starvation is likely the greatest, but least documented" factor. Another cause of eagle deaths across the country is "lead poisoning due to scavenging, especially in winter, on game killed with lead bullets."

IN THE CRYSTALLINE blue morning, we drive along Route 570 in Pilar while keeping an eye on the ducks in the river—scaups and goldeneyes with a pirate-like patch behind the bill. After we have crossed into the Rio Grande del Norte National Monument, I see a person in jeans along the side of the road, looking at something. At the same time Michael thinks that he's seen a speck of white. In the next instant, he spots a bald eagle atop a massive bare ponderosa pine. In this brilliant light, the bird looks ethereal, a creature from another world.

We stop in a dirt patch, near a US Geological Survey gauge station, and walk across the road to the other side. The pine tree is some two hundred feet away from the road. Snags are believed to be an important part of bald eagle habitat in the state. For a few minutes we take in views of the bird who is growing unsettled by a couple who has hiked up to the base of the tree. The eagle tilts into a horizontal position and rises into the air. For such an enormous bird, it flies effortlessly, as though weight were no consideration.

It is the eagle's stealth flight that allows it to swipe fish from an osprey's beak. "The eagle appears as from nowhere, and the chase that ensues is likely to end far beyond the observer's range of vision," wrote Royal Dixon more than a hundred years ago.

On some occasions, however, it may end where the watcher on the beach can see the osprey's final defeat. It will drop the fish when the eagle is at last upon it, and before the flashing object has fallen more than a few feet, the eagle has seized it. This last instant in the pursuit is well calculated, for it is invariably noticed that the eagle flies lower than the osprey, as if in perfect readiness for what it knows will be the last resort of its victim.

The eagle flies toward the cliffs of volcanic rock that flank the south side of the river, glides against this stunning backdrop, and crosses the river again, perching momentarily on some brush high on the other side before sailing out of sight.

The woman who has been exchanging eagle notes with us shows us a harrowing photograph she took of this bird's mate—its left eye is hollowed out, whether because of disease or injury it's hard to tell. A veteran eagle watcher, the woman comes here regularly from Albuquerque. She has seen only one pair this year (though the woman at the visitor center had suggested that maybe six birds have been seen in the area this year).

We face the cliffs of dark volcanic rocks, the shade of coffee grounds, and the woman points out a group of bighorn sheep, *Ovis canadensis*, on a ledge of a steep hill, halfway up the cliffs. The impressive size of these animals—males are three feet tall and can weigh up to three hundred pounds—and their curled horns, which alone weigh some thirty pounds, lend them a wild mystique. Two bighorn sheep stand with stately profiles against the rock; one begins to climb down and I see the milky-white rump of a third animal sitting with its back to us. I stay for a while gazing at their ingeniously curled horns and stirring profile. Mia borrows my binoculars. Pika says that she can see the sheep with her eyes.

We drive on, undeterred by snow this time, to the Taos Junction Bridge, which turns out to be an uninspiring metal structure. A couple with waders stands in the water, fishing. We turn around and on our way back we pause again to marvel at the four bighorn sheep—two in profile and the white rumps of two others—easily navigating the high, precarious cliffs. Even these sizable sheep are dwarfed in this ancient landscape. Some thirty million years back, when magma caused the Earth's crust to buckle, a rift was formed beginning in the Southern Rockies and tearing all the way south to Chihuahua. The Rio Grande, formed by this rift in the Earth's crust, is one of maybe five rift valleys in the world. Over the last three hundred years, a rift has similarly

occurred in our hearts that has sundered us from our landscapes and the magnificent animals that roam wild. We rarely
look to these splendorous gifts for succor. What a radical shift
it would be if we sought to live in concert with the natural
world and grew intimately acquainted with the inscrutable
landscapes and the resourceful creatures who inhabit them.
As we drive away, it's still cold enough near the entrance of
the national monument that the river is frozen white. Our
spirits, however, are blazing.

WE HEAD NORTH to Taos where Wheeler Peak, the highest mountain in our state, gleams with snow. The children
draw in sharp breaths when I tell them that Michael has
climbed it. Many of the surrounding ranges are also snow
peaked. We stop at the Hanuman Temple, an ashram inspired by the Indian sage Neem Karoli Baba, who taught that
we are all one and added: "Feed everyone." Here, the wafting
incense and singing, against the backdrop of an organic farm,
evoke the silent rhythms and fervent songs of my childhood.
As my children gaze at the enormous statue of the monkey
god Hanuman, who was Rama's greatest devotee, their eyes
light up perhaps because Hanuman is a lovable god who lifts
the veil on the complex mythological stories I sometimes tell
them. The son of the wind, Hanuman is said to have once
carried an entire mountain, on which a healing herb grew,
to save the life of Prince Rama's brother on a battlefield.
Sometimes I wonder when my children will lose interest in
these mythological tales. But whenever I stop in the middle
of a story, Pika says, "Keep on telling."
Reversing the damage we have done to the Earth

sometimes feels as impossible as carrying a mountain in our arms. There is no magic herb that can heal the wounds caused by the inexorable march of industrialization. What remains in our power, however, is to alter how we see the natural world and to appreciate that this finely tuned biome (what's left of it) sustains numberless creatures, including us.

LATER IN THE afternoon, we drive back toward Santa Fe. After two robust eagle sightings, I have still not given up hope of seeing an eagle on the way back. I dream of seeing it flying in the canyon, as the El Gamal waitress and the businesswoman did. Is the bird in this area the one with a shattered left eye? I'm all anticipation but once we pass Sugar's, my hope begins to wane. We stop at the Embudo gauge station and drink in sweeping views of the green river. No sign of an eagle.

The station, established in 1888, was the first US Geological Survey training site for hydrographers, under the leadership of John Wesley Powell. Some of the earliest hydrological studies in the country were conducted here and the newly trained hydrographers went on to gauge and evaluate the country's rivers and streams. Lakes and rivers are said to make up only .002 percent of New Mexico's total surface area—we have the lowest water-to-land ratio of all fifty states.

We drive on. The sun is in my eyes now, blinding me from my right, where the river flows, so that it becomes impossible to scan the trees.

Just then Michael says, "There's one."

The eagle is flying in the canyon, flapping its wings recurrently, and flying more laboriously than the others I have seen. No doubt it is flying up the green river toward Pilar. Is this the injured bird? I can see only its right eye. The striking white-and-chocolate pattern of its body makes it stand out in the deep canyon, like a comet in the amaranthine-blue sky. Watching the eagle fly is like experiencing a poem taking off. "People come to see it for obvious reasons," a ranger at the Bosque had told me with a smile. No wonder it's the emblem of our country. I concede that there is no way to adequately describe a bald eagle. The only thing to do is to drink in your fill of this arresting bird. Sunbeams caress me, filling my bones with amber warmth; I feel included in the landscape. I always carry the eagle's indelible image within. It's obvious that we must return to the eagle the habitat we have foolishly snatched away by draining rivers and watersheds and cementing them with dams. If more souls wandering by a river were to glimpse this extraordinary bird, they might see that the bird is not a symbol of American aggression; it is a sentient being who goes on flying against relentless odds.

II.

The Sangre de Cristo Mountains in Colorado are glittering white. It has been a long drive to the Maxwell National Wildlife Refuge but soon after we enter the 3,700-acre mixed-habitat area, I know we won't be disappointed. In the distance, I see two bald eagles soaring. At half past noon, we approach Lake 13 and a massive extinct volcano, Capulin Volcano, is right before us. To its left is a second volcano, likely also dormant, with an elegiac mesa top. The mountains north of here, including a couple of fourteeners in Colorado, are like ice maidens, decked head to ankle with snow. The eagles flying over the water are actively using the wind to their advantage. The water level is lower than when we were here last August but the wildlife doesn't seem to be suffering for it.

In the lake, a common merganser, when faced with a massive slab of ice, stops floating, flutters, takes off, flies neatly over the slab, and lands at exactly the right spot from where it can swim forward. I gasp when I see a bald eagle standing at the edge of this ice slab. How does the gaggle of Canada geese just a hundred feet away know that it's all right with the eagle standing nearby? Something about this scene, with predator and prey sunning themselves on the same ice slab, touches the source of life. You experience a heightened sensitivity toward the vulnerabilities we all face, how we are nestled against death, and must continually hone our intuition to stay on this side of life.

Along the farthest beach of Lake 13, two adult eagles and a juvenile stand watch, with a small colony of gulls standing just thirty feet away, once again not rattled by the presence of the eagles. I am astonished by their close proximity. The lake—all the waterfowl in it and the eagles hovering over or watching from the shore—is a microcosm of a highly intelligent system. There are complex relationships here, with staunch allies and foes, but on this sunny February afternoon, the lake is as symphonic as though *The Magic Flute* were playing above.

The eagles are more lively and playful than I have ever seen them. Two circle in the sunny air and a parent chases a juvenile, a white patch developing on its tail, into a cottonwood tree, where they both settle—the parent in the center of the tree and the juvenile on an outlier branch. This grove of bare cottonwoods is well beyond the water.

Over the lake, one adult dive-bombs another in the air but the other skippers away and is no longer molested. Two adult bald eagles circle over the water—one is almost an adult, with some mottling in its feathers—before they go their separate ways. There's an ease to the movements of these eagles; they are clearly content.

An adult eagle hovers over half a dozen common goldeneyes and mergensers, who calmly stay put until the eagle flies away. A gull races in the air. The sapphire water lends a sparkle to the dashing ducks floating in it.

"We get only transient and partial glimpses of the beauty of the world," Thoreau wrote in his journal. "Standing at the right angle, we are dazzled by the colors of the rainbow in colorless ice. From the right point of view, every storm and every drop in it is a rainbow. Beauty and music are not mere traits and exceptions. They are the rule and character. It is the exception that we see and hear."

The children are seeing and hearing and they are activated by this scene. "The juvenile is still on the snag," Mia calls out. But the mother has flown. All at once, five eagles, including the juvenile, soar over the lake. Lower down, ring-billed gulls fly over the heart of the lake. The water is dotted with black-and-white buffleheads. Horned larks, the color of sand, skitter up and down the beach.

A little later, among the five eagles standing on the farthest beach, three, including the juvenile, take off. A flock of a few hundred redheads and coots mingle in the water, arrayed like a footbridge, with a couple of goldeneyes floating nearby like sentries.

Taking a last look at the eagle standing on a mud island, some hundred feet away from a gaggle of seventy geese, I wonder if the geese are unruffled because eagles attack from above, not from the ground. A massive slab of ice skirts the island of mud. The scene is more reminiscent of Alaska than New Mexico. Two mergensers float by with crayon-orange beaks. Past the ice, horned larks dart across the beach.

What if not only this refuge, but also our planet were a safe haven for birds like eagles, if they could live as playfully as they do here, without being poisoned by lead bullets or starved because of warmer temperatures and droughts in the Southwest? Some may dismiss this as wishful thinking but the iconic scientist E. O. Wilson has argued that if 50 percent of the Earth's surface were to be conserved, we would no longer have the tragic phenomenon of mass extinctions and many diverse animal and bird species would have the habitat they need for their populations to stabilize.

In the eagle standing on the island, I see myself: watchful, patient, making no sudden moves, soaking in the February afternoon. Both of us come from someplace else, are content to winter by the lake that is offered, and will sail away when it's time. While watching the eagles, I simply am in the present. The lake is a blissful canvas of pale blues, like a sky come alive with ducks of different shades, bobbing up and down in a blue shard of the cosmos.

17

DESERT BREEDING GROUNDS

When I observed my first long-billed curlew in the Elkhorn Slough near Santa Cruz, I focused on the otherworldly outline of the bird and its monkish pace, not on the perils curlews face. Threats have been mounting steadily since. These large shorebirds are not alone in facing habitat loss but the consequences have been stark in their case. Like other members of the *Numeniini* tribe, long-billed curlews rely on native grasslands, especially short-grass and mixed-prairie habitat, for their breeding grounds. Ground nesting birds such as curlews benefit from big blocks of habitat where predators have to comb large swaths of land before finding the birds. Across the continent, however, what were formerly grasslands have been transformed relentlessly, decade after decade, into agricultural land and human habitat. "Grassland birds have experienced steeper population declines between 1966 and 2015 than any other bird group in the North American continent," write Jay Carlisle and colleagues. The starkness compounds: curlews are being "accidentally" shot in areas where target shooting of ground squirrels is allowed, such as in southwestern Idaho where a population of two thousand curlews in the 1970s is now down to fewer than a hundred birds. When you consider this localized impact of recreational shooting, along with larger anthropogenic impacts such as habitat conversion and degradation in the curlews' range across the western United States, it's no wonder that curlew numbers are plummeting.

"Uncontrolled hunting during the late 1800s and early 1900s and widespread conversion of native short-grass prairie grasslands to agricultural fields up to the 1930s severely reduced curlew populations, and in many regions eliminated them entirely," acknowledges one US Department of Agriculture publication. "There is also evidence that curlew populations may have been adversely affected by organochlorine pesticides in certain regions."

It is through my quest to delve into the lives of birds that I have come to understand the plight of the larger natural world. While researching long-billed curlews, I learned, to my surprise, that they breed in New Mexico and since then I have been in contact with rangers at three wildlife refuges about their whereabouts. In the summer of 2020, I hoped to be able to observe them in their breeding grounds. My queries led me to curlew biologist Jay Carlisle, who invited me to join him or one of his colleagues while they tagged migrating long-billed curlews at the Rio Mora National Wildlife Refuge in New Mexico. Jay is the research director of the Intermountain Bird Observatory in Boise, Idaho, and he is leading a historic effort to track curlews by tagging them in their vitally important desert breeding grounds. The satellite data will be used to determine threats and conservation priorities for this species.

In December 2019, when I asked Jay about the weight of the transmitters the curlews are tagged with, he said that they are 3 percent or less of the bird's body weight—9.5 grams (or

11 grams if you add the harness). Over the phone, I asked Jay if he'd noticed whether the transmitters bother the curlews. He recalled one bird who, soon after being tagged, kept preening as though to take the tag off; he had worried all night about whether the bird got back on its nest. But the team has mostly seen "normal survivorship patterns" after tagging curlews.

A charismatic biologist, Jay admits to "living and breathing curlews." Near the Boise area where he works, recreational shooting is popular on National Conservation Area land and the curlew ends up as "incidental take." Jay believes the illegal shooting of adult curlews is a significant factor, locally, in their declining populations. "In places where target shooting of ground squirrels is allowed, seven out of sixteen curlews with transmitters end up being shot," Jay told me. "We see the bullet wounds or bullet bits embedded in them. . . . Birds such as burrowing owls, ferruginous hawks, and other protected birds also get shot. Recently there was a report that a bald eagle was shot but by the time law enforcement got there, all traces of the bald eagle had been removed."

Hesitating to use the word *rampant,* Jay settled for saying that we live in an "uncontrolled shooting culture." While he doesn't want "responsible gun owners" to feel attacked, he said, "I obviously can't support the minority of gun owners who illegally shoot or kill protected wildlife species, adding insult to injury for species already facing other threats like habitat loss and degradation."

Jay and his team are the whistleblowers but they need law enforcement to arrest the culprits swiftly in order to dissuade other recreational shooters from slaughtering protected birds. "Law enforcement here in southwestern Idaho have really stepped up efforts in recent years so I don't want any of the blame to be on them," Jay said. "In reality it takes a few seconds for an illegal shooting event to take place and it would be very difficult to be in the right place at the right time to catch someone in the act."

In 2009, when Jay began to research long-billed curlews on BLM land in southwestern Idaho, the population was down 85 percent in the last thirty years. By 2019, 95 percent of the population had been lost in the prior forty years. If that isn't a jaw-dropping decline, I don't know what it.

THE CORONAVIRUS COMPLICATED everything. The banding trip was canceled at the last minute and it seemed that my preparation over the course of several months to observe the curlews in their breeding site would come to nothing. After some discussion, one of Jay's colleagues at the Migratory Bird Division of the US Fish and Wildlife Service, Kelli Stone, said that she might take me to a curlew site.

In May, while I waited, Kelli grew unexpectedly busy and then her vehicle broke down. She explained that due to the pandemic, federal workers faced "massive bureaucracy" to go out into the field and two rangers or biologists were not allowed to drive in the same government vehicle. May slipped by. It took all my patience to wait for Kelli to get back to me about a date. By the middle of June, I was fretting about when the curlews would leave the state. Finally, Kelli offered to take me to a site on her own time, on July 4, and I was grateful for her generosity but to wait that long was also to risk not being able to see the curlews. I began to wonder if I might go see the birds on my own.

I hadn't asked Kelli about the exact location of the breeding grounds in case this was confidential information; curlews are especially sensitive to human intrusion during their breeding season. I imagined that the curlews were breeding in the refuge, which was closed during the pandemic, and thus I needed to go with Kelli in order to get access.

When I inquired further, Kelli told me that the birds were not actually in the refuge. Last summer, the biologists from the Intermountain Bird Observatory saw only a couple of curlews on refuge property and they suspected that these were "either passing through or nesting across the fence on an adjacent private property," as Jay later told me. The biologists had funding to tag five curlews. At the time, neither the US Fish and Wildlife Service nor the biologists knew how many curlews used the area. As the study progressed, they found two nest sites along Highway 161, west of the refuge, and they tagged one bird per nest site for a grand total of two birds. The biologists were fortunate that a graduate student at New Mexico Highlands University, a local, put them in touch with the owners of a ranch in Watrous, where they tagged three more birds.

My chances of observing the curlews that summer were narrowing; the chicks must be growing up and their mothers leaving (the fathers stay behind until the chicks can fly). At last, I summoned the nerve to ask Kelli for directions. To my surprise, she encouraged me to go by myself. "It'll be an adventure," she said.

ON SATURDAY, JUNE 20, Michael and I drove over an hour north to Rio Mora, where we checked out a list of sites that Kelli and a couple of other rangers had suggested. As we drove up and down deserted roads alongside the bleached tan-and-olive short-grass prairie, meadowlarks, like molten drops of gold, serenaded us from fence posts, adding a dollop of hope to my quest. Elsewhere, black-tailed jackrabbits with distinctively long ears raced from one piñon pine to another, holding some wildness in them that seems missing in the cottontails in our backyard. As the hours wore on, the landscape seemed to grow more desolate. I felt as though I were looking for a phoenix. I brightened when a leggy roadrunner skittered by, flashing its blue eye shadow. I tried to open myself simply to what the day had to offer. After several hours in the area, I almost shrugged off my disappointment at not finding the curlews. The ranger who ran the refuge had said that if we didn't find the curlews, she hoped we could at least get some coffee and pastries from the Watrous café. But it turned out that the café was closed on weekends.

"The living world is in desperate condition," writes E. O. Wilson in *Half-Earth*. "It is suffering steep declines in all the levels of its diversity. . . . Only a major shift in moral reasoning, with greater commitment given to the rest of life, can meet this greatest challenge of the century."

The habitat loss that curlews face is part of an intensifying pattern that has devastated biodiversity all over our planet and landed us squarely into what is now called the sixth extinction. We clearly need the major shift in moral reasoning that Wilson prescribes. It won't come until we get to know the spectacular animals we are losing daily; this is one reason why I spend so much time understanding the lives of birds. A major shift in our perspective also won't come until we recall that animals once roamed the land where we now live—they rely on the land for their survival and have as much right to it as we do.

On June 27, exactly a week after my unsuccessful attempt to observe long-billed curlews at the Rio Mora National Wildlife Refuge, I tried again, waking up at 5:00 a.m. The curlew is such a distinctive bird that Mia and Pika also grew engaged in this quest; during the car ride, I promised to get the children ice cream if we found the bird. Shortly after 7:00 a.m., we were at Rio Mora, driving past an artificial lake fed by the river when I saw the silhouettes of two shorebirds. They weren't curlews but the morning felt more promising. We drove along the fields, past the auspicious mile markers near where a ranger had seen a pair of curlews heckling a hawk in the past month. After once again coming up empty all along Loma Parda Road and back, where the curlews had supposedly been "hanging out," I struggled to fight back a feeling of frustration, even doom. I wished I had asked Kelli earlier about the location of the breeding sites. Perhaps the chicks and their fathers were already flying toward their wintering grounds.

We got back on Highway 161 and drove west. The previous Saturday, we had turned back on mile marker ten, thinking that we had driven far enough west. This time, because a retired ranger, Brian Miller, had passingly mentioned mile marker nine, we went on driving. Here and elsewhere, cattle had chewed the ground almost to the bone. Perhaps the curlews are used to that—the thinking goes that they evolved here with bison. Though it's now believed that bison grazed in unfenced grasslands in ways that were less extreme and damaging than how cows are grazed. In the grazing field, curlews have been known to flip cow dung to look for insects and they also favor water sources such as overflow ponds created by water tanks for cattle.

Between mile marker ten and nine, I spotted the tawny body and telltale überlong, eight-inch bill of a curlew. I feared I would see this bird I had searched so long for only fleetingly. It was impossible to stop the car, just past a curve; a vehicle coming from behind wouldn't see us in advance. I jumped out of the Honda and Michael drove on in search of a safer place to park.

The curlew was in a grazing field across the road, alongside a small gray chick with a stubby bill, who would have been camouflaged if the grass weren't so stunted. I watched the chick walk directly in front of the adult, in the shadow of the chopstick legs of its parent. Now a second adult appeared, larger in body, and with an even longer bill—a female.

Both curlews lost no time trying to squawk me out, though I stood across the road. My arms were faintly trembling; it was a wonder I could keep my binoculars in focus. It had been so long since I'd last seen this bird, who had catalyzed my falling in love with birds of all stripes. The curlews' undulating lines, their small stippled tawny-brown heads, the slightly elongated neck, the teardrop-shaped body, and the exceptionally long bills conveyed to me the tenderness and vulnerability of these relatively large shorebirds. The male, who stood closest to me, was slender and its bill was shorter but still like a colossal needle curved down at the end. I saw both adults in a single view through my binoculars and the difference in the size of their bodies and bills was clear.

When the male curlew cried out, its bill opened and quivered and I could see the pink insides of its mouth. It is this piercing *cur-lee* cry that gives the birds their common name. The bill extends out like a miracle, a crescent moon. That a bird with a relatively small head should have such a lengthy bill is an enigma. The bill is the inspiration of its genus name, *Numenius*, meaning new moon or the first of the month, *néos* being Greek for "new" and *mën* for "month." The bill is fully functional; it is essential to forage and to nourish chicks. Here in their summer grasslands, the birds feed their chicks beetles and grasshoppers. With their dexterous bills, curlews can snatch a grasshopper out of the air. "The grasshoppers go down easy," Brian Miller, who studies grasshoppers, later told me. "They don't last long in the bill."

Last August, when we had been observing burrowing owls in Maxwell National Wildlife Refuge, fat grasshoppers kept catching rides on our windshield. We were amused to see them because it was an unusual sight. "When I was young in the 1950s," Brian told me, "sometimes cars would overheat because there were so many grasshoppers on the radiator." But times have changed. I wonder if the curlews in Rio Mora have enough grasshoppers to eat.

Fall grasshoppers help get curlews to their wintering grounds but with our irregular rains, I wondered if there had been a noticeable decline in grasshopper numbers. The insect base is generally better near wetlands. However, if they aren't drained already, wetlands, like grasslands, are only getting drier. Fall adult grasshoppers lay eggs in September; the eggs overwinter underground and hatch the next summer in the rain.

"Twenty-five years ago, gentle rain was regular; it rained almost daily for a few minutes in the monsoon season," Brian told me. "Now, there is one large rain and then nothing for ten days or two weeks. Then there might be another large rain. In conjunction with drought, the ground bakes hard and the runoff is larger."

Last June, during a grasshopper count, Brian and his colleague David C. Lightfoot, Senior Collection Manager at the Museum of Southwestern Biology, counted 1,058 individuals. By mid-September, the number was down to eleven individuals. A September 9 snowstorm, when temperatures fluctuated from ninety degrees to twenty-four degrees, would be the culprit. This time frame also coincided with the largest bird die-off in Southwest history. The early snowstorm stressed small migrants, like violet-green swallows, who died by the hundreds, and the birds who survived had no food to eat. Scientists confirmed that the birds died of starvation.

With climate change, freak events such as the September snowstorm are growing more common. After studying twenty-seven years' worth of grasshopper data at the Sevilleta National Wildlife Refuge, David concluded that the grasshopper species who are ecological generalists, with regard to their diets, habitats, and large geographic ranges, seem to be increasing but ecological specialist species—opposite traits of generalists—are declining. "I expect that these grasshopper trends do affect curlews by creating more annual variation in food resources, depending on how typical or unusual the preceding year's weather, plant production, and insect production were," David told me. "That variation is increasing with global warming. That makes breeding success less reliable for birds in any given year. I imagine the brood success of curlews and other birds is becoming more variable over time due to global warming."

IT WAS GETTING bright enough that my eyes smarted in the sunlight. Where was the chick? At first, I had seen it distinctly walking with the male but it had now vanished. The chick was smaller than I expected. Perhaps the pair's first attempt at breeding had been foiled and this chick was the fruit of a second attempt. Michael had U-turned somewhere ahead and parked the car on the other side of the road, next to the grazing field where the curlews stood, but a respectful distance away. The road was narrow and he was halfway parked on it. Time was short. We were on a straight stretch of road, adjacent to a depression where the road descended and climbed up again, and there was a danger of getting rear-ended by cars climbing out of the dip.

Eyeing a strip of grass between the road and the field, Pika said, "What a pretty flower!" And the children busied themselves picking a handful of sparkling white bindweed.

Soon after, the male curlew moved away from me and shuffled east, closer to the car, where Michael stood. The underside of the male was tawny or a pale russet, the marbled back was slightly darker, and the head also appeared tawny in the sunlight.

The curlew inclined its head toward Michael and the children and it screeched intently and vociferously, deploying a trilling *ki-keck* call. The grazing field consisted of strips that were scorched ocher or barely green. Behind the curlews, the land dipped and rose slightly again and on the rise a pronghorn antelope stood watching. The previous Saturday, one young pronghorn in the field by the road grew spooked by our car and tried to outrace us, sprinting for fields on end; its speed and stamina were staggering.

To the far right of the mature pronghorn stood a handful of cows: four in burnt caramel, including a calf, and one raven-black adult. In the blue distance were rolling mountains. Impatient with our presence, the female curlew flew directly over us three times. Both curlews went on screeching vigorously though we maintained a studied distance. In addition, we remained immobile or minimized our movements to create the least possible disturbance. Once, through my binoculars, it looked as though the female was flying straight at me. Having squawked assiduously, the female flew over me like a bomber plane. I found myself hunching. I knew we would leave very soon. Once, the female flew behind the car and landed on the other side of the road, away from the grazing fields where the chick was, likely to distract us from the presence of the chick.

I needed this experience to get my head around what Jay had said: in Idaho when curlews mob people who get too close to their chicks, some people shoot them. What a brutal response to the paternal love of these devoted birds. And we consider ourselves the superior species?

Now the pair wisely shifted strategy; they weren't squawking so much anymore and instead were moving farther back into the field. The male stayed on, nearer to the edge of the

road, to divert us, or to keep an eye on us, while the female
and the chick moved farther back. The male, its head cocked
and one eye tilted in the direction of the car, now squawked
only occasionally.

A little later, Michael, who had walked to the west, saw the
female curlew fly over and barely clear a midsize juniper tree,
shaped like a fulsome upside-down cone. Shortly after, I saw
the female walking about near that tree. Two pickups hauling
trailers packed with logs sped by. The noisy interruption was
jarring not only for us, but also for the male curlew, who visi-
bly stepped back, while the antelope spun around and strode
away.

It was around 9:30 when we got back into the car. As we
drove away, I caught a glimpse of the slate-gray chick, moving
against a sun-drenched rock, adjacent to the side of the tree
that faced away from the road. The female curlew patrolled
vigilantly at the base of the juniper.

NEW MEXICO IS believed to be the southernmost range of
the curlews' breeding grounds. In this species, males and fe-
males have different wintering grounds—the birds Jay's team
tracked from New Mexico migrate to the western Mexico
coast between the mouth of the Colorado River and an area
south of Mazatlan—but, amazingly, they arrive at their summer breeding grounds at the same time.

We drove past the refuge, which was closed due to the
coronavirus, and were deciding whether or not to drive up
to the Maxwell National Wildlife Refuge, an hour north.
Between mile markers seventeen and eighteen, atop another
fulsome juniper tree I saw the luminescent rufous wings of a

large bird, which began to follow our car, its wings gleaming in the sun. I glimpsed its giveaway decurved bill.

The curlew flew to a scorched grassland area to our right. I jumped out of the car and soon spotted a sizable chick, almost double the size of the first chick I'd seen, and another, only slightly smaller, walking east along the horizon with a studied pace, as though deep in conversation. Michael stopped the car on the side of the road and the curlew landed on top of a juniper tree next to us; from this post, it watched us, occasionally flying over the Honda in order to squawk us out.

Through binoculars I was observing the curlew, just a few feet away, when Pika's crying interrupted me. I returned to the car where she was eating a muffin I had brought with us.

"My scone dropped!" she cried.

I picked up the "scone" and returned it to her, though I would normally have composted food that had met the floor of the car. It took her a few moments to stop crying; turning around, I sensed from the way the curlew had cocked its head and how one eye was focused on us that the curlew was also listening to the child.

The chicks in the sunny field beyond were hidden occasionally by the shrubby juniper that punctuated the landscape and now their devoted parent began to follow them at a distance of some twenty-five feet.

The male curlew's instinct served him well. Abruptly, a Swainson's hawk flew in swiftly from the southwest and landed on the ground near the chicks. Directly, the male curlew began to screech and, as the hawk lifted into the air, the curlew dove west into the hawk's path, using every tool at its disposal—speed, bill, and call—to warn off the hawk. The two birds pirouetted in the air as one body, twice, thrice, with the curlew heckling the hawk unceasingly. This time, the curlew prevailed. The hawk, repulsed, glided away, at a slower pace than it had arrived, its white forewing a stark contrast to the wing's black border, its wings wide open and sunlit as it retreated from sight.

Some six feet away from where I stood was a mess of gray feathers. One was half white and half black. Chick feathers, maybe. They looked fresh somehow. But no blood or body. I wondered whether a hawk had carried off a chick here recently. Later, Kelli and I spoke about curlew predators. She told me the story of a female they had banded in this area last year. Her partner disappeared one day and the female alone couldn't incubate the eggs. Then her two eggs went missing. The culprits were likely crows or ravens who are particularly hard on ground-nesting birds. Other curlew predators are raccoons, skunks, foxes, and coyotes. Kelli admitted that a curlew wouldn't be able to hold its own against a coyote— who would be more interested in an adult curlew than its chicks or eggs.

As we drove away, I observed that the parent had resumed its post devotedly following its young, continuing its raw, primal watch to defend them from life's unending calamities.

Driving past the artificial lake, we saw hawks perched on three successive telephone poles. Large, impressive raptors, the first two were red-tailed hawks and the third had the chocolate brown head of a Swainson's. I felt keenly how vulnerable the curlews and their chicks are, how small the strip of grassland that they are breeding in is. Power lines or poles near their nesting sites are easy perches for predators.

As we left, a lark sparrow remained perched on the wire fence that bordered the grazing field and a pair of turkey vultures soared above, searching for carrion.

A few days later I learned that a female curlew tagged near Rio Mora last year had just reached the border between Sonora and Baja California, at the mouth of the Colorado River. What a fearless, intrepid traveler! Soon the males and the chicks who have survived the threats of predation and the ever-shrinking, drier grasslands in New Mexico will follow. May they all return here next summer to begin once again the wild, capricious cycles of their lives.

18

MI CASITA

Aldo Leopold lovingly designed this Forest Service cabin so that after he and Estella Bergere married, their east-facing porch would command an arresting view of the Southern Rocky Mountain range in Tres Piedras, New Mexico. The long, undulating blue line of the Sangre de Cristo Mountains is as eloquent as it was 108 years ago when the Leopolds lived in this cabin. Their mornings, though, were less marred by the grating noise and sight of truck traffic along the arterial Route 285 that runs just beyond this Forest Service property.

It was the first Sunday in August and, amid the tragic hullabaloo of the pandemic, I felt ready to leave civilization for a rural area; having admired the ecological consciousness in *A Sand County Almanac*, it was an honor to do a five-week residency in the Leopolds' cabin where, fortunately, there is no Wi-Fi. I was eager to study the birdlife in this area; of particular interest was a goshawk nest that Sheila Davis, a Forest Service wildlife biologist, had promised to take me to, in the surrounding Carson National Forest. Our first evening here, from the porch that runs the length of the cabin, I peered at a massive hill of tan-and-clay-colored granite boulders piled up to my right. The name of this village, Tres Piedras, means "three boulders" and there are boulders here the size of cars. On the porch, Michael and I settled on a graceful seat that Aldo and Estella designed and which is now called the Leopold bench. All at once, Michael said, "A bobcat, look!"

I glanced through binoculars at the shadowy outline of two erect ears, two eyes, and an amorphous catlike body. The children ran out to the porch and begged to borrow the binoculars. As they were looking, I saw a chunky squirrel slink down from the topmost sand-colored boulder and, in the same instant, the bobcat vanished. We soon realized our mistake. The tawny squirrel atop a similarly colored rock outcrop, roughly in the shape of a big cat's body, had created the illusion of a bobcat. Earlier in the day, Sheila had told us that a family of bobcats had been seen in the area, which had only stoked our delusion.

Over the next three mornings, while writing at a desk that faced the hill of boulders, I observed the large buff-colored squirrel sun itself regularly on the topmost boulder, occasionally vanishing into a small cave-like opening scalloped under the second-highest boulder. I nicknamed this squirrel Bobcat.

ESTELLA LEOPOLD WAS startled one day when a mountain lion materialized behind her kitchen and took up residence on a nearby boulder. After their wedding in October 1912, Estella had left her sprawling adobe house in Santa Fe to move two hours north to a Forest Service supervisor's cabin in Tres Piedras. Her ardent Aldo had overseen the cabin's construction on Forest Service land that backs onto boulders piled high into hilly cliffs. Leopold poured into this place the tender hopes of a young man in love; he finished the ceiling himself, he created the front path, and he paid carpenters out of his pocket after Forest Service funds ran out. Inside the cabin, space flows—one room yields to another. In only his midtwenties then, Aldo designed this place with a sure hand. Had he learned from his maternal grandfather, who was trained as an architect? This grandfather had died when Aldo was only thirteen; a bright student, Aldo spent his childhood in his grandfather's compound where he also inherited the old man's love for birds. So it was that when Aldo, the forest ranger, fell hard for Estella, he not only deployed his literary skills to woo her, but he also designed and oversaw the construction of a cabin where they could start their married life. Estella named the cabin Mi Casita, my little house, and she learned how to cook and even how to shoot a rabbit for dinner. Still, to have a mountain lion stalk her kitchen porch was a situation the former belle must have felt unprepared for.

The kitchen porch leads to a root cellar, which backs onto the boulders, and from here you can walk out into a modest pine grove. At the base level of the Tres Piedras tree line, Mi Casita is flanked by stringy Gambel oaks, lofty ponderosa pines, and huddled piñon-juniper stands. If you clamber up the boulders in the back, a short steep trail spiked abundantly with cacti leads to a curious cement square, an overlook of sorts. From up here you can see swifts wheeling overhead. A desire comes over you to wander higher among the granite boulders. At dusk the boulders blush enticingly with a pinkish glow. "The rock's rosy color comes from feldspar minerals which have turned reddish due to bombardment by radioactive decay particles," writes Halka Chronic in *Roadside Geology of New Mexico.* Among the mature ponderosa pines that grow miraculously between these boulders, you feel wrapped in an ancient landscape. It's as though you're wearing your great-grandmother's shawl to see what she saw on a late summer evening. But you also tune in to some charge in the air that leaves you unsettled. A mountain lion could surprise you here from one of the boulders piled above. Mountain lions, or pumas, feel at home in precisely such rocky areas. Sheila, the wildlife biologist, had confirmed that this is mountain lion country. She'd added that we are right at the edge of (as in across the road from) rattlesnake territory. There are no real trails out here and you had better watch where you step.

ONE AFTERNOON I sat facing the cabin's south windows when all at once I saw a bobcat outside, no more than a dozen feet away. "Look, a bobcat!" I said quietly to Michael, who was working at the adjacent dining table. It was around four in the afternoon and the bobcat was headed toward the boulders that the squirrel who shares its name rules, but on hearing me it turned to look. It's not the first time that I have met a bobcat's penetrating gaze. The beauty of this animal, its light-russet coat and the saturated black lines etched on its face, never fails to move me. The bobcat disappeared into a thicket of Gambel oaks. Mia was on the living room sofa reading Beatrix Potter to Pika. We all poured out onto the porch, hoping to see the animal again. We stood near the south side of the wooden railing and our eyes scoured the landscape, but the bobcat had seemingly vaporized. A few moments later, Pika, lately turned five, said: "There it is."

The bobcat had evidently decided to turn around. It

emerged from behind a Gambel oak, next to the old Cow Creek Ranger Station, a historic one-room structure to our right, and ambled down a grassy slope. As the bobcat crossed the gravel road, it looked warily over at us once, then a second time, after which it picked up speed and passed through another oak thicket and into the meadow beyond.

LATE ONE EVENING, toward the end of my first week at Mi Casita, I hiked up to the cement square, then turned left and kept on going up. I heard a bouncing *pik-pik-pik*, like a bushtit's beat, but different. I looked through binoculars at a little blue-gray back and a milk-white underside. Before I looked again I scanned the boulders above me. I wouldn't want a big cat to jump on me while I was observing. . . . Yes, pygmy nuthatches, *Sitta pygmaea*. Highly social birds, these tiny epsilons travel in flocks. I followed one pygmy nuthatch for a few minutes as it scoured the tip of a pine branch, then flew to another large pine and repeated the procedure. Pygmy nuthatches meticulously comb entire pine trees, including the needles, for insects, as opposed to white-breasted nuthatches who mainly explore tree trunks. I looked over to the east; the Sangre de Cristos were pinkish tangerine in the glowing light of the setting sun. I decided to hike up farther. I was eager to explore the trail I had discovered early that morning. I scampered up using stones here and there as ledges. Above me loomed a solid mass of boulders. I wondered for a moment whether to weave through the boulders or go around them. I decided to go through. Climbing up, I felt sure I was nearing the top. Abruptly, some fifteen feet ahead between two boulders, I saw movement, something slinky with fur. A chipmunk? But my heart knew it wasn't. It was darker than chipmunk fur. I took two more steps forward to look. In a twinkling, I was staring into the fiery eyes of a bobcat. The sizable animal stood behind a modest boulder but its head and torso were clearly visible. What I had first seen must have been its tail. The bobcat looked at me with a slightly pained expression as though it were saying: "You! Again!"

I felt my heart turn liquidy. And my body froze. I was little more than ten feet away. I found that I couldn't shout or make myself appear bigger, all the things you're supposed to do if you run into a wildcat. If the bobcat had a den among the boulders here, which was plausible, it might charge at me. Even one forceful swipe of its paw could maul me painfully. Being above me, the bobcat undoubtedly had the strategic and muscular advantage. It was standing its ground—its posture and look were tensely assertive. I don't think that bobcats commonly charge at humans but I didn't want to stay here and find out. Its gaze was so piercing that not only my heart but also my legs felt less than solid. I must be the one to give in.

The boulder the bobcat stood behind was flecked with gold in the evening light. The animal looked darker than I would have imagined; the black lines on its face etched into my soul. Its ears erect, its gaze unwavering, its feral energy was focused on me. We were utterly alone, high among remote ocher boulders, as the sun dipped and the bluish-tangerine sky against the pines grew so sublime that something hurt inside me. I felt the earth's pulse beneath my feet and the barrier between the universe and my body melted. I was devoured in a liquescent whirl. Then, all my primal instincts kicked in: Beauty be damned, where is the door to that cabin?

I turned around and began to scamper down. But I couldn't help turning my head in an Orphic gesture. Oh, how I commiserated with Orpheus in this moment! Yes, the bobcat was still staring, bullet-like, at me. I must not be perceived as a threat but I mustn't run for my life either—for that would only flash my potential as prey. Instead, I must gracefully sail down into the violet darkness, unmolested by this hauntingly beautiful animal.

Despite my resolve not to run, my legs picked up pace and some mud and a pine cone skittered down with a distressing sound. I descended the cliff as though I were in an electric dream. Once again I looked back to make sure that the bobcat was not following me. I sensed that I had lost my way and my mind was screaming, "You cannot get lost now!" I scanned the area, spotted the cement square, and reoriented myself. The cabin, when it came into view, had never looked dearer. The evening's shadows were deepening. As I walked the last few paces toward the back porch I was no longer on any semblance of a trail. In the slate-gray darkness, I came upon a black hole in the ground and fully expected a rattlesnake to spring up from it. I parted two Gambel oaks and walked through, as twigs snagged and tore my hair. I approached the closed back door. Not feeling up to knocking, I went around the side, past an old mousetrap, which now seemed puny and not worth bothering about, and toward the front door. Out of the corner of my eye I saw a bird fly eastward but I didn't lift up my binoculars. I have observed quite enough birds for one day, I thought.

The rest of the evening, I sat in a daze, all pins and needles; I had experienced some catharsis, everything unwanted had fallen off. I felt very relaxed, even intoxicated. I had come face-to-face with a predator, an elemental force on Earth, on its turf. The chasm of separation had narrowed; only one boulder had separated us. Our eyes had locked, pupils melting; we had sized each other up and both of us had walked away unharmed from the encounter. What more could I ask for?

IN APRIL 1913, Aldo Leopold traveled on horseback and train to the Jicarilla Ranger District to resolve Forest Service disputes with sheep herders in northern New Mexico. While there, he was soaked by rainstorms and, on his way back, Leopold had a near-fatal attack of what was likely Bright's disease—his face and limbs were painfully swollen and a misdiagnosis of the condition may have precipitated kidney failure as well. A couple of months later, Leopold, along with his pregnant wife, returned to his childhood home in Burlington, Iowa, to recover. In his absence, a ranger in Tres Piedras killed one bobcat and three mountain lions in a matter of three November days. Leopold, still an employee of the Forest Service, was on leave without pay and he continued to edit the Tres Piedras district's newsletter, *The Pine Cone*, from Burlington. In the next issue he noted the fact of the killing of the bobcat and the mountain lions but he did not condemn the act—that would have been contrary to his thinking at the time. The next year, when Leopold began a desk job at the Forest Service's Albuquerque office, he also took on the position of secretary of the Game Club, whose mission was to exterminate predators—so that the forests would have plentiful deer for hunters to kill.

In hindsight, Leopold's backing of predator control in his day was misguided. In the late 1920s, Leopold himself began to question his previous enthusiasm for killing predators. Writing in 1929 to his former Forest Service supervisor about the overpopulation of deer in the Gila Wilderness, Leopold conceded in part when he remarked: "Concentrating the predatory animal work on coyotes and letting the lions alone for a while might be a better remedy." Today we know that by taking out predators such as big cats, wolves, and coyotes, we cripple ecosystems, the most common consequence of which is an overabundance of deer who overgraze the land and cause catastrophic soil erosion.

Only later in his life did Leopold come around to understanding the centrality of wolves in the ecosystem and, ironically, he then became the target of the ire of other ill-informed people in Wisconsin—the self-proclaimed deer lovers. In his masterly essay, "Thinking Like a Mountain," Leopold wrote, "I now suspect that just as a deer herd lives in mortal fear of its wolves, so does a mountain live in mortal fear of its deer." He added that though a "buck pulled down by wolves can be replaced in two or three years, a range pulled down by too many deer may fail of replacement in as many decades." When we unthinkingly shoot down predators, we precipitate habitat degradation, and drain the land of its wildness. Writing about the last grizzly bear on the mountain of Escudilla, in Arizona, Leopold noted ruefully, "The government trapper who took the grizzly knew he had made Escudilla safe for cows. He did not know he had toppled the spire off an edifice a-building since the morning stars sang together."

Though predator control has today become a textbook

example of how not to manage the land, reality has not yet caught up to science. The New Mexico Department of Game and Fish continues, astonishingly, to be steeped in the misconceptions of Leopold's day and still allows trophy hunting of mountain lions and the trapping of predators like bobcats using near-medieval traps such as a neck snare that not long ago drew condemnation only because it strangled an eight-year-old dog. In many cases, political pressure is still too strong against allowing ecosystems to regain a healthy balance. During my stay at Mi Casita, I interviewed Francisco Cortez, the wildlife biologist at Carson National Forest. At the time, there was a ballot measure in Colorado about reintroducing wolves into the state (it has since passed with a razor-thin margin). "When will it be New Mexico's turn?" I asked Francisco.

"The ecosystem here could take it," he said. "But it won't happen. The pressure from ranchers is too great."

ONE SATURDAY AFTERNOON at the end of my second week in the Leopold cabin, I was in the living room, reading out to Michael the instructions in the *Taos Hiking Guide* on what to do if you have an encounter with a mountain lion.

"Oh, a bobcat!" he interrupted.

It was past five and the sun sizzled through the late-afternoon clouds. For once I was grateful that it hadn't rained—our laundry hung out back on old metal wires tied to wooden posts. The bobcat strolled under our wet clothes, the sun caressing its silky, lustrous, buffy-chestnut coat, and the black trim on its ears glistened. The metal clothesline looked like Leopold or a successor might have rigged it up. The wood of the clothespins is so old, it has turned splintery gray and the springs are rusted through. There is no washing machine here and we wash everything by hand in the claw-foot bathtub.

The children rushed to the master bedroom window to watch the bobcat and it threw them a sidelong glance. Then it strode on and when I came up to the window, I saw its muscular, ink-splotched back turn right and climb up the steep boulders with such ease, it might have been walking on a sandy beach. The bobcat strode exactly parallel to the area strewn with pine needles, within a few feet of where I walk up daily. Abruptly, I felt gladdened that a bobcat still passes under the clothesline where Aldo and Estella once hung their clothes. Despite the assaults that bobcats and other predators have suffered in the last century, this magnificent species still electrifies the space behind the Leopold cabin with its feral walk.

19

THE MOUNTAIN LION OF BIRDS

"I don't have many superpowers," Sheila Davis said, "but this is one of them—I can find a goshawk nest."

I cracked a smile from the passenger seat as Sheila steered her Toyota Tacoma on Forest Road 42 in Carson National Forest. A wildlife biologist, she has worked for the Forest Service for three decades. She had picked me up from Mi Casita and we drove to American Creek, where a timber sale had taken place over 450 acres of Forest Service land in the summer. Both the goshawk nests Sheila and I planned to check up on were in the area of the timber sale. A late August rainstorm had just let up and the cool dove-gray air shimmered in the late afternoon. We got out of the pickup and waded into a forest of spindly ponderosa pines with dark-brown bark that lacked the majesty of the old ponderosas with scaly, terra-cotta bark behind Mi Casita. We were in a second-growth forest. Sheila estimated that the trees here were between eighty and a hundred years old. Felled trunks crisscrossed the forest floor, which lacked a robust understory layer, causing the prostrate logs to stick out eerily, like bodies in a battlefield.

With the canopy cover slashed down considerably, this portion of the forest scarcely resembled goshawk territory. Large, territorial birds, goshawks like to claim approximately a 700-acre area for themselves and they aren't shy about defending their territory against other goshawks.

"They're a mountain lion of a bird," Sheila said, as we walked up to the first nest site. "They'll hit you on the head if they see you as a threat." She would know; she's been studying these birds for some twenty years.

High up on a ponderosa pine, thirty feet ahead, a prodigious nest constructed out of large, coarse twigs was visible to the eye, not least because the area had been heavily thinned during the recent timber sale.

"I was driving by here last May," Sheila said, "when I first saw this nest. . . . I called up Francisco [Cortez] and asked—'Do we have a goshawk nest in American Creek?' He said, 'Not that I know of.' The next time I stopped here, an adult goshawk was sitting on the nest!"

This year, it seems the nest was used only as a decoy. Sometimes a goshawk will have three to nine nests in its territory, though it's not known exactly why the bird goes to this trouble. Perhaps to stake its claim to an area more firmly? Or to confuse a predator? Goshawks are monogamous birds and they also return to their old nesting territory, where they might add sticks to an old nest like bald eagles do or construct a new nest, lining it with pine needles.

The goshawk nest sat fairly high up, just under the live, needle-bearing canopy of a tall but slender ponderosa pine. On the ground below, we found ash-gray pellets with tiny intact bones in them. "This is pretty cool." Sheila picked up the pellets. "Would the girls like to take these apart?"

I nodded, gratefully accepting the pellets. But I felt confused. The goshawk is one of four sensitive species in Carson National Forest. The Forest Service defines sensitive species as "plant and animal species identified by a Regional Forester for which population viability is a concern."

The *Forest Service Manual* Section 2672.1 further states that sensitive native plant and animal species "must receive special management emphasis" to ensure their survival and prevent an endangered status, which leads to a need for federal listing. Any impacts to sensitive species must be preceded by an analysis of the "adverse effects on the populations, its habitat, and on the viability of the species as a whole."

So why was the integrity of this grove, with an established goshawk nest site that was active last year, not protected during the timber sale? What puzzled me even more was that this particular timber sale was initiated by the US Fish and Wildlife Service, using reserve funds, for the stated purpose of restoration.

Sheila acknowledged that she was blindsided by how much the area had been thinned out. "But I wouldn't say that I'm devastated," she added. She owned that her time in forestry school at Virginia Tech and her work for the Forest Service since 1989 had inured her to timber cutting. "What they cut in the Pacific Northwest is on a much larger scale than what they're cutting here!" The Forest Service generally explains away thinning as a way to make forests more resilient to wildfires and climate change but scientists reporting in *Conservation Letters* in 2020 found in a study in Oregon and Australia that thinning made little difference to "fire severity, irrespective of stand age, forest type, or fire zone."

AT AMERICAN CREEK, Sheila had marked the goshawk-nest-bearing tree with a small metal WILDLIFE sign. Some of the trees around it were spray-painted with orange rings around the trunks—a signal to leave them standing. But the area to the right of the nest-bearing tree was all but clear-cut.

"The goshawks might not use this site again," Sheila admitted, looking out into the distance.

I stared gloomily at the near clear-cut: the area was so exposed now that it seemed very likely the goshawks would no longer feel safe here. When I asked Sheila about the latter point, she simply said that the birds would find another site. I nodded but a spatter of indignation welled up inside me.

BACK IN THE Toyota Tacoma, we put on our masks and Sheila dropped the goshawk pellets in a little ziplock bag for me. We headed to the second nest site. It was raining again— the dirt road turned slick and the tires of the Tacoma grew coated thickly with mud. "Like soccer balls!" she exclaimed when we got out.

We turned into Forest Road 91, marked with the tiniest of signs, and stopped at a slight fork. "They haven't skidded this unit," she remarked, meaning that the contractor hadn't piled the cut logs into a deck yet. Strewn everywhere, logs traversed the forest floor, even more densely than at the first site. A chill permeated the air. I nudged a translucent white cover-up across my tank top. We hiked into the forest, hopping over tree trunks at almost every step, so many had been felled.

Sheila carried a device that looked like a huge gray flashlight. "I really enjoyed your book," she said with a mischievous smile. "I'm not sure how you feel about my using this."

In the novel I criticize birders who use call devices for their birding pleasure.

Before I could respond, Sheila confessed that she uses a call device regularly while surveying sensitive species. "For my work, I harass animals," she joked.

"In order to protect them," I added. I told her that I was fine with limited use of call devices as long as it was for research.

We reached a cluster of pine trees with orange rings painted around their trunks. A cold breeze blew and the rain picked up a little. From here the goshawk nest was easily visible; it was characteristically positioned just under the live canopy of a ponderosa pine. Once again, around the nest-bearing ponderosa pine, there was barely an intact circle of skinny trees. I felt perplexed. How could two active nest sites of a sensitive species have suffered the same wretched fate? Had certain lines of communication broken down? Sheila turned on the device and played the plaintive call of a juvenile goshawk asking for food. The robust, emotional squeal, undulating and continuous like a bouncing ball, is designed to fetch a parent from the depths of the forest.

A three-toed woodpecker responded instead and began to peck away at the bare upper trunk of a nearby ponderosa. The bird cooperated when I took a long look at its jaunty black head with a white stripe running down from behind the eye.

Sheila played the juvenile goshawk's call again. A little later, from the distance, from the depths of a grove to our north, we heard something promising. But the response didn't come any closer. The rain was smacking us. Our hats were soaked. Next Sheila played the goshawk's alarm call—a high-pitched, staccato call.

"When I've surveyed all day long, I hear this call in my sleep or just as I'm about to wake up," she said.

The three-toed woodpecker remained impressively unfazed by the alarm call and scooted over to a tree even closer to us. The rain was getting into our clothes. Sheila offered to loan me the device so that I could return later to this spot on my own.

As we turned back and hiked away from the second site, the forest was being drenched. It is rare in New Mexico to experience moist, wet forests. I didn't feel exhilarated, however. Encountering felled logs at every step, I hopped over them continuously, like a cottontail, while my conviction grew that something was strangely awry. Sheila's Tacoma was now in sight. The ink on my notebook was running and I tucked it under my wet cover-up. In the distance, a neat, grim pile of logs was decked at the side of a dirt road. It would serve as a marker for when I returned. I asked Sheila if this area was open to hunters.

"The entire forest is open to hunters!" she said. "But at this time of year, when they're looking for antelope, you'll only encounter hunters in American Creek if they're very confused or lost."

IN THE TACOMA, with rain pelting the windshield, Sheila showed me a video she had taken of a female goshawk when she had gone to the second nest site with a couple of foresters to spray-paint orange rings on the trees. There were three chicks in the nest then. Observing the spray-painters, the female goshawk flew up to the tip of the tree and squawked loudly, hoarsely, and incessantly at them. This particular bird wasn't a head-thwacker but she was clearly very stressed.

Sheila also showed me a photo of a chick poking its

white head out of the nest. With its unkempt tuft of feathers, the chick was the definition of adorable. When we'd been standing under the nest, Sheila had pointed out the twigs at the base of the tree. "The young kick them down over the course of time," she'd said. The large, coarsely made nest can sometimes be confused with the nest of an Abert's squirrel, *Sciurus aberti*, also called the tassel-eared squirrel.

As we drove out of the forest, we came upon an Abert's squirrel with a magnificent, bushy pearl-gray-and-white tail, perched on a small ponderosa branch. Spotting us, it leaped to the ground and began to glide away. Sheila pointed out that this squirrel is common goshawk food, along with birds such as flickers and Steller's jays. The latter bird is also talented at mimicking precisely the goshawk alarm call. The animals of the forest listen closely to one another. "Sometimes when I'm playing a spotted owl call at night," Sheila said, "in the darkness a cow will low in response."

IT WAS A chilly evening but I found myself simmering after I returned to the cabin. I was astonished that the Forest Service did such dramatic "thinning" ostensibly for "restoration." What made the American Creek timber sale more surreal was that the US Fish and Wildlife Service had paid a contractor to cut down the trees. The total amount paid out was approximately $450,000. From my conversations with forest rangers, I had gathered that going to forestry school, where trees are seen as a crop (which is presumably why the Forest Service remains under the umbrella of the US Department of Agriculture), desensitizes them to clear-cutting operations. In the end, $1,000 per acre was spent to "thin" 450 acres, in a partnership between the US Fish and Wildlife Service and the Forest Service. Once all the lumber is stacked into decks that can be loaded onto trucks, the Forest Service will auction it.

Driving back, I had asked Sheila if timber sales such as this one make up the gap in the Forest Service budget, between what Congress allocates them and what is needed.

She paused to think, and then she said that it helps, but "it doesn't even come close" to bridging the gap.

If sensitive species such as the goshawk are being given short shrift even when no commercial interests are involved, in what ways are bird habitats being hacked down when lumber companies *are* involved?

Prior to NEPA being passed in 1970, the Forest Service was an industrial freight train, gorging on heavy grazing and clear-cutting operations. Widely acknowledged as the first major environmental law with a broad national framework, NEPA is said to be the Magna Carta of our environmental laws. NEPA requires "the federal government to use all practicable means to create and maintain conditions under which man and nature can exist in productive harmony." "Productive" and "harmony" can be at odds with each other, however. A productive forest (presumably a forest that yields a satisfactory amount of lumber) usually isn't a harmonious forest (its fungal network is disrupted, its understory layer is disturbed, and its bird habitat is decimated).

After NEPA was passed, the Forest Service got some pushback from environmentalists. "NEPA forced the Forest Service to become more holistic," Sheila said as we drove back to Tres Piedras. For instance, they now had to hire wildlife biologists. "Federal laws such as the Endangered Species Act are why I have my clout," she added.

Environmental laws also obliged the Forest Service to consult with the US Fish and Wildlife Service. The Clean Water Act is why the Forest Service had to hire hydrologists and they had to consult with the Army Corps of Engineers on waterways. NEPA supposedly steered the Forest Service toward an ecological, restorative approach. But judging by the shorn forest I had just experienced, better and more thoughtful steering is needed. A Forest Service veteran, Sheila didn't fail to add the standard phrase that the service uses to defend itself—that they are "still multiuse."

"But now they don't clear-cut," she added.

I stared pensively at the windshield of the Tacoma. The timber sale I'd surveyed behind Mi Casita had looked awfully like a clear-cut.

OVER SEVERAL TRIPS to Carson National Forest, I grew troubled by the trash heaps I saw lying about in the timber sale areas. One morning I happened to have a bag in the car and Michael and I collected beer cans and sundry bottles. If these loggers—the companies, the contractors, the workers— can leave trash lying around so callously in a hundred-year-old ponderosa pine forest that they have just plundered, how can we believe that they have any respect left for the forest?

The next time I saw Sheila, I asked her about the trash.

"The rangers get used to seeing trash around here," she joked.

I asked if cleanup requirements could be more explicit on the permit forms and she said wearily that they already are.

I have a nagging suspicion that the Forest Service needs to shore up its own respect for the integrity of the forest ecosystem and also do more outreach in the community. I feel torn about criticizing the Forest Service because at Mi Casita I was, in a sense, their guest. This wasn't how I was raised, to criticize my hosts. Moreover Sheila is a caring, knowledgeable, and hardworking professional—a person I had admired from the start—and it is not my intention to criticize her. Still, a recalcitrant streak makes me question why the goshawks weren't better protected.

The funereal piles of branches, piles and piles on end, gathered along the sides of another part of the forest had me questioning if these weren't a wildfire risk. Sheila later told me that the Forest Service was being sued by WildEarth Guardians for not better protecting spotted owl habitat, so whereas the rangers would have burned these piles by now, everything was on hold until the lawsuit was settled. I wondered why the Forest Service is always on the defensive against environmental groups, why it clings so damagingly to its utilitarian credo. What prevents us as a people from reexamining the role of the Forest Service and how they tend to our forests? Why not prioritize the health of our forests, and the wildlife that inhabits them?

WHILE I WAS wrestling with my dilemma, a few days later, I ran into another employee of the Forest Service. I began to question him and soon he was telling me about how powerful commercial interests bang every day on the doors of the Forest Service, asking for access to cut trees for timber and for unlimited pasture for their cows. "The voices of people like you and me who respect the forests for their aesthetic and spiritual benefits are without a doubt being drowned out," he said.

What I learned is that lumber companies and ranching corporations wield their power to relentlessly exploit our national forests. "The cattle, timber, and mining barons are still barons," he said. "The cattle ranchers for instance are wealthy—they own a lot of land; their families go way back in this area—and if they are unsatisfied [about Forest Service policy] they can call up the governor's office or the DA's office or almost anyone else. They are that powerful and they can get their voices heard."

"Is the public at large getting its voice heard?"

"No."

I let out a long breath. It seemed clear to me that in order to protect the integrity of our forests, our fervor must be greater than corporate greed.

"At any given time the Forest Service here is being sued by one of the commercial interests in the area—the local lumber company, for instance, if they can't get access where they want it. Their argument is that the forests are public land, and they're a member of the public and should have access to the land.

"When a year back there was an injunction on logging because of the New Mexico spotted owl, I received death threats. At my office, at the grocery store, and at the barbershop when I was getting my hair cut."

I gasped.

"These people don't care about owls!" he added.

Or any other birds, I thought dolefully.

This meeting emboldened me to speak up. Even though I cannot name this employee, who told me that he would lose his job if I did so, I will never forget the sun-soaked afternoon when we stood under the shade of a tree and talked. How quickly and astonishingly the gap between us bridged. In the end we were both concerned children of the land and it grew clear that stifling my voice in the interest of politeness would be unconscionable.

ALDO LEOPOLD DEFENDED the term *beauty* in its fullest biotic sense—that is, with a nod to the complex links between soil, plant, and animal communities—and he ardently believed that there is spiritual value to being in a forest. Even the utilitarian Gifford Pinchot, architect of the Forest Service, supported the concept of arboreal beauty as a young man and he inserted the term *forest ecology* into the latest edition of *The Training of a Forester* shortly before the book's reissue in the twilight of his life. His growing sympathy in favor of ecology is further illustrated in other corrections he made to his iconic training manual. He encouraged classes in wildlife management as part of a forester's training. As Char Miller points out in *Gifford Pinchot and the Making of Modern Environmentalism*, Pinchot wrote that what "birds and animals do to and in the forest is not yet fully known," but he added that the survival of these birds and animals is essential to the forest's health. The father of the Forest Service proclaimed his newfound understanding to the world before his death in 1946. Today, some seventy-five years later, how can the Forest Service be so cavalier about cutting down the nesting habitat of a sensitive species like the goshawk? What kind of restoration denigrates goshawk habitat? Who is this restoration for?

ONE MORNING IN early September, Michael and I returned to the site of the goshawk nests. It was raining as our Honda headed into the forest and we wondered if we should turn around. The mud roads up in the area of the nests turn slick fast and ours is not a four-wheel drive. The rain let up a bit and we kept on going. We drove past the Valdez ranch that leads into the forest and crossed the Tusas ("corn husk" in Spanish) Creek. A female kestrel, the black vertical markings on its face shining in the bright morning, watched us from a post. Northern flickers flew ahead of us, flashing glowing rufous wings and the milk-white bar on their backs.

We easily found the first nest. It hadn't been in use this year and was in disrepair with some twigs hanging out. I once again considered the vast swath of trees to the west that had been cut. Not only the nest but also the habitat was in shambles. It was somewhat challenging to find the second nest but Michael and I hopped over numberless fallen logs until a cluster of trees looked familiar and I spotted the nest high in one of the ponderosas.

The tree the goshawks had picked was so skinny that I could put my arms around it and clasp my hands on the other side. Now that it wasn't pouring, I counted the trees around the nest-bearing tree. Eleven, including saplings. We stayed for an hour but there was no sign of the goshawks. I imagined how the mother must have felt, seeing the trees around her being felled one after the other, her three chicks still in the nest, the chain saws unrelenting, the men loud, trashing the forest with their deeds and their waste (I saw an ugly mound of empty fuel canisters, scrunched beer cans, and water bottles). No doubt the mother goshawk could barely wait for the last chick to fledge before whisking her family away from this wreckage. Earlier in the summer, I had visited a Cooper's hawk nest in my neighborhood and I grew aware that the adults were stressed. We were in an arroyo and it was early evening. The male hawk flew close to the base of the nest-bearing tree, perhaps to flush me out of the area. The female stayed in a tree across and farther back from the nest-bearing tree in order to keep me in a straight line of sight or perhaps to confuse me about the location of the nest. They squawked repeatedly at the juvenile, who chose to be recalcitrant and went on devouring a rodent. When Pika, curious about the juvenile's dinner, took a step closer, the parent hawks scolded with such screeching calls that the juvenile reluctantly abandoned the rodent and flew over to them.

Let's say that the "restoration" in American Creek was done to make the forest resilient in the future against wildfires. In that case, why not wait until the end of the breeding season? A study of snow geese in the Bosque showed that stress causes cortisol levels to rise in birds and has serious physiological effects, causing them to lose body weight and ultimately impacting their mortality. Having seen the video of how stressed the female goshawk was when its nest-bearing tree was being spray-painted, I can only imagine how the goshawk's stress levels must have rocketed as the trees around it were being cut down. This was an experience the nesting goshawk had no framework for. If the Forest Service does not harvest timber on special time lines, as Sheila had said, why hack down goshawk habitat during the breeding season? The Migratory Bird Treaty Act, a federal law, protects the tree the nest was on. All the foresters did was to protect ten more trees (including saplings) around that tree, which didn't provide anywhere near the 70 percent canopy cover or shaded buffer zone that scientific studies show the goshawk needs.

Where the forest had been brutally thinned out, near the goshawk nest sites, there remained only wet, fragrant sap oozing out of tree stumps. We counted the rings on one such stump: there were about eighty. Eighty years of wise, considered growth, eviscerated by chain-saw-wielding persons who didn't even care enough about the forest to remove their trash from it. When the lumber decks were auctioned off, the goshawks' home was auctioned off as well.

On the way back to the cabin Michael stopped to get us coffee at the Chili Line Depot. He ran into the co-owner Debbie, who asked what we had been up to. When he told her that we had been out looking at goshawk nests, she was surprised that the nests existed.

"I thought that was just an excuse to halt the timber cutting," she said.

Alas, no timber cutting was halted long enough to allow a sensitive species to raise its young in peace. Debbie's comment, however, speaks to general public ignorance about how vulnerable sensitive species can be. The Forest Service really needs to educate the community about their work. A few newspaper ads and radio interviews don't seem to be doing the trick. Debbie's disbelief about the existence of the goshawk nests is significant. She comes from an old Tres Piedras family and is something of a hub of information dispersal in the community.

In 1911, President Taft fired his chief of the Forest Service, Gifford Pinchot, for insubordination. Still, Pinchot didn't abandon the Forest Service; for three more decades, he fenced away its enemies, notably a procession of secretaries of the Department of the Interior who wanted to reel the Forest Service back into their department. The canny Pinchot knew that if the forests were signed over to the Department of the Interior, they would soon be opened for drilling, mining, and other aggressive forms of exploitation. Pinchot may have been utilitarian but he had his limits, and he seemed to have been a reasonable man. In a Forest Service publication titled *The Use of the National Forests*, Pinchot wrote that public forests "exist to-day because the people want them. To make them accomplish the most good the people themselves must make clear how they want them run."

The last time I returned to the goshawk nest, I hiked through the area for two hours and was about to give up again when at last I saw a goshawk—flying with deft, swift flaps of wing, like a secretive, mysterious, luminous, glowing spirit of the forest. It was already flying when I saw it, flying in an arc along the rim of the forest, to the beyond where the trees were still one organism. The goshawk was one with the deep silence that permeates hillsides and valleys pulsing with trees. It was a juvenile with a whitish-brown head, chocolate-brown body, and a long tail with white showing on the undertail coverts. Minutes earlier we had heard a hoarse, unfamiliar call and, soon after, we saw a flicker dart away with an alarmed mew. Michael had walked up to the rim beyond where the land slopes down into a valley. When he returned without seeing anything, I said about the call: "That was exciting."

The children started to get into the car, and I said, "Bye, goshawks, we'll see you next year." But I lingered outside my door. And lingered. That is when I saw the juvenile. How strange. That after four extended field trips to the area, I saw the goshawk just before I was getting into the car, on my last try.

The wings of the juvenile I had seen seemed to be beating continuously, short and hard wingbeats, with only short intervals of gliding, so that the sense of speed was unbroken. The goshawk flew just over the tree line. Since I was looking up at it, the white undertail coverts made its tail glitter in the late morning sun. Similarly the white streaks on its head gave it a milky glow, whereas the body and the wings were distinctly chocolate brown.

Sheila's argument was that the timber sale was done over only 450 acres in an 800,000-acre forest. However, timber sales go on and, if every few months, year after year, 450 acres is chipped away from this forest, and others, that adds up to substantial destruction. Our bar for species is too low: they should not only be surviving, but thriving. Of course if we slash down all the old-growth, thick-canopied areas, which scientific studies show that goshawks strongly prefer, the birds will find other thinner trees with anemic canopies to nest in. But will the goshawk thrive under those conditions?

That weekend I called Sheila up to describe my juvenile goshawk sighting. She was charmed by my description and I questioned her further about what happened around the active goshawk nest during the American Creek timber sale. In the end, she characterized it as "an unfortunate series of events."

The goshawk is a feral top predator; its eye has a glint of wildness. Isn't it awesome that when it's incensed by our intrusion over its territory, it thwacks us on the head? We see trees as crops, we plant tree saplings in clean rows, and we have chopped down magnificent old-growth stands, which grew exuberantly in asymmetrical groves. We are draining the last remaining wildness out of even the forests. The goshawk has every right to thwack us.

20

CLIFF TOP

I.

Michael asked why I continue to go to the cliff top behind Mi Casita. One still afternoon I took him and the children to the area where I encountered the bobcat and he sensed how isolated it is here. He experienced the same sensation that I first had, that these boulders could easily conceal a mountain lion who might surprise one from above. Being a naturalist involves some risk and being a female naturalist is something else. From the top of the cliff, when one morning I heard a male voice in the forest, I shrank momentarily. I had no idea who lives beyond the forest, who roams in it. In three weeks, I had never seen another person here, only animals. Michael has been anxious ever since he heard at the Chili Line Depot, the sole food stop in this rural community, that a drug cartel had allegedly murdered two people who worked for them in this community, days before we arrived in Tres Piedras. Still, I feel compelled to go on exploring here. The cliff is the only place within walking distance of the cabin where the habitat seems continuous, where the ubiquitous wire fences, though I can see them, are not in my face.

After having three bobcat sightings in two weeks, I took a two-day hiatus from hiking. I also needed to recover from the dozens of mosquito bites that dotted me painfully. But early one morning, I hiked again to the cliff top and yearned to keep on going. I squeezed through a sliver of a gap between a barbed wire fence post and a boulder and then descended into the forest below, walking down a slope strewn with cacti and deer droppings. After weaving past some ponderosa pines, I came upon an abandoned wooden shack. A No Trespassing sign was posted on the front door and the dilapidated condition of the cabin made it clear that no one had lived in it for some time. But maybe vagrants still slept in it from time to time?

Another morning I returned to explore this northern edge of the forest, which had been leased recently to a lumber company; the community had been unhappy about the clear-cutting that resulted and the Forest Service knew this. I soon came upon a wide area where the lumber company had sawn down ponderosa pines. I stood at the edge of this forced clearing, staring at the stump of a ponderosa, limestone yellow on top where it was severed. Many such limbless stumps squatted beyond, bearing witness to the mindless destruction of almost all the trees in the vicinity. This was no informed, selective culling. A chill went through my heart, the chill you might feel at a crime scene. We are still clear-cutting our forests; we go on gouging holes into the forest's ecology. I wanted to flee from this location where arboreal slaughter, spurred by our greed, had been carried out. A dusky flycatcher glumly flitted from a wire fence to an extended branch of a lone ponderosa. Life had forsaken this area. Feeling profoundly blue, I turned around.

Back near the fence I saw two juvenile dusky flycatchers calling for food. One opened its mouth so wide, I could see the inside, the color of orange juice. They began to flit between a handful of pines and I took in their soft white undersides and ash-gray backs. With so many trees cut down, the insect biodiversity of the area has probably also declined. What food would their impoverished parent bring them back?

Just before I clambered up to the high point, where I could squeeze through the sliver gap between fence post and boulder, a tiny grove of intact pines surrounded me. I heard tap-tapping and saw a bird fly from one pine to next. Through binoculars I first saw the wing bars, a vertical streak of white, then the bird's dark glossy back; as it curved around the tree trunk, its laughing-yellow belly and crimson nape came into view. A male Williamson's sapsucker! *Sphyrapicus thyroideus.* A tonic for the heart. If a bird is an archetypal symbol of the spirit, the sapsucker truly raised my spirit out of the dreary place the clear-cutting had taken me to. Sapsuckers favor conifer trees—they drill holes in them and return to sip the sap or eat the insects trapped therein. My brilliant bird soon flew to an adjacent pine and I once again gazed with wonder at its lustrous back before it flew away.

THE CACTI-DOTTED SLOPE that led back to the boulders was rich with droppings—deer and horse, mainly. The high density of deer droppings, and my sightings, pointed to the presence of deer in the area, which only made it more likely that one of the mountain lions in the surrounding Carson National Forest also roamed here.

I regularly saw deer droppings on my side of the boulders too, along the cliff face where I daily observed birds. Why did I keep clambering up this cliff when bobcats and probably even mountain lions hunted here? Something draws me up here. Climbing up, there is the crunch of dried pine needles under my shoes and the heady scent of pine. The habitat feels intact, though that is an illusion. The silence pulls me in but that is also an illusion for trucks drone along the road below. Still, there's a kind of silence that pulls you out of the everyday world of breakfast and dishes and when you settle into this deeper silence, its surprising punctuations—the *pik-pik* of a Virginia's warbler or the tintinnabulations of pygmy nuthatches—signal which direction it might be rewarding to take next.

The pygmy nuthatches became my familiars along with a dusky flycatcher who acted like a sentry and perched on a dramatic, bare ponderosa adjacent to where the nuthatches did the meticulous work of gleaning insects from pine branches thick with needles. The ponderosas that have met a natural death look strikingly handsome: their pale limbs stretch out against the backdrop of salmon-pink boulders and azure sky.

At the very top, where you feel closer to the sky, there is pure solitude, without a drop of loneliness in it. The embrace of ancient boulders, venerable ponderosas, and petite nuthatches mingles with the crisp air and light breeze. It deepens the sense of being alive. You inhabit the present while recalling that you rose out of the past.

Aldo Leopold also sought solace from these boulders. When he proposed to Estella in the late summer of 1911, she told him that she would answer him in October. In the interim, she wrote him that she'd already promised another beau (who had also proposed) that she would be his date for the season's social highlight, the upcoming Montezuma Ball. After reading her letter, Aldo, desperately in love, feared that he would lose his Estella to the other beau and he strode out back to the boulders to pull himself together.

THE LAST THREE times I have been up among the boulders, in the solitude, out of nowhere came the new realization that early deaths notwithstanding, my parents and my brother had lived rich lives—they lived rooted in communities teeming with old friends, extended family, and warm colleagues. My überintelligent older brother had had *rasa* to spare. Recently when a childhood friend from our Assam days tracked down my phone number, he remarked how my brother "always had a smile." He left this world early, at twenty-six, but in that short time he forged extraordinary friendships all over the world. Such friendships that when Michael and I went to Paris a few years later, my brother's college friend lovingly invited us over to her condo and cooked us a sumptuous dinner. I donated bone marrow to my brother but it didn't work out. I said yes to all the blood and marrow the surgeons asked to take out of me, I said yes though they cautioned that they weren't sure what all this taking out would do to my body years later. But my brother's body didn't accept my gift. The universe assimilated him back into its womb.

It is painful to stray out of our safety zone and to look at death but if we endure, an experience opens up that can be called spiritual; we see the edges of the universe because we have grieved there and then returned to live again.

The time has come for me now to walk among these boulders in peace.

"The last *rasa* is *shanta rasa*—peace, tranquility, and relaxation," writes Ravi Shankar.

The Indian sage Sri Nisargadatta Maharaj encourages us not to be immersed in our experiences—past or present—but to move beyond them. "When you stand motionless, only watching," he says, "you discover yourself as the light behind the watcher."

II.

A ranger who stopped by told me that the Forest Service had approved renting Mi Casita out as an Airbnb and was waiting only for clearance from some obscure board. It's true that the Forest Service is often on the receiving end of budget cuts and they need to look around for additional monies. But some places are sacrosanct and must be excluded from the coarseness of market forces. A few days later, I spoke on the phone to Chris Furr, who once was the district ranger in Tres Piedras and now works for the Forest Service in the Cascade Range in Washington. Chris genuinely appreciates Leopold but one of the first questions he asked me was about the mouse problem in Mi Casita. He also pointed out that the cabin's roof would need to be replaced soon and it would cost $25,000.

As August wore on, I found myself writing at my desk, to the music of a dozen mice dancing between the boards of the staircase. But in the late afternoons when colorful birds began to flit outside the cabin, an hour would mysteriously vanish.

Seeing a female western tanager from my desk, I would think, Ah, now I can do a visual comparison of the size of this bird with the juvenile tanager I'd seen this morning. But the lemony-colored female ducked into the glossy leaves of a south-facing Gambel oak thicket. To locate the bird, I ambled out to the porch, but felt compelled to look first at a dusky flycatcher diving admirably for flies in the shimmering afternoon. The female tanager at last showed herself and I observed that it was significantly larger than the juvenile I'd seen on the ground this morning.

As the tanager took off from a scrawny oak, behind the thicket was some rustling movement. A magnificent set of chocolate velvety antlers appeared. I glimpsed the mouth of a buck munching oak leaves but when I approached the screen door to softly call Michael, the buck disappeared. I slipped on my shoes and rushed around to the back to look for the buck. No luck.

Now that I was outside, I couldn't resist climbing up the boulders to the overlook. As I reached the cement square and gazed at the trucks on the road below and the mountains beyond, two swifts wheeled above at just the right pace so that my binoculars kept up with them. A nighthawk with prominent white bands on dark-brown wings bolted past. This was an ideal vantage point from which to peer at the barn below.

Seeing bird activity behind the barn, I naturally headed down there. A Townsend's solitaire flew up to last year's mule-ears flower stalk. Beyond the fence, a Steller's jay was smacking a nut on the bark of a ponderosa pine. A house finch dared the solitaire and perched on an adjacent dried mule-ears flower. The solitaire stubbornly out-perched the finch and me. I finally wandered over toward the meadow out front, noting some female finches along the way. But what was that? A coyote racing past the meadow. I quickened my pace, wondering where the coyote was headed. The animal vanished like the wind. Instead I got close views of a pair of dusky flycatchers and the elusive female tanager flew by, adding a streak of color to the sun-bleached afternoon.

Around the Leopold cabin, fifty-five species of birds, to be precise, have whispered in my ear and roguishly prodded me away from my desk. The only other place where I have experienced such a current that obliged me to spend my waking hours outside is when as a child I lived in remote northeastern India. Mi Casita is of course more than simply any old cabin.

In the evenings, as I delved deeply into the battles for conservation before and after Leopold's time, I felt sure that we need more spaces like Mi Casita that foster careful ecological thought, the ethics of how we live on Earth, and evolving ideas about how we can cope with the climate crisis. Leopold was a master of evolving thought—consider how he pivoted after he realized that his initial ideology about predator control was misguided. Today, when biologists and naturalists are called upon to decipher ever-stranger mysteries such as this summer's bird die-offs in the Southwest, Mi Casita is a refuge—an edifice rich with symbolism, where we can ponder our fast-changing relationship with the land. Preserving an old structure may pose a unique set of challenges but this is one cabin that must remain shielded from commercial considerations. Mi Casita has already survived 108 years and, if we'll go on repairing its cracks and listening to birdsong from its porch, what it can teach us won't be exhausted in the 108 years to come.

III.

If Pika finds a moth or a large ant or a baby lizard in Mi Casita, she guides it into her hand and cries out, "Help, somebody open the door!" so that she can release it beyond the porch, where she stays to observe moths in a variety of colors—milky white, emerald green, and chocolate brown. "Oh, here you are, moth!" she says, sometimes bringing a moth inside to show us before releasing it again. When I took the children and Michael to the cliff top to show them where I had seen the bobcat, that afternoon, up top, the children crouched over a treasure trove of what they called "crystals"—white rocks with shiny elements in them. They were so smitten by the magic of their crystals, they disregarded a cluster of prickly pear cacti thriving at their heels.

It made me think that when we experience the richness of what it before us, we don't need some corporation to come along and entertain us. An acquaintance with the natural world grows and deepens until it permeates our cells; it re-awakens primal memories. It is only when we grow disconnected that we need to be entertained.

During a phone conversation about Mi Casita with Francisco Cortez, to my surprise, the staid biologist admitted that "the place has a positive energy" and hinted that the Forest Service may not go down the road of renting Mi Casita.

He told me about the recent history of Mi Casita, in the decade before its 2011 restoration. A district ranger had moved in here and he all but raised his family here. "The kids were mischievous," Francisco said. "One day they took a horse inside the cabin and got it upstairs. Once the horse was up there, it didn't want to come down!"

This prank seems to have made an impression on some people in the Forest Service. I wonder if this was the same family who painted the fireplace pink and screened in the porch that was always meant to be wide-open. After this ranger moved out, the Forest Service stopped using the cabin for long-term employee housing and, from their Centennial Fund, money was found to restore the cabin. Volunteers from around North America did most of the work.

A HUNDRED MOTHS flutter about here at any given moment at twilight and bats boldly whiz through the now open porch to snag the moths before fluttering into the night. The bats come one after the other and I feel that if I were to take one more step forward, their black, flying bodies would smack my cheek. After the procession of bats has thinned, I walk out into the night and look up at the inky sky. There are over a hundred billion stars in our galaxy. Under pristine conditions one can see a few thousand in the night sky. From the cabin I see a few hundred glittering stars and I think that the night is a singular shimmering creature when you experience it as a whirl of stars, a spray of the Milky Way, a procession of bats, and a congregation of moths.

In his journal, Thoreau writes, "We wake the echo of the place we are in, its slumbering music." I listen to the cacophony of crickets, coyotes yipping, and, once, the insistent *pwick* of a nighthawk. Venus shines down on the porch; this must have been a good omen for Aldo and Estella—she conceived their first child here. At last I return to the bedroom and lie down. I can't help gazing at their wedding photograph on the wall—sheer joy emanates from Aldo's face; he can't contain his smile. She looks sprightly and happy, at the cusp of the grandest adventure of her life.

The song of this cabin is the chipmunk's chirruping mixed in with the *phee-phee* of the flycatcher, the scolding of the Steller's jay, and the rustling of yellowed oak leaves as a spotted towhee scratches under them. A truck grumbles by on the road; there's no avoiding that. The *thuk-thuk* of the woodpecker as it excavates a cavity on a nearby pine. The song ebbs and flows, it begins at sunrise and quiets somewhat when the sun blazes at noon. But at four, a pair of warblers begin pik-picking again and, by sunset, if your ears are tuned in, the "slumbering music" turns into a swell. Darkness brings an interlude before the nachtmusik begins in earnest: an orchestra of crickets, the solo of a nighthawk, the screech of a great horned owl or a catbird's scream, and the clear yipping of coyotes ring out into the night.

A STORM IS in the making. Thunder sounds cataclysmic here, as though the boulders were cracking apart under tremendous pressure. The sky is soft gray, the air thick with mist; the undulating line of the Sangre de Cristos can no longer be seen. Still, some scrub jays remain perched on the high, pinnacle-like boulder to the southeast. Only when rain begins to fall do they commence diving playfully from the boulder and dip up and down in the air just for fun before belatedly taking shelter in a cottonwood tree. Soon it will be time for us to leave the forest and return home to Santa Fe.

IT WAS BOUND to happen. I was high up the cliff, observing a solitary Virginia's warbler as it emerged from the foliage of pine needles and, on seeing me, the bird issued a quick series of *pik, pik, pik, piki, piks* before returning into the heart of the tree to scour the needles for insects. I usually spot the Virginia's warbler by itself at around eye level in a tree, unlike the orange-crowned warbler I had seen earlier in the morning squatted on a stone among a flock of chipping sparrows who pecked at the sod nearby. The Virginia's is more resilient than the flitting yellow warbler who lets out a *tchk, tchk, tchk* call in scrub close to the ground and quickly flits from one shrub to another. I was so surprised by the secretive warbler's alarm call that I only noted the soft rustle I heard. The Virginia's warbler was hidden now but I could still see it flitting about through the pine needles.

Then I heard another rustle. This time I took the binoculars off my eyes and stepped two paces to my right to determine the cause of the rustling. Ahead on a pine tree, a juvenile bobcat was hanging off a short branch—the third branch up from the ground—its limbs holding the branch where it connected with the trunk. It arched its russet back, checking how far it could extend itself—I have seen my own children execute this very move. I was so charmed and absorbed by the playful movements of the little bobcat, suspended in the piney air, that I experienced a forgetfulness of sorts and lost myself in this sublime scene. Involuntarily, I stepped back and all at once I saw the young bobcat's mother seated upright on the ground, staring at me with her luminescent foresty eyes. Her ears were erect and the black tips at the ends of these ears glistened in the morning light.

The mother's glance was a question mark and also a wary I'll-brook-no-nonsense look. I felt suspended between the charm I had just experienced and the hypnotic, warning stare of the mother. When you lock eyes with a bobcat, the past melts away. What is left is the essential part of yourself. I no longer saw the juvenile but I didn't try to look either. I simply backed up and spun around and headed back down. I knew better than to exercise my curiosity while a predator was guarding its cub.

The bobcats and us and even the goshawks have this in common: we do our utmost to keep our young safe and we give our young a relatively extended childhood; we also care to provide our young ones with safe spaces to play in. The juvenile goshawks kicking sticks off their nests—is that not a form of playing? I empathize with the bobcat and the goshawk, and I don't want the former trapped or shot and I don't want the latter to have its home clear-cut while it's raising its young. A handful of times as I wandered around the cabin, a hummingbird thrummed right up to my heart or my forehead and, for a microsecond, I experienced the sensation of life fusing with life. The hummingbird is as much an expression of life as I am. The claims animals have on the land are as compelling as our own. Yet there are precious few places left where we can be "in place," as Thoreau writes, where we can see not just the path but what lies beyond, where the electric mystery of a bobcat can thrill us rather than manufactured entertainments that often pale on second viewing. Who we will be (and whether we will continue to be) tomorrow depends on whether we have the vision to see the treasures we already possess. And if we truly own this treasure-filled vision, we will naturally want to heal the damage we have inflicted upon the earth and heal our relationships with the animals who are one with the land, more eloquently than we can ever hope to be.

SOURCES

Allinson, Tris, ed. *State of the World's Birds*. Cambridge, UK: BirdLife International, 2018.

Barber, Mary. *Bird Wins Reprieve in Battle of the Bulbul*. Los Angeles Times. Dec 29, 1985.

Bharata-Muni. *The Natyashastra*. Translated by Manomohan Ghosh. Calcutta: Asiatic Society of Bengal, 1951.

Campbell, Joseph. *Myths of Light: Eastern Metaphors of the Eternal*. Novato, CA: New World Library, 2003.

Cartron, Jean-Luc E., ed. *Raptors of New Mexico*. Albuquerque, NM: University of New Mexico Press, 2010.

Chronic, Halka. *Roadside Geology of New Mexico*. Missoula: Mountain Press Publishing Company, 2005.

Coates, Stephanie E., Wright, Benjamin W., and Carlisle, Jay D. *Long-billed curlew nest site selection and success in the Intermountain West*. The Journal of Wildlife Management, July 2019.

Colwell, M. A., Millett, C. B., Meyer, J. J., Hall, J. N., Hurley, S. J., McAllister, S. E., Transou, A. N., and LeValley, R. R. *Snowy Plover reproductive success in beach and river habitats*. Journal of Field Ornithology 76 (4), 2005.

Coomaraswamy, Ananda K. *The Essential Ananda K. Coomaraswamy*. Bloomington, IN: World Wisdom, 2004.

Cornell Lab of Ornithology. "All About Birds." allaboutbirds.org/news.

Cornell Lab of Ornithology. "Birds of the World." birdsoftheworld.org.

Darwin, Charles. "Darwin's ornithological notes." In *Bulletin of the British Museum (Natural History). Historical Series*, edited by Nora Barlow, vol. 3, no. 7, 201–278. London: British Museum, 1963.

Dixon, Royal. *The Human Side of Birds.* New York: Frederick A. Stokes Company, 1917.

Dunn, Jon L. and Jonathan Alderfer. *National Geographic Field Guide to the Birds of North America, Sixth Edition.* Washington, DC: National Geographic, 2011.

Eakle, Wade L., Bond, Laura, Fuller, Mark R., Fischer, Richard A., and Steenhof, Karen. *Wintering Bald Eagle Count Trends in the Conterminous United States, 1986–2010.* Journal of Raptor Research, 2015.

Ehrmann, Max. "Desiderata," www.desiderata.com.

Erdoes, Richard, and Ortiz, Alfonso, eds. *American Indian Myths and Legends.* New York: Pantheon, 1984.

Exupéry, Antoine de Saint. *The Little Prince.* Translated by Katherine Woods. New York: Harcourt Brace Jovanovich, 1971.

Fergusson, Erna. *Dancing Gods: Indian Ceremonials of New Mexico and Arizona.* Albuquerque, NM: University of New Mexico Press, 1957.

Johnsgard, Paul A. *Crane Music: A Natural History of American Cranes.* Lincoln, NE: University of Nebraska Press, 1998.

Kale, M. R. *The Meghadūta of Kālidāsa.* Delhi: Motilal Banarsidass Publishers, 1999.

Kaufman, Kenn. *Lives of North American Birds.* Boston: Houghton Mifflin Company, 1996.

Lake-Thom, Bobby. *Spirits of the Earth: A Guide to Native American Nature Symbols, Stories, and Ceremonies*. New York: Plume, 1997.

Leopold, Aldo. *Aldo Leopold: A Sand County Almanac & Other Writings on Ecology and Conservation*. New York: Library of America, 2013.

Maestas, José Griego y and Anaya, Rudolfo A. *Cuentos: Tales from the Hispanic Southwest*. Santa Fe: The Museum of New Mexico Press, 1980.

Maharaj, Sri Nisargadatta. *I Am That: Talks with Sri Nisargadatta Maharaj*. Edited by Sudhakar S. Dikshit. Translated by Maurice Frydman. Durham, NC: Acorn Press, 2012.

Martin, K., Aitken, K. E. H., and Wiebe, K. L. *Nest sites and nest webs for cavity-nesting communities in interior British Columbia, Canada: Nest characteristics and niche partitioning*. Condor 106 (1), 2004.

Meine, Curt. *Aldo Leopold: His Life and Work*. Madison, WI: University of Wisconsin Press, 2010.

Miller, Char. *Gifford Pinchot and the Making of Modern Environmentalism*. Washington, DC: Island Press, 2004.

Ortiz, Alfonso. *The Tewa World: Space, Time Being & Becoming in a Pueblo Society*. Chicago and London: The University of Chicago Press, 1972.

Page, G. W., Stenzel, L. E., Warriner, J. S., Warriner, J. C., and Paton, P. W. *Snowy Plover* (Charadrius nivosus): Birds of the World. Edited by A. F. Poole. Ithaca, NY: Cornell Lab of Ornithology, 2020.

Pinchot, Gifford. *The Training of a Forester*. Scotts Valley, CA: CreateSpace, 2016.

Pinchot, Gifford. *The Use of the National Forests.* US Department of Agriculture: Forest Service, 1907.

Sams, Jamie, and Carson, David. *Medicine Cards: The Discovery of Power Through the Ways of Animals.* Rochester, VT: Bear & Company Publishing, 1988.

Shankar, Ravi. *My Music, My Life.* New York: Mandala Publishing, 2007.

Sibley, David Allen. *The Sibley Guide to Bird Life and Behavior.* New York: Alfred A. Knopf, 2001.

Singer, Emily. *How Dinosaurs Shrank and Became Birds.* Quanta Magazine. June 2015

Souder, William. *Under a Wild Sky: John James Audubon and the Making of* The Birds of America. Minneapolis, MN: Milkweed Editions, 2014.

Taylor, Chris, Blanchard, Wade, and Lindenmayer, David B. *Does forest thinning reduce fire severity in Australian eucalypt forests?* Conservation Letters D, Sept 2020.

Thoreau, Henry David. *The Journal of Henry David Thoreau: 1837–1861.* Edited by Damion Searls. New York: New York Review of Books, 2009.

Wiebe, K. L. and Moore, W. S. *Northern Flicker* (Colaptes auratus): Birds of the World. Edited by P. G. Rodewald. Ithaca, NY: Cornell Lab of Ornithology, 2020.

Wilson, Edward O. *Half-Earth: Our Planet's Fight for Life.* New York: Liveright, 2016.

Young, Stanley P. *The Bobcat of North America: Its History, Life Habits, Economic Status and Control, with List of Currently Recognized Subspecies.* Lanham, MD: Stackpole Books, 2017.

ACKNOWLEDGMENTS

This book is a song of gratitude for birds. I wrote it over a few years and I am grateful to Daniel Slager from Milkweed Editions for spirited conversations and for shining the light.

I visited a wealth of national forests and monuments, national parks, state parks, and wildlife refuges staffed by dedicated rangers and volunteers. I would like to thank two refuge managers in particular—Debbie Pike (and her indelible pig, Princess Fiona) at Las Vegas and Chris Lohrengel at Maxwell. Wildlife biologist Jay Gatlln and forester Erica Enjady at the Carson National Forest graciously answered many owlish questions.

Thanks to the Army Corps of Engineers for organizing the Midwinter Bald Eagle Survey at Abiquiu Lake where I volunteered. Alex Patia from the New Mexico Wildlife Center generously offered me his spot on the patrol boat. Kirsten McDonnell, eagle biologist at the US Fish and Wildlife Service, answered queries on eagle numbers.

Curlew biologist Jay Carlisle offered warm encouragement and generously reviewed some chapters in this book. Kelli Stone at the Migratory Bird Division of the US Fish and Wildlife Service made time for a wide-ranging conversation and encouraged me to keep looking for curlews. Brian Miller and David Lightfoot shared their research on grasshoppers and grasslands.

Anthony Anella, Steve Fox, and Jeff Pappas offered support and friendship during my Aldo & Estella Leopold Residency. In Tres Piedras, I had stimulating talks with wildlife biologist Francisco Cortez and ranger Chris Furr. Sheila Davis (not her real name) is wildlife biologist and person extraordinaire— thank you for your intelligence, dedication, humor, and humility.

An essay on cranes appeared in a modified form in the *Los Angeles Review of Books*—thanks to Boris Dralyuk. A nuthatch essay appeared in the *Pasatiempo*—thanks to Tracy Mobley-Martinez. A fledgling piece on Mi Casita ran in *El Piñon*.

Carol Petersen closely read a draft of the manuscript—thank you for your beautiful friendship. Deborah Winslow read my final draft and floored me with her enthusiasm; what a joy to be your friend! Thanks to Amy Bianco for her readiness to help and Richard Ian Greene for asking about my "birdy book." The late Ravi Shankar and his family welcomed me to their home and musical world and brought to life the concept of *rasa*.

I thank my parents for gifting me with a childhood like no other and my older brother for being the rock of my childhood; you will always live on in my heart.

My gratitude to the entire Milkweed team, especially to Helen Whybrow for her sensitive editing; Mary Austin Speaker for the gorgeous cover; Broc Rossell for his dedication and cool California vibe; Joanna Demkiewicz, Morgan LaRocca,

Shannon Blackmer, and Katie Hill for their zeal; and Jordan Koluch for her thorough copyediting. Any errors are mine alone.

I deeply appreciate the countless hikes and birding trips and the life that Michael and I have shared. Michael took notes on our trips to Cape May and Lassen Volcanic National Park, which I drew on for the chapter on flickers, and he carefully read the manuscript. Our daughters Mia and Pika (nicknames) never fail to add *rasa* to our birding expeditions.

Molly Wagoner

PRIYANKA KUMAR is the author of *Conversations with Birds*. Her essays and criticism appear in the *New York Times*, the *Washington Post*, the *Los Angeles Review of Books*, the *Huffington Post*, and *High Country News*. She is a recipient of the Aldo & Estella Leopold Writing Residency, an Alfred P. Sloan Foundation Award, a New Mexico/New Visions Governor's Award, a Canada Council for the Arts Grant, an Ontario Arts Council Literary Award, and an Academy of Motion Pictures Arts and Sciences Fellowship. A graduate of the University of Southern California's School of Cinematic Arts and an alumna of the Bread Loaf Writers' Conference, Kumar wrote, directed and produced the feature documentary *The Song of the Little Road*, starring Martin Scorsese and Ravi Shankar. Kumar has taught at the University of California Santa Cruz and the University of Southern California, and serves on the Board of Directors at the Leopold Writing Program.

milkweed
EDITIONS

Founded as a nonprofit organization in 1980, Milkweed
Editions is an independent publisher. Our mission is to
identify, nurture, and publish transformative literature, and
build an engaged community around it.

Milkweed Editions is based in Bdé Óta Othúŋwe
(Minneapolis) within Mní Sota Makhóčhe, the traditional
homeland of the Dakhóta people. Residing here since time
immemorial, Dakhóta people still call Mní Sota Makhočhe
home, with four federally recognized Dakhóta nations and
many more Dakhóta people residing in what is now the state
of Minnesota. Due to continued legacies of colonization,
genocide, and forced removal, generations of Dakhóta
people remain disenfranchised from their traditional
homeland. Presently, Mní Sota Makhóčhe has become a
refuge and home for many Indigenous nations and peoples,
including seven federally recognized Ojibwe nations.
We humbly encourage our readers to reflect upon the
historical legacies held in the lands they occupy.

milkweed.org

Milkweed Editions, an independent nonprofit publisher, gratefully acknowledges sustaining support from our Board of Directors; the Alan B. Slifka Foundation and its president, Riva Ariella Ritvo-Slifka; the Amazon Literary Partnership; the Ballard Spahr Foundation; *Copper Nickel*; the McKnight Foundation; the National Endowment for the Arts; the National Poetry Series; the Target Foundation; and other generous contributions from foundations, corporations, and individuals. Also, this activity is made possible by the voters of Minnesota through a Minnesota State Arts Board Operating Support grant, thanks to a legislative appropriation from the arts and cultural heritage fund. For a full listing of Milkweed Editions supporters, please visit milkweed.org.

Interior design by Mary Austin Speaker
Typeset in Bulmer

Bulmer was created in the late 1780s or early 1790s.
This late "transitional" typeface was designed
by William Martin for William Bulmer,
who ran the Shakespeare Press.